Wannabee Rock Star Who Finally Found the Rock

A Story of Trial, Faith and Triumph

FULL COLOR EDITION

by
James Michael McLester

Photo credits
Exquisite Photography, Cindy Williams
Marty Perlman Photography
Amanda Lewis, ACLEW Photography
Robert Reddy
Hartsart Photography
Brent McKinley, Photographer
Mitch Moore
Alexandria Quinn
Karen Overstreet
James Bland
Eric Younkin
Front book Cover: Chris Jones @ C Chris Jones
Back book cover: Jill Cross

Cover and interior layout & graphic design: Gary Taylor

Web design for www.jmclester.com provided by Todd and Teresa Jungling of WSI. www.LeadingWSIwebsolutions.com

Edited by Gary Taylor

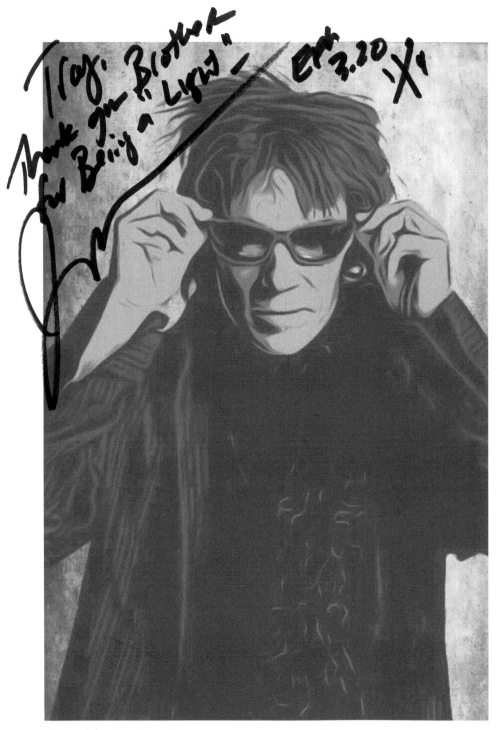

Artwork by Joey Spector

Contents

Dedication

This book is dedicated to the Lord who saved me and is gracefully restoring me to health—in spirit, soul and body. And to my loving mother, Susan Howeth, to my father, the late James Morris McLester, Jr., and to all my wonderful family and friends.

Following is a letter from my dad to me, Christmas 1990:

Dear Son,

Well it's a new year now. I hope and pray you're doing ok. I love you and I always will be proud of you. Good luck with whatever you endeavor to do with your life.

I miss you very much. Wish we could see each other more and maybe talk more often, but I guess you're busy and with being so far away it's hard to stay in touch.

It sure was good to see you Christmas. You look real good and it was a pleasure to spend some time with you.

Everybody is doing fine, except Granddaddy and Nanny have had the flu. I haven't been sick with it yet. I hope I don't get it.

Write me and let me know how you're band is doing. Call me anytime collect. I'd love to hear from you, 817-523-7023.

Marilyn will be 18 years old Jan 11. She is really growing up. Nanny and Granddaddy said Hi. They love you and miss you. Granddaddy said to come help us with the computer, ha ha! They're pulling for you too, and pray for you daily.

Well, this is short but I don't have much time before I go to work. Write me or call!

Love,

Dad (POPS)

Acknowledgements

A special thanks are in order for two generous men, who were instrumental in helping make *Wannabee Rock Star Who Finally Found the Rock* a reality. First, my heart goes out to Dr. Bob Bard, OD, who, after a long day at the office, sat through a loud night of Christian rock, hip hop and worship and endured hundreds of kids bouncing around and getting excited. His decision to approach me regarding the creation of this book at the end of my Hearts on Fire fundraising concert had a profound impact on my life.

Dr. Bard's gracious offer to assist me on my personal health journey and with my mission to impart Godly wisdom to mankind in spirit, soul and body is what I like to refer to as "paying it forward." I am forever grateful. Dr. Bard, who is a published author, organic farmer/rancher and excellent eye doctor, previously worked with Gary Taylor, a talented writer and editor, and called to see if he would lend his editing skills.

Second, and equally important, I extend a sincere "thanks" for the tireless efforts of my editor, Gary Taylor, an accomplished freelance writer in Gainesville, Texas. I simply was going on faith that a door was open to share my story. Little did I know at the time how blessed I would be to work with a gifted but humble editor.

Gary spent many hours editing and proofreading copy and testimonials (which are the book's "heart and soul"). My hope is that you will be touched deeply by all who shared their heart during the story. Gary edited the photos and developed the overall layout and design. Gary did the cover layouts, using artwork provided by Chris Jones and Jill Cross, and finalized the camera-ready digital files for publishing. Finally, Gary encouraged me to keep digging for the best, most relevant content.

I spent months typing manuscript revisions one-handed on my cell phone at dialysis treatments, with my right arm in a blood pressure cuff for four hours and my left forearm connected through lines to the machine. Gary and two generous people helped me acquire a new Dell laptop to create the remainder of the book. Returning from our May 2012 House of Blues concert in Houston with Stryper and getting an email to visit my local Best Buy to pick up a new laptop, provided by strangers, strongly affirmed my faith in a God that provides.

If we step out in faith, the Lord provides. Dr. Bard, Gary, and others, recognized a need and were moved to seek provision, and, hence, a few compassionate souls met the need and made this book possible.

Dr. Bard, Gary, the artists, photographers, musicians, saints and music industry insiders, all the precious ones who shared their testimonials, and those who will be touched by our story are all rock stars in my book.

Foreword

So, you want to be a rock star! Really?

Isn't it great to have dreams? You remember as a kid you wanted to be a fireman, astronaut or maybe an explorer to discover new worlds yet to be revealed. You would dream about them day after day, night after night. Your whole world was consumed with that dream. But you were only 7, thinking,"Man, I wish I were older."

Then life invaded. Things changed, priorities were altered, life began to take strange turns and you wondered, "What in the world is going on? Now, what do I do? Hey, it's 4th and 40—time to punt!"

Life happens to all of us. It rains on the good and the bad (and the ugly). In those moments when our lives deviate from the "plan," the real you shows up (or shows off). Time and time again, I've seen the "characters" show off and make some very bad choices. Anger, bitterness and resentment become your constant companions. They color your choices and counsel your deep subconscious. Justification becomes your daily alibi or drug-of-choice for those decisions. You spiral down, down, down.

But I've also seen the character of the person rise to the occasion. This is when life gets good. Character doesn't look for the easy way out; it looks for the best way through. Genuine solutions emerge and float to the top to become the chemical reaction of answers. With good choices come good consequences (Gal. 6:7). A revelation for us all to realize is that the principles of life and the scriptures are a sure-fire way of staying out of the ditch while cruising on the center-line of the road to success. All of a sudden, you realize that, even though "the plan" has changed, life just keeps getting better and better. You begin to believe that miracles *still* can happen.

What you're about to experience is the journey of one man who made those discoveries and how his life so dramatically changed. His discovery of those life principles and his faith in the Author of those principles has brought him from the dream to the reality. He has truly reached the pinnacle of his dream to be a rock star. He's living life out loud, and if you listen very carefully to what he has to say to you, you too will know that his heart's on fire. He really is a "wannabee rock star who finally found the Rock."

Bill Bishop

Pastor

Introduction

Why did I title this book *Wannabee Rock Star Who Finally Found the Rock*? Well, it was something I had been praying about. And I thought, you know, so many times in life we take ourselves far too seriously. In fact, those who know me would say that about *me*. When you're pursuing something, you have to be focused, you have to be serious and you have to be motivated. All these things, of course, are a part of success, but I finally realized that you have to lighten up, enjoy the ride and have a sense of humor, too.

Looking back at all the time I spent in pursuit of the glitz, the fortune and the fame—and the dream of becoming a rock star—I can say that it was what I always wanted. I wanted to become something or become some*body*. I longed to escape the dysfunction of my youth and find out where I belonged. But after the music faded, my dream appeared to be long lost at the age of 36 when I went through a near-death experience.

I was flat on my back, alone in the cold hospital. There were no drum risers. There were no screaming girls throwing themselves at me. There were no accolades. It was all gone. It was me, in the basement of a hospital, away from the "White Noize," when the Lord spoke to me on the seventh day of an eight-day "Valley of the Shadow of Death" experience. I was listening to the *Braveheart* soundtrack (one of my all-time favorite movies), to drown out the symphony of alarms in the dialysis unit and find some peace. This was when the Lord clearly said to me, "James you will live and not die, and you will declare the works of the Lord."

From that moment forward, I knew my life's purpose. All the years, all the tours, all the traveling— and all that went along with it—none of it really mattered much when I realized that I had finally found the Rock that I could build my life on. I surrendered my pursuit of becoming a rock star to the epiphany that God wanted my heart. He wanted all of the warrior heart that he had placed in me. He wanted me to lay down the gift of music that He had given me and really get to know Him.

First Peter 5:6 says "Humble yourself under the mighty hand of God, and He will exalt you in due season." True surrender requires faith, because we do not understand or fully grasp what the Lord is doing or what the road ahead will look like. I realized that, without an absolute dependence on his Word and promises for restoration, I was just a man who had poured my heart and soul into becoming a rock star. I spent my life trading all my failures and disappointments, including my dysfunctional childhood, for a chance to make music and give people some relief from reality.

I was discharged from Presbyterian Hospital in Dallas, Texas, on Valentine's Day 2003. I left with a glimpse of hope that outpatient treatment would continue to improve my condition, while remaining optimistic that a kidney transplant or stem cell therapy might one day restore my health. The doctors required that an arteriovenous (AV) fistula be installed in my left arm, and as a professional drummer I was concerned about the risk of injury. The surgery was initially mildly successful and, with some hesitation, I agreed to let it be revised, by vascular surgeon Dr. Cannaughton, MD, who has performed a few minor revisions to keep my dialysis access free and clear of clotting. Despite these procedures, I play drums at a higher level today. The music I play with the Crossroads Praise Team, and Supernova Remnant in various churches and in venues such as House of Blues and Trees, is at a higher level today than ever before in my 18-year professional music career. God has restored so many things to me and blessed me in so many ways! I am so excited to see what the next part of this journey is going to hold for me. So, *Wannabee Rock Star Who Finally Found the Rock*? Yeah, I think that says it best.

Chapter 1
War and Chaos

I called this first chapter "War and Chaos," because I came into the world at a very tumultuous time. In 1967, the Arab-Israeli War was going on, and Vietnam was right around the corner. Sandwiched in the middle of these catastrophic world events were the destinies of two high school sweethearts: my father, James Morris McLester, Jr., and my mother, Susan Jane Landrum, from Haltom City, Texas.

He was a football player who loved working on cars; she was a cosmetologist and a cheerleader. They hooked up. They did the things high school sweethearts do, but my dad also had a wild side. He started drinking alcohol at an early age, but my mom was raised in a home were alcohol was rarely around. She dedicated her life to the Lord at 9 years old, and she just didn't get in trouble. So, my dad was getting in trouble, and my mom was trying to keep the peace. Somehow, they managed to ride it out, and, at a very young age of 17, my mom said, "Yeah, I'm going to get married."

My parents were married on September 3, 1966 at Chanute Air Force Base in Illinois. My grandfather inspired my father's enlistment in the Air Force, because he served as a pilot and flight instructor in World War II. Soon after moving to Luke Air Force Base in Glendale, Arizona, my mom became pregnant. Suddenly, on September 4, 1967, amidst this very tumultuous time, I opened my eyes for the first time into a chaotic world.

I remember spending a lot of time with my grandparents early on in my childhood. While my father was away in Vietnam, my mom and I would visit with my nanny and granddaddy, and my nanny and my mother would spend a lot of time with me. I remember my father would send pictures from the Air Force base and write, "I love you, Pookie," to my mom, and, "I miss Jimbo." It was always cool seeing my father pictured in uniform—but I longed to see *him*.

Finally, we did have a chance to see my father. We moved to Laredo, Texas, when I was very young, and my grandparents drove up to see us. We lived in a duplex near the Air Force base until housing became available, and we moved into a trailer on the base. While living in Laredo, my father was dealing with the stress of being in the Air Force. My mother kept the peace as a "homemaker." She came from a modest home, but now she was in the middle of Laredo with no friends, no family and no one around her. My father, under all the stress, was drinking alcohol heavily. My father's alcohol addiction ignited several episodes of violence and abuse toward my precious mother. One night, my father in a drunken rage, threatened to severely hurt my mom with aggressive physical force. My father would corner her and trap her and she feared for her life. One night in a drunken rage my father came home and became very angry and told my mom, "Get out!"

My mom grabbed me in her arms and we ran into the street, and when she noticed he was getting in his car to follow us, we hid in the trees until a military police car came by and my mom flagged them down to take us to safety in their office. My mom hid me in a hotel that night, and we called my grandparents to make them aware of the dangerous situation. Things would settle down, and then the chaotic episodes would replay over and over.

Nobody really understood what was going on. Imagine being my father, fighting an unpopular war in Vietnam, volunteering to fight for your country, only to come home and have people spitting on you and calling you a baby killer. He was only trying to defend his country. I know that was tough on my father, but the alcohol was how he was dealing with it at the time.

Finally, around 1969, my father received an honorable discharge as a USSGT Staff Sergeant in the United States Air Force. My parents left Laredo and moved closer to their hometown, initially settling in Richland Hills, in a little house they rented. It was just my mother, my father and me in this rent house. Although I did not understand the turmoil, I knew in the depths of my heart that I longed for safety and love, priorities for all of us. They cannot be purchased at The Room Store. No matter how much my father offered to do for me, it would not pacify the longing in my heart to feel safe and loved.

I was an only child, and I did not have very many friends, but I had a next-door neighbor named Greg Mayes, who was my best friend. My father's drinking problem and extreme jealousy escalated the fighting, —so there wasn't much else to remember.

The only semi-fun thing I remember was when I would go into my parent's bedroom and crawl into bed with them and we would listen to songs on their clock radio by artists like the Beatles, the Rolling Stones, The Who, and Simon and Garfunkel. They loved music, and I loved music, and that was sort of a happy time we had together—a time to bond and feel safe—but it only lasted for so long.

My mother could see that my father's mental state was far beyond having really come back from Vietnam. There were many episodes in my childhood where my mother literally would tell me that we were fleeing for our lives, with my father coming after her in a drunken rage. Then he'd come back and make up with her, and then the next thing you'd know she would be at her parents' house trying to hide out. After a period of time, it just got to be too much. I didn't understand these crazy nights of my father screaming obscenities. It almost seemed as if this war raging overseas had come to torment me at home.

Then my mother became pregnant with her second child. My little sister, Marilyn Sue McLester, was born on January 11, 1972. We lived as a family together for about 13 months, and we even took an Olan Mills family picture—and then Valentine's Day came. It was supposed to be a day of love, but it wasn't that way at our house, so my mother said, "enough is enough." No more abuse, no more bruising, no more shaking—no more. I resented my father for what was happening. I wanted him to love me and make us feel safe, but the alcoholism and the war had bred rage, anger and dysfunction. After my father threatened mom in a drunken rage, my mother packed up my sister and me on Valentine's Day 1973. We sped away and went to live at my grandparents' house in Hurst, Texas.

Chapter 2
Second Chances

Valentine's Day, 1973, my mother and I, and my baby sister Marilyn, were speeding away from my father, because my father just wasn't right. It's nothing personal. It's just that war will change a man. Nobody understood what my father went through back then, but my mother knew that she could not allow us to be in danger any more. Alcohol when added on top of unresolved anger is a recipe for disaster. We know today (from watching Fox News specials on post-traumatic stress disorder, for example), that this can be a brutal force against peace in the home.

Life was very strange not being together as a family. It was almost like the hit song "The Way We Were." There we were, the McLesters, in our Olan Mills family portrait, and now, all of a sudden, we were not together. Only the photograph remained. I would have given anything to have our family restored.

We moved to Hurst, Texas, for a brief time with my grandparents. I attended West Hurst Elementary, and all the things that I wanted at home—the attention, and the love and the acceptance—I tried to find in school. My parents did many loving things for me, but I guess I never really felt safe with all the chaos, early on. I tried to be the model classmate, and I tried to be the teacher's pet. I did all of these things because I wanted the attention that I craved at home.

At home, I always felt unsafe, and I felt that I had to hide. At least when I was in school I could do well in my studies, and I could be the teacher's pet. That's just what I did.

My mom's sister, June, my dear aunt (she's gone now to be with the Lord after a fatal car accident with an 18-wheeler), was married to Billy Almonrode, from California. Billy was a really laid back guy—the kind of guy that always cracked jokes and tried to keep life on the lighter side. He worked at Lockheed Martin as a machinist, and he had a good friend who was single. In 1973, my Aunt June set my mother up on a date with Billy's friend, and soon after that my mother married him. Mom married for the second time, and that's one of the reasons I call this chapter "Second Chances," because many people try something once and it fails, but yet they have the courage try again. In Proverbs, the Bible speaks of a righteous man falling seven times, yet he rises every time to try again by faith.

So my mother *was* trying again, and now, all of a sudden, I had a stepfather in my life. We had visitation with my real father (I think it was every two weeks), and my father would pick us up and take us to Six Flags, The Texas Rangers ballgame, SeaWorld (or whatever it was called at the time)—he was always taking us somewhere and doing something, trying to make up for the lost time. I am certain he was living with regrets of how things ended in divorce to my mom, whom he always loved even though he did not understand love in a kind manner. My father likely felt very insecure, like many of us have before realizing God's abundant grace.

By contrast my stepfather was really passive. He might have had a beer on occasion, but I don't ever remember him being crazy with alcohol. He was passive, so, in other words, my mom was pretty much saying how things should go in our home. This is what it appeared like to me as a 7 year old boy who had been through war and chaos since the day I opened my eyes. Living for so long with my father being the domineering figure, which my mother resented, I think she felt safer and more in control in her second marriage. And that also went for the fact that she gave her life to the Lord at 9 years old and regularly attended church, and she felt like we needed to be there. My father was also raised in a Christian home, but somehow—maybe it was the need for approval or internal questions—he was drawn to alcohol.

I remember my stepfather used to work some crazy nights and we would rise early in the morning and drive down Highway 183 in the Mid-Cities to pick him up from the machine shop. We would drive our blue Subaru wagon through this long tunnel (no longer there) and come out the other end in the very early hours of the morning. Life was good, at least for a moment, with our donuts and chocolate milk, driving down the road listening to the car stereo.

We had those kinds of memories, and as a family we did the best we could, but things just weren't the same without my father. And, after a while, of course, my mother found out she was pregnant from her second husband. Soon, my brother Richard was born October 17, 1974 (my mother's birthday), and now it was me, my sister and my little brother Richard, living and trying to adapt. It was tough for me. When I would visit my father on the weekends he would tell me one thing and when I returned home I was told another. And I know that deep in my mother's heart, she wanted to have that extra chance to believe that it would work this time. They stayed married, and things went along. But, no matter what, I knew that my father felt this deep sense of guilt in his heart for not being the father he wanted to be. He was certainly disillusioned and hurt after returning from war.

My father volunteered for the Vietnam War, returning home alive, and then, instead of being treated with respect for serving his country, he was called a baby killer. I know that was hard for him to process.

Our stepfamily moved to North Richland Hills, and I started school at Holiday Heights Elementary. Ours was a modest home on Sybil, only three houses down from the school. My third grade teacher, Mrs. Lecroix, was the coolest teacher ever. I was selected for a gifted arts program called LAMP (Language Arts for the Mentally Proficient) and was privileged to take field trips to art museums, enjoy delicious meals at Red Lobster (we sampled *langostinos*), and even traveled to San Antonio. At last, it seemed like there was more to life than hiding away at home or hoping that our family would be restored.

Mrs. Lecroix was a creative arts teacher, and she eagerly encouraged us to listen to music in class. This was long before the release of the iPod, which we have the leisure of taking everywhere today. We had a record player—the old LP style, the kind you had to replace the needles on, and she would say, "Hey, Jimmy, you want to go home and grab some of your records and come back, and we'll listen to music during class?" I would run over to the house, pick up my albums, like K.C. and Sunshine Band, the Bee Gees, Barry Manilow—all the Top 40 music of that time—and bring it to the classroom, and we'd play my records with the windows open and just escape in the music. We had a great time in class. I thought I was Mrs. Lecroix's favorite student, and we enjoyed a great relationship during my school years.

A traumatic thing occurred while I was enjoying going to school. Some things began taking place in our home. I'm not going to go into the details, but there were some family issues. I was full of anger deep inside from my parents separation. I thought I was to blame somehow. Yes, it's true that my stepfather put a roof over our head and helped coach me in Pee Wee sports and my baseball team, but it just wasn't the same; it wasn't me and my father. Now that my mother had all that abuse in her first marriage, this was different. I sought to find the acceptance and love at school and hide from the emotional pain in my heart. I wanted to spend time away from home. As an honor student, proud of my near perfect attendance, I fell more in love with school.

I recognized around the fifth grade or so, like most kids, I didn't think much about what I ate. Mom often cooked a delicious pot roast with stewed tomatoes, onions, carrots and potatoes. She even taught us how to make a Chef Boy-Ardee homemade pizza, back when pizza delivery meant "create your own."

On Sundays, on occasion after church, she would let Sun Garden cafeteria in The Northeast Mall serve my favorite meal of chicken fried steak with cream gravy, mashed potatoes, kernel corn and a dinner roll with butter. I cannot forget the heavenly slice of strawberry cheesecake with golden graham cracker crust. Yum!

Sometimes the menu was Sloppy Joes, Swiss steak or Hamburger Helper. We were happy to have something to eat. Sometimes, not knowing any better we wanted Spam or Vienna sausages. If you don't know what Spam is, it's a potted meat product, so let's just say it's definitely not grass fed beef.

Through the SAD (Standard American Diet) and not really paying attention, I fell in love with *sugar* as most kids do. I consumed Kool-Aid, loaded with real cane sugar, soft drinks and candy. Pez, Fun Dip, Pop Rocks, Lifesavers and Pixie sticks were a part of my diet. In fifth grade, I remember taking a trip to Dr. Cooke, our family dentist at the time, and after examination, I was told that I had 11 cavities. Dr. Cooke's answer to "fix" my 11 cavities was silver mercury amalgam fillings. Not knowing what silver mercury amalgam fillings were, or the damage they could do, we allowed Dr. Cooke to drill out my teeth and fill them up with this silver-mercury alloy. I was 11 years old and terrified, but I trusted that Dr. Cooke knew best. It was 1978, and very little research had been done at the time to suggest that silver mercury amalgam fillings were unsafe.

In contrast to this health dilemma, I lived and breathed sports. I played soccer, baseball and ran track, but I loved football the most. And there was a point in 1979 where I also began to fall in love with music. My older cousin, Steve Smith, turned me on to bands like Journey and AC/DC. I'll never forget, we went to our first Rock concert when I was around 12 years old. Picture this: Tarrant County Convention Center, Fort Worth, Texas. The dome-shaped main concert arena was overrun with fans wanting to see Hard Rock Band AC/DC from Australia and Journey from San Francisco. My uncle Ron dropped us off at the concert, and I heard avid rock fans screaming as loud as they could.

Jet black concert tees proudly displayed the names of the bands they lived and breathed for. Many fans were walking around with large plastic cups of beer, and others were smoking these cigarettes that "smelled very peculiar." I kept asking my cousin, who was about 15, "What is that smell?" If there is such a thing as a contact high, I probably acquired it as the smoke filled the arena.

Watching these famous, professional musicians take the stage and "kick #$@ and take names" had tremendous influence on my youth. This is exactly what I wanted to do with my life. Hearing songs pierce my soul like "Wheel in The Sky" and "Winds of March" from *Journey Live* and experiencing the late AC/DC vocalist Bon Scott with guitarist Angus Young on his shoulders playing "Whole Lotta Rosie" was unforgettable. We were out until 1:00 a.m. I bought the concert T-shirt, and as an adrenaline-starved youth, I thought, "Wow, what an experience!"

I had once loved sports and school, but now I was in love with the music of the 70s and early 80s. I discovered bands like the Cars, Cheap Trick, Van Halen, Foreigner and Boston, and several others emerging on the music scene at the time, and, somehow, I just knew that music would be my first love.

During this transformational period, I kept going back to Dr. Cooke for my dental checkup, and that drill kept coming at me. I was really traumatized by this—not just the sound that it made, but I can remember it digging in to my teeth—not knowing that what was going in to my mouth would later affect my health.

After my first concert, I began to think seriously about becoming a rock musician, a rock star. That's what I wanted to do with my life. But all the while, my mother had us going to church and Sunday school. I was in this organization called the Royal Ambassadors, and in Boy Scouts trying for the Eagle Scout. I was seeking a solid upbringing and leadership. I enjoyed the mentorship of my youth pastors, but I knew deep in my heart that rock music had a whole different kind of lifestyle attached to it, and I wanted the freedom it represented more than the regimentation of the Scouts.

I remember going down to Camp Goddard with the First Baptist Church of Richland Hills where I accepted the Lord. I was born again under the oak tree, singing

Seek ye first the Kingdom of God

And His righteousness

And all these things shall be added unto you

Hallelu, Hallelujah!

I will never forget when I felt the Lord walk into my heart and cleanse me from those fears and traumas I had as a young child. But Camp Goddard didn't last long, and although I was saved, it wasn't long until a major episode severely struck my life. In 1980, just two years after getting my cavities filled with "silver" fillings, my knees began to swell like grapefruits. Now, mind you, I ran track, and I played football, and I was one of the fastest guys on the team. But now my knees were swollen like grapefruits, and my hands began to swell like link sausages. I could not bend my hands, and my inflamed joints screamed with excruciating pain. At 13, I was crippled like an elderly rheumatic.

Dr. Golden, our family doctor, didn't know what to do, so he ordered some blood tests and concluded that I needed see a specialist. He referred me to Dr. Claudio Lehman, M.D., a rheumatologist. He examined my inflamed areas and my immune markers suggested Reiter's Syndrome, a juvenile form of arthritis.

Reiter's Syndrome literally crippled me. Soon, I reluctantly handed Dr. Lehmans' note to Coach Sales. The words were painful. I was instructed to stop participating in all sports until the Reiter's syndrome went into remission. I will always remember, in 1980, walking up to Coach Sales, as an NRH Junior High Falcon and then walking off the football field crying because I couldn't play sports any more. Despite this heartbreaking news,

I had faith that I was going to get better. My mom was a seasoned prayer warrior and I began to study nutrition.

Dr. Lehman prescribed Tolectin, a strong anti-inflammatory medication, and six aspirin per day, but nothing helped. At the same time, Dr. Lehman asked me if I had had homosexual encounters, because he wanted to rule out STDs or AIDS, or some other kind of autoimmune disease. I was beside myself. I thought to myself, "This is not a good place to be, not being able to run, not being able to play sports—what can I do?"

After Dr. Lehman prescribed medications to provide relief, I began to learn about nutrition, protein powders and vitamin pills. Back then, these mammoth multivitamins would choke Mr. Ed the talking horse (a popular television show from the 70s), and they smelled like horse pills, too. We've come a long way now. I began to study and incorporate nutrition into my diet. I became more careful with what I ate. I abstained from sugar, and the Reiter's syndrome went into remission. Hallelujah! I received my first bona fide miracle. I was excited. I had been shown the love of God. This debilitating illness that came against me at 13 was now gone from my life. I could move my hands freely and bend my knees.

Since I no longer participated in sports, I auditioned for the sixth grade concert band. I had the right embouchure to play trombone. Part of me wanted to play percussion, but I guess in the band director's assessment I was best suited for the trombone. My parents agreed to buy a concert trombone to see if I would pursue learning to perform and read music. I came under the tutelage of Mr. Fred Allen. I learned how to play the trombone proficiently. Soon, I was elected president of the concert band. Routinely, Mr. Allen left me in charge of the band hall, and during these precious moments I ditched my trombone and bolted for the percussion pit. Even though I had felt the exhilarating pulse of the sheepskin cover of a marching snare, I diligently practiced my trombone until my lips were swollen blue from blowing the #$%^ out of my horn. I competed in UIL competitions, and I sat first or second chair in the school band.

I pursued music. All of those bands from the 80s—Cheap Trick, the Cars, Van Halen, Foreigner, Boston, Styx—they all made an impression on me. But part of me just wanted to be in a rock band. I wanted to be in the school band to learn music, yet I yearned to become a rock star and live out the freedom that captivated my heart during my first concert at Tarrant County Convention Center. I was in love with music.

After this whole journey, from war and chaos to my second chance of being born again, I wanted to find *it*, the sweet spot, the place where I belonged.

Being healed of Reiter's Syndrome was a step in the right direction and forever changed my course. This turning point helped me move my passion from sports to music. Although these childhood events significantly shaped my life, my truest desire of all was to have my family back. I focused all my energy into my dream. I connected with a couple of like-minded guys that believed we could conquer the world and become rock stars. Now, my long-lost hopes of my family being restored were fused into the band—and I was determined to make my way to the top of the music business.

Chapter 3
I'm with the Band

At this time, most of my church experience was limited to just having a sense about the Lord. I had a sense about these things that people talked about—the miracles in the Bible, blind eyes being opened, deaf ears hearing, the mute being able to speak—but I was questioning whether these things were really happening in the church? Did these miracles really pass away? Or did some pastors just believe they had passed away? Was it a new dispensation? What did *I* know about dispensation?

I didn't understand it as a child, but I did know my mom was praying. Reiter's Syndrome was the first problem with my health that I experienced. Aside from having chickenpox or mumps (having swollen cheeks and being thrown into an ice-cold bathtub), I was a healthy child.

Nobody had any idea back then about silver mercury amalgam dental fillings. As I said before, I learned about nutrition and started reading about vitamins, coenzymes and fatty acids and how they affected the body. I did this because a) I wanted to get better, but b) I had family members around me who were sick, and I asked myself, "Why are they always taking drugs? Why do they always have a headache? Why are they always complaining? I don't want anything to do with that." Most any teenager would probably feel the same.

Thank God, though, that through prayer and the promises in the Word, the Reiter's syndrome was in remission. And now I had found a new calling in life: music.

In 1980, after seeing the Journey and AC/DC concert, and playing the trombone for a year or so, I thought, "Wow, it's time to get my money for nothing and my chicks for free." MTV was big, and this Dire Straits song came out and it really blew up to number one on the Billboard Charts. My older cousin Wade played drums and was an influence early on. I would drum on the dashboard of his Chevy truck to Rush's "Tom Sawyer," and I wanted a drum set. I kept telling my band director, "Look, you need to let me play drums and percussion."

But he would say, "No, I need you in your first chair position."

I told him, "I don't want to play trombone any more—I want to play the drums." Luckily, as president of the band, I would take over when Mr. Allen would leave the room. I would jump over to the drums and percussion and I would jam. I knew that's what I wanted to do.

Soon enough, I talked my dad into purchasing private drum lessons at Grants Drum city in Irving, Texas. I needed to learn to play the drum rudiments and read sheet music. He bought me my first drum set, which was a five-piece blue CB700 kit, and I was ready to *rock*. I practiced for hours and hours to 45s and LPs by various artists, from the Beatles and Aerosmith to Van Halen and Top 40. My inner circle of friends and family began to wonder if I was born with headphones attached to my ears.

After I became proficient on my drum kit, some of my friends suggested that I meet Eric Younkin. I had heard about Eric being a good guitar player, so one day I went to his house in Meadow Lakes, which was a nice neighborhood. Eric's dad was a car salesman, and his mom Debbie was just very sweet. I always felt like I was around family with them. Being from a broken home, I was always searching for that "mom-and-dad-are-in-love-and-everything-is-happy-in-the-household" thing, and it seemed to be that way at the Younkins. After school, I would bolt to Eric's house to listen to him play guitar. North Richland Hills Junior High (NRJH) was literally five minutes from his front door.

Eric's friend, James Martinez, played drums, and James had his black Ludwig drum kit set up in Eric's little bedroom, which he used as a studio. On one of these visits, my friend Robbie Gustin, whom I will tell you much more about later, also happened to be there. After James Martinez finished playing a song with Eric, I said, "Hey, Eric, can I have a try?"

Eric said, "Sure." This was about the time when Van Halen had really blown up, and everybody wanted to emulate them— look like them, sound like them, play like them, live like them. Van Halen were a four-man hard rock band from Sunny California who turned the world of hard rock music upside-down.

Van Halen blazed a trail across North America with their "over the top" showmanship by lead vocalist David Lee Roth and the fiery fret board antics of Eddie Van Halen on lead guitar, along with the thunderous drums of brother Alex Van Halen, and the low-end thump and high backing vocals of bassist Michael Anthony. At a time before the 80s glam rock emerged on L.A.'s famous Sunset Strip, Van Halen ruled the late 70s (78-80) with their infusion of blues and metal.

James Martinez got up, and I sat down behind the drums. After four stick clicks, we broke into Van Halen's "Runnin' with the Devil." The room felt electric. The air seemed to almost explode with the excitement we felt. It was just pure teenage testosterone. Our instinct drove us, and it was obvious to everyone in the room that we had just created something raw and edgy.

After I finished, Robbie said, "Jimmy, you just took it to another level!" I don't mention this to brag, but I knew I had a gift, and I was ready to spend my life perfecting it. When Eric and I played together, it was like *fire*.

It was from this impromptu jam session that our first band Vengeance was born. Eric Younkin and I recruited John Phillips on bass guitar and vocalist Peter Nepo.

Nepo was a Greek kid from New York who lived down the street from me on Sybil—a good looking kid who played piano.

At that time, locally, everywhere you looked there was a teen club, a skating rink or a night club where we wanted to play. Next thing we knew, we were playing at all of these places and garnering attention. Eric was known for his David Lee Roth antics as a frontman, but he could also play his guitar with blazing speed, like a young Eddie Van Halen. Eric had long blond hair and sported sunglasses, parachute pants and his trademark bandana. The girls loved him.

Younkin had the rehearsal room (a spare bedroom), the four-track recorder where we crafted our songs and the PA system. His parents were cool. They let us jam and swim in their pool. They took our promo pictures out on the gazebo in their backyard, and Debbie, Eric's mom, would frequently treat us to Taco Bueno. This was back in the day before major fast food chains could be found on every major intersection.

John Phillips, a musician's musician, was John Paul Jones of Led Zeppelin in a teenage frame. He was laid back and shy, comfortable in blue jeans, a Member's Only jacket and maybe a pair of shades if he was feeling brave.

Nepo, with his long, flowing black locks, had an athletic build. He usually wore a sleeveless concert tee and jeans, with black leather boots. Being from upstate New York, he was a fan of Billy Joel ("Piano Man"). He liked to rock, and he was a big Van Halen fan as well.

I was influenced by Alex Van Halen and John Bonham of Led Zeppelin. I hit the drums hard with fury and passion, channeling my angst into the drum kit and smashing cymbals. I frequently wore white leather signature gloves, a sleeveless shirt and parachute pants. I have to admit, as I began growing my hair out it looked a bit like the actor's hair from the television show "James at Fifteen." I knew it was important to be a solid musician first, but I also knew that the flashy stick tricks would get lots of attention. I would put flash paper I bought from the magic shop on my cymbals, and when I hit them they would "spark."

Even though the gigs paid very little, Eric's parents were very supportive of him and the band with the equipment and the PA system. We would show up and play—we were very good—and it was on.

As Vengeance, we took our promo pictures at the mall, and we would walk around Musicland at Northeast Mall in parachute pants, our lean muscular frames outlined by our sleeveless shirts, with combs in our back pockets, and always making sure the girls were checking us out. We played that whole game until we got to a point that they let us play in the North Richland Junior High talent show. Everybody knew about it, so there were hundreds of teenagers there. While every act before us was just somebody playing a flute solo, doing a King Tut skit, or who knows what, we took command of the stage and started playing Def Leppard and all of the popular rock music of our time.

There I was, behind my CB 700 drum kit, shirtless and wearing the famous "British flag" shorts that Def Leppard drummer Rick Allen made popular in their "Rock of Ages" music video from *Pyromania*. My mom hated those shorts, and she let me know it. I wore them anyway.

We likely had rented a fog machine from a local costume shop. Most people don't know this, but behind the curtain on the upright piano was my band director Fred Allen, playing the opening line to the rock anthem "Rock n Roll Party in the Streets," by Axe. We stole a play out of Aerosmith's playbook, known to have a keyboardist off side-stage to enhance their sound.

We were amazed at the power our music had on the crowd. We felt invincible. Literally, it was like *Beatlemania*. The girls bum rushed the stage, and Principal Henserling actually got up and shut down the concert in the middle of it. It was total pandemonium.

So we said to each other, "Look, we're good at this, we can get attention doing this and it's fun doing this—so we're going to *do* this." But after a series of shows with Vengeance, which made an impact on the North Texas music scene, Younkin and I were growing in separate directions.

At this point, I was still doing well in school, and as long as my grades were up my mom was okay with it. I wasn't playing football anymore, but I was still an athletic trainer, and I was running for treasurer of the Student Council. I was involved in school activities like choir, drama and, of course, band. I was popular with all the freaks, the jocks, some of the cheerleaders, the music guys and the band nerds. I had a lot of friends. Since we were friends with all different pockets of people, anywhere there was a party we were the band. Many times, after football practice, the jocks from NRJH would come over to my garage and listen to us play ZZ Top, Judas Priest, Iron Maiden and Motley Crue.

I was 16 years old and still in high school, so now there were tensions mounting between me and my mom. She found out I was skipping classes and going to set up in these Dallas/Fort Worth nightclubs, and she became very concerned.

At home, I was thinking, "God, I don't want to be here. I *so* don't want to be here in this boring, conservative, Christian home." I resented my stepfather. I just wanted to go do something with my life.

All of this came to a head one day when my mom said, "Look, I'm concerned. You stay in your room for hours playing your drums. You've got posters of Judas Priest and Iron Maiden and Motley Crue on your wall, and these guys look like gang members. You're playing this metal music, you're rebellious and, under my roof, you're going in the wrong direction, James. You need to be studying. You're a smart kid. You're a good student. You need to prepare for college, and instead you're out there hanging out with this rock 'n' roll crowd."

And I thought, "Oh, man, you're an old-fashioned prude. I want to go out and rock. I want to do this thing, and nobody is going to stop me!"

At the same time, I was missing my dad, and I was only getting to see him every two weeks. I felt like if I lived with my dad I'd have a little more freedom. Now, I tried to justify in my mind that I just missed my dad and wanted to see him, but, looking back, I really was just trying to use the situation for my own freedom.

But, at any rate, my mom said, "Listen, no more of this!"

And I said, "Yeah, there's more of this."

So I packed my drums, and I packed my things, and I said, "Mom, I'm leaving to go live with my dad." I never looked back to my mom's astonishment. I had no idea what I was doing. I was following my heart at the time. My mom remembers me wearing my favorite red-and-white OP Hawaiian shirt, holding my drum sticks, and off I went.

Next, I joined Outright, with Chad Burroughs on vocals, Bryan Taylor on bass, Ruben Aguirre and Brad Spalding (my best friend) on guitar. I played drums. We were playing Top 40 from Journey, The Romantics, Cheap Trick, AC/DC, the Cars, etc., in the teen clubs, and now they were paying us a couple hundred bucks. We hired David Bell as our manager. David was well spoken, astute and a perfect fit.

I had just received a yellow Mazda pickup truck with a camper and sleeper with yellow and orange striped mattress and pillows (what were they thinking?), which my dad and grandfather had designed for me. They had also built and installed a rotary engine in my truck. My dad had a diesel mechanics background, and my grandfather was a pilot, flight instructor and engineer. The truck, with its bulldog hood ornament, would be handy for moving our gear, and, being the drummer, I usually had the most gear to move.

To get the best paying gigs we needed a great PA system and top-notch musical gear. We had been burning money renting from sound men, but we finally found a bargain on a good PA system. The day I received the keys to my truck, bassist/vocalist Bryan Taylor and I set off for Strawn, Texas, more than 90 miles from my home at 3333 Edith Lane in Haltom City, Texas, to go pick up our new PA system. Without the modern conveniences of GPS or cell phones, we were lost for hours trying to find the location of our future PA system. We finally found the right location and loaded the black Peavy PA system into my truck. It was well past dark when we finally arrived in Haltom City, where an irate Mr. Taylor (Bryan's father) waited on our porch, wondering where his son was. As soon as we pulled in the gravel driveway that led to the mechanic's shed my grandfather had built, Mr. Taylor voiced his displeasure with me, ordered Bryan to get in the car, and they sped away.

My dad was furious with me, too. "Son, where have you been?" I responded weakly that we needed the PA system so we could play more gigs and make more money. I will never forget that day. My grandfather asked me, "James Michael, do you know why we gave you that truck?"

I said, "No, why?"

"To drive it." he said calmly. I knew that was his way of saying that on life's open road to adventure, sometimes you have to take chances. That day, I felt he was on my side. And, as a teenager, getting this kind of attention and having this much fun playing in a rock band, I didn't want it to stop.

In time, my dad graciously upgraded my little CB700 kit to a TAMA Brazilian wood Rockstar kit. He took me to C&S Music in Duncanville, Texas. The kit was $2,000–$3,000. It had all the bells and whistles, including Zildjian cymbals. I really had the tools to craft my drumming now. I left C&S with a big smile on my face. My dad made sure I had the best Riddell football helmet and cleats and the best Shakespeare fishing rod. He did many wonderful things for me, but nothing could top this. I mean, a gorgeous seven-piece TAMA Brazilian wood drum kit with Zildjian cymbals and LP percussion—wow!

Brad Spalding and I continued playing cover songs anywhere we could set up. We listened to music and wrote songs at his parents' home behind the North Richland Hills Police Department. Brad had an incredible stereo system for the time. We would sit in the living room floor and read the liner notes for Motley Crue's *Shout at the Devil* or Stryper's *Yellow and Black Attack*, and we would read *Metal Edge* magazine and dream of being famous rock stars. We also had copies of *BAM* magazine from Hollywood through our mutual friend Charlie Spradling, who had ventured to Los Angeles during high school to become an actress. We would thumb through page after page of LA bands with the "look" that every record company wanted at the time and were hungry to make it.

The Spalding's had a quaint home, fostered by a loving mother, Karen, and a stepfather, Mike, who was a psychiatrist. They were always "spot on" with the cookouts, making us hamburgers and cultivating an environment for us to hang out and work on our songs. We soon converted their garage to our rehearsal studio and spent countless hours "woodshedding" our musical skills for bigger stages.

I was 16 years old in 1983 when we formed Teazer and hooked up with an older bassist named Rusty James, from Carrollton, Texas. Now, Rusty James was from the rough side of the tracks. He was tall and intimidating and had the number "13" tattooed on his shoulder. Rusty rode motorcycles. We wondered what we were getting ourselves into at 16 years old, but Rusty was "cool" and had a street sense. By this time, the major-label rock band WASP had made an impact on rock music, and Rusty was a huge Blackie Lawless fan (WASP's frontman and bassist). WASP were over the top in their giant black boots on fire, long manes of hair and roughhouse image. They were loud and aggressive.

Rusty was hooked up with a guitarist, Dennis Keyes, and they needed another guitar player, so Brad and I joined the band. Teazer needed the right frontman, and we discovered this singer, Chad Haynes, who was a sort of spinoff of Vince Neil of Motley Crue—one of the biggest rock bands at the time.

So Brad and I joined Teazer and began playing at free beer night at the Ritz in downtown Dallas. We would go over to the Ritz on school nights, with 1,000–1,200 people in this club. We were surrounded by beautiful blonde women wearing miniskirts, alongside rockers with earrings and mullets. Upstairs, in the balcony, DJ Chaz Mixon from KZEW 98 FM was spinning the rock music that Ritz patrons loved (the Ritz's infamous second-story stage was amazing).

People from all over the Metroplex came in droves to hear Teazer. We would go out to the Gemini drive-in movie theater on Highway 75 in Dallas, get drunk, get high and pass out flyers to a thousand people to try to amass a following. It was our Sunset Strip.

We played all the metal music of the time: Motley Crue, Anthrax, Armored Saint—even Metallica before they were wildly popular. We were doing songs like "Four Horsemen" and "Creeping Death" off Metallica's *Kill 'Em All* album before anyone had heard "For Whom the Bell Tolls." I had to really practice at getting the double bass drum rolls down, as Lars Ulrich of Metallica was lightning fast. Vinnie Paul of Pantera had also become a great double bass drummer from all the gigs Pantera played locally at Joe's Garage, Matley's Phase 2 on Skillman in Dallas and at Savvy's in Fort Worth.

Soon, KZEW 98 FM and KTXQ 102 FM were playing Teazer's demo, which we had recorded and self produced. Teazer's first demo featured songs like "Guns for Hire" and "On the Run." We were actually pretty good for that era. We would stay out playing until 2 a.m., and then we would drive home to North Richland Hills, go to bed and get three hours of sleep. Then I would get up, throw on some clothes and go to class.

Teazer booked a road show, opening for Armored Saint in Wichita Falls, Texas. Money was scarce, but we were stoked to be in another city opening for a red hot band like Armored Saint. Wichita Falls is a big military town (I think we were on a military base), and I remember seeing a sea of sweaty guys with clenched fists in the air, symbolizing "metal."

Since there were five band mates in Teazer (and a few roadies, of course), feeding the band required ingenuity. Most of our humble earnings wound up on our bar tab. We were known to light up the bar and sell plenty of alcohol for the club owners. The shots flew—Lemon Drops, Jagermeister, Crown Royal, Colorado Bulldogs—one by one, until the combination of head banging and booze gave us menacing headaches.

One night, we had about $10 in the band's "kitty," so Rusty walked into the local Pizza Inn with his empty bass guitar case. Dressed in his trademark black fishnet, tattoos on his sleeves, head band, leather pants and shades, he strolled in, paid for the buffet and wolfed down his meal. Then, on his way out, he crammed his guitar case full of pizza and returned to the band headquarters to feed the rest of us. We were in heaven. At other times, we would buy a loaf of Wonder bread and a jar of peanut butter and survive on sandwiches to satisfy our hunger pangs.

I remember crazy summer nights, still a teenager, sneaking out to the parking lot in my Mazda truck and getting into some convenient mischief between sets. Boy meets girl, boy asks girl to come along, temptations rage, and in between our set and the headliner I began to sleep with women or have sexual interactions.

One night at The Ritz, I went home with an attractive older woman, probably about 29 years old (I was only 17). She was beautiful and had a chic apartment. I woke up about 5 a.m., not really knowing where I had been. I saw on the woman's nightstand a picture of the late, great Led Zeppelin vocalist Robert Plant, which, somehow, I rationalized into feeling that I had been in the company of greatness. I scrambled to get to school, stopping to change clothes in the McDonald's restroom on Rufe Snow. I went on to class disheveled but grinning and thinking, in my schoolboy brain, that I had really done something macho.

I was 17 years old, right around the end of my time with Teazer. Brad and I had earned a strong reputation on the scene in Dallas, and there were several popular bands like Pantera, who went on to sign with ATCO Records, tour the world and sell millions of records, Sweet Savage, the biggest draw on L.A.'s Sunset Strip when they inked a record deal, and the Molly Maguires, DFW's own most popular band, playing all the top venues. The Molly Maguires were a big draw in a Fort Worth club called Savvy's, which was one of the larger night clubs. At that time, the Ritz was open, and there was also Matley's Phase II in Dallas.

Meanwhile, Dirty Blonde, a touring rock band travelling regionally, was going outside of Texas into Oklahoma, Louisiana and other states. Dirty Blonde's agent was Mike Hyrka, with Greater Southwest Talent. Bryant Hunter, lead guitar player with Ricky Lynn Gregg, put Dirty Blonde together, and they were playing an average of six nights a week. They were making around one to three grand a week, which that meant each band member was making $400–$500 bucks, plus the free drinks, the perks and the lifestyle.

Dirty Blonde held auditions for guitarists and drummers, and Bryant heard about Brad because he consistently placed in the top three at Texas guitar player competitions judged by "Diamond Darrell" Abbott of Pantera. Brad was extremely gifted. Bryant approached him and said they also needed a drummer because their drummer, Craig, was leaving. Brad and I interviewed with Bryant Hunter and a friend of ours, Chad Allen, who was already in the band, and the four of us became Dirty Blonde.

Dirty Blonde went on tour when I had only one semester of high school left. I had an A average in all subjects, with honors in everything, and I went to my dad and said, "Dad, I need your permission. I'm going on the road. I'm leaving high school with one semester left. What do you think about that?"

Well, Mom was livid. How could my dad possibly do such a thing and allow me to get away with it? My mom wanted to see me walk across the stage with my graduating class, as any parent would, but thanks to my persistence and my dad's passivity, she was denied a milestone in my life.

My dad, on the other hand, said, "Well, Son, you know, if you want, pursue your dream, but you have to make us this promise: You have to promise that after the tour's over you will go back to summer school and knock out the rest of your high school."

I said, "Sure," and then we took off on one of the greatest adventures of our lives. We were 17 years old, and they were sending us to Doc Livingston's club in Corpus Christi, one of the highlights of the city, right there on the beach. We were there for two weeks. We were the house band, so we would set up our gear once, and we didn't have to tear down for 14 days. We would walk in, play music during the day, do our sound check and play at night. We were playing three sets of Led Zeppelin, Deep Purple, Alice Cooper, KISS, Ted Nugent—all of these bands that really rocked, and we just *nailed* it. We were a great band, they wanted us and we were in demand. They fed us, the hotel rooms were awesome, the pools were awesome and, of course, the girls were always there. It was normal to have our hotel rooms flooded with tanned beauties who didn't mind sharing their wares. I was learning the ropes early on and taking full advantage of the opportunities. It was an incredible experience for a young man full of wonder.

About nine months into Dirty Blonde, there was a little dissension in the band. Brad and I were saying, "Look, we're not going anywhere playing cover songs. Yeah, we can get up here and play four 45-minute sets and rock it out, but this band is nothing but a cover band. We're making a few hundred bucks a week, but we need to venture out on our own."

So, after Dirty Blonde, I said, "Okay, Brad and I are going to do something original," and we parted ways. Then, about 1987, Brad and I formed a new band that would really change things as far as writing original music and seriously pursuing becoming rock stars.

Chapter 4
Marching to the Beat of a Different Drummer

As of 1982, I had played in junior high and high school bands, metal bands and rock bands, and graduated to the top of the Dallas-Fort Worth music scene. My musicianship carried me to the regional scene, and I learned a lot about the music business early in my career. Dirty Blonde founder Bryant Hunter and Mike Hyrka from Greater Southwest Management taught me to think like a business man, which proved to be very valuable to my music career.

Before the reformation of ChazaRetta in 1987, my dad bought my TAMA Brazilian wood drum kit, and, as I mentioned earlier, I practiced, practiced and practiced. I knew my drum kit inside out. My next drum kit was a TAMA Superstar, with a white acrylic finish. My white Superstar drum kit boasted two 24- inch kick drums, a 12 x 14 rack tom, a 14 x 14 rack tom, a 5 ½-inch TAMA maple snare, a 16 x 16 floor tom and an 18-inch floor tom. Erik Skjolsvik, my good friend from high school, became a famous artist designing backdrops for major label bands all over the world.

Erik helped me design decals, which he airbrushed to accentuate my white glossy kit with all shades of purple and blue. No one had ever designed anything like it before. We also airbrushed my name "Jamie Powers" on my double bass drum heads. It was visual, it was cool, and after the show someone always appreciated our design. Erik deserves all the credit for creating a new reality on my drum kit.

During ChazaRetta, "Jamie Powers" was my stage name. As a youngster, everyone called me Jimmy, but I thought that sounded like a farmer's name, so I decided to change it to Jamie. In Teazer, my stage name was "Jamie Blaze," and in Dirty Blonde and ChazaRetta, "Jamie Powers." So, at every performance, the lead singer would announce, "Ladies and gentlemen, welcome, on the drum kit, Mr. "Jamie Blaze," or "Jamie Powers." Wow, talk about show business! Most of the rock icons we idolized had names like "Nikki Sixx," "Blackie Lawless" or "Vik Foxx."

As a child, Elvis was my greatest influence. I used to mimic the King of Rock 'n' Roll at Christmas parties and reunions, gyrating around on my grandparents' floor singing "Hound Dog." I wasn't sure I wanted to *be* Elvis, but I loved the beat, the rhythm and the freedom in his music. When I fell in love with the drums, I was studying Gene Krupa and Buddy Rich, quintessential musicians first, but ultimately drummers who were spectacular showmen. Then I watched Tommy Lee, who came out flashy—twirling his sticks in the Motley Crue video "Looks That Kill" on MTV—and his drums were on fire. Alex Van Halen intrigued me with his four bass drums on Van Halen's "Fair Warning" tour when "Unchained," a heavy driving rock riff showed up on MTV. I found interesting poly rhythms in Stewart Copeland's drumming from The Police, who incorporated TAMA octabons, strange cymbals and Jamaican percussion to create his precision reggae. Terry Bozzio, drummer/musician with Missing Persons and for guitarist Frank Zappa, was a real clinician. I was influenced by Dennis Chambers, who could play serious funk. Old-school guys like Papa Joe Jones, who influenced John Henry Bonham from Led Zeppelin, also found a place in my drumming vocabulary. There were so many influences, and all of them were shaping me as a player.

I loved listening to my influences on vinyl, cassette and 8-track, but I also loved watching the performers on video, and I loved the freedom of the drums. Initially, I played guitar, but I found it boring to sit there and pluck on six strings. During a guitar solo, you can go up and down the neck and make these cool sounds with the pedals, but with the drums your imagination can create anything such as a stunning visual with the sound. Just think of John Bonham or Tommy Aldridge fervently bashing their drums and cymbals with their bare hands, Dave Grohl of Nirvana and the late Keith Moon of The Who demolishing their drum kit at the end of a scorching performance, or Tommy Lee's Roller Coaster drum kit that catapulted him 360 degrees around the circular track where he plays suspended upside down. All of these musicians and their artistry and creativity were stirred up inside me.

In all my early bands, we were doing cover songs and not thinking like original artists. As a result, Brad and I revamped ChazaRetta, from the original lineup (1983) of Eric Younkin (Eric coined the name), John Phillips and Peter Nepo. Brad and I became the *new* ChazaRetta. We took the name, and now we had to actually find the band.

Chad, bassist/vocalist in Dirty Blonde, joined us, so now all ChazaRetta needed was a new singer. I phoned Nepo, my schoolmate. Nepo had the look, and he was a good frontman, so he was in. We began rehearsing and writing original material to blend in with our cover songs that would get our foot in the door at the top DFW clubs. Pantera and Sweet Savage, the top two local draws were the bands we needed to open for to build our following.

In addition to their own songs, these bands played AC/DC, Dokken, RATT, Motley Crue and Van Halen to keep the nightclub partiers happy with music they heard every day on the radio. Both Pantera and Sweet Savage had massive followings and played Savvy's and Matley's Phase 2 every weekend. ChazaRetta worked up our show and began networking in all the clubs and gentlemen's clubs. I remember we built about 30 amplifier cabinets without speakers, just for the visual. Skjolsvik crafted a professional banner that matched our amps and my drum kit. Our musical gear was top tier, but we still had to compete with Pantera's and Sweet Savage's monstrous back line. We would hang out behind the chain link fence at Savvy's, which fenced off the minors, while partying and watching the bands. We knew what flasks were and how to sneak the alcohol into our sodas or take a straight shot of whiskey or tequila.

In those days, any opening band with Marshall half stack amps against the headliner's eight amplifiers per side looked frail on stage. Most hard rock bands were "over the top," from the moment Van Halen launched it's Fair Warning tour, which displayed maximum opulence, featuring Alex Van Halen's drum kit with four bass drums and a never-ending staircase of toms, nestled between hundreds of speaker cabinets per side for Eddie Van Halen and Van Halen bassist Michael Anthony. Given this scenario, we not only had to write great songs people could rock out to, but we also had to build a massive stage show that would attract the audience and hold our own against the most popular acts of the time.

ChazaRetta were fortunate to open for Pantera and Sweet Savage on several shows. I confess, there were a few funny moments, like the time Joey C. Jones walked into Savvy's and saw our massive back line of purple amps set up and my drum kit standing proud upon Savvy's drum riser. He said with his laid back vibe, "Surely all the opener's back line is not staying up there is it?" ChazaRetta was Savvy's house band during the week, and our gear was already in place. Pantera and Sweet Savage were a few years older than we were, and had both already released their own records, so we knew all we had to do was work hard during the week, craft our own songs and open for the headliners on the weekends, and we would attract a following.

ChazaRetta were playing week nights, three sets per night, Tuesday through Thursday, and then on the weekends, when the main headliners came in, we would strike our gear to make room for theirs. It was all about who had the best musicians, the biggest hair and the most gear, as it is today in music—very competitive.

ChazaRetta enjoyed our days as the house band at Savvy's. We continued opening for Pantera and building our fan base. Once, I recall playing at Matley's Phase 2, opening for the original Pantera line up, and I had to play Vinnie Paul's electronic drums, which sounded killer, but, of course, I preferred to play my own drum kit. I wanted the audience to know who I was by seeing my name displayed on the double bass drums, but, sometimes, when you're the opener, you play the headliners drum kit and bring your own cymbals. Life was full of surprises, and I always tried to be a good sport and recognize the opportunity to learn from great musicians like Pantera. Pantera's sound man, Ambrose, loved us as musicians and was always kind to us. We hired him when Pantera wasn't performing.

Pantera parted ways with original vocalist Terry Glaze (Lord Tracy) after blazing the trail across the Southwest playing a more straight ahead rock style. Interim vocalist Donny Hart subbed several shows until Phil Anselmo from Razor White was selected as their new lead singer.

With Phil, Pantera had a much edgier, hardcore sound. I was at the first show that Phil did with Pantera. Pantera quickly changed its straight ahead rock style to hardcore Texas metal and inked a solid record deal with ATCO Records. Soon, *Cowboys from Hell,* Pantera's first release, went on to sell millions of records worldwide.

ChazaRetta continued playing shows with Sweet Savage, the biggest band on the LA circuit, and Brunette, the biggest rock act from the East Coast, along with Mannekkin, the best from Maryland. All these bands traveled with major productions: 64–128 Par 64 lighting rigs, concert sound and amazing gear. It raised the bar for us.

I started playing night clubs at age 17. Savvy's had a chain link fence in the club to separate the minors from the drinkers, and they would put a big X on the minors' hands. We thought we were having so much fun. We would drink in the parking lot before the show. Any shots of alcohol that came our way were a bonus, and, of course, someone always had a joint to smoke or a line of cocaine. It was one thing to be in the audience and behind the chain link fence partying, but it was a whole other dimension when playing on stage six nights a week—making $600 a week with a killer production—at 17 years old. We had an "in" with the club owner Rick Miller (drummer and founder of Savvy the band), so we started opening for people like Pat Travers and Blue Oyster Cult, Eddie Money and all these big names that came through.

Soon, a music agent named Buck Judkins, artist relations for Pat Travers, Greg Almann, Black Oak Arkansas, Blue Oyster Cult, Ted Nugent, and all kinds of bands in that vein, approached us and said, "Look, I think you guys have something- I can help you."

I asked him, "How can you help us?"

Buck said, "Well, I work for *Performance Magazine*, and we place all the artists we represent in the magazine. I think I can get your ad in there. The only stipulation is we're going to move over offices, and I need you guys to show up with a Ryder truck and help us move some furniture."

I was thinking, "No big deal, we'll just go over there to help this guy move some furniture around, and we'll get a half-page ad in this magazine. And all these agents will know who we are and what we're doing, and it will be awesome." So we put out this ad that said, "Get your Rock Hot on Cha-Cha Records." In our promotional picture we were all dressed up to the hilt. The 80s were all about "eye candy," and you also had to be able to actually play your instrument, or you were a poser. We practiced rigorously to ensure we were respected as musicians.

Buck called and said, "It's time to move the magazine offices in downtown Fort Worth." But what we thought might take an hour turned out to be a long, arduous day. They had desks coming out of the basement of their offices. It was desk after desk, and boxes of books, that were very heavy, and we had to go up and down stairs to load them in the truck. We were all laughing at the pain we had to go through just to pay the price for this magazine ad.

ChazaRetta was wildly popular from 1987-1988. Chad eventually joined another band. We recruited Dennis Keyes from Teazer to play bass, and this lineup lasted another year.

ChazaRetta released our EP *Get Your Rock Hot*, which did very well, and we were reeling from our success. Laura Church (owner of Church's Fried Chicken) managed The Cause, represented by our agent Buck Judkins, and considered backing us. We staged a massive production at the Irving Cultural Arts Center; we were the house band at Savvy's; we were doing bigger and better things.

1988 brought about a "cool change" (a lyric from the Little River band). Brad and I decided to move on to the next chapter of our music. Although ChazaRetta accomplished many of our objectives, such as improving our songwriting, musicianship, stage presence and following, we were looking to do something different musically. We still had solid relationships with the clubs in Dallas and Fort Worth, so Brad and I decided to find a new bass player. Dennis was gone, and we soon parted ways with ChazaRetta's lead vocalist, Nepo.

Brad attended TCC (a junior college in North Richland Hills), taking music classes, where he met a laid back musician Steve Thompson. Steve played trumpet in high school and was studying bass guitar and music theory. Steve and Brad quickly became friends. Brad told me, "I've found the perfect bass player. Man, this guy looks cool, he's a great writer and he has a good sense of melody."

I said, "Bring it on," and the three of us scheduled a jam session. I felt that of all the bands I had been in, this one had superior potential as far as what we could do musically. Brad and I continued to write songs—this was back when we would stay up late and get the four-track out and try to ping-pong all the tracks and get as much out of the tracks as we could, and after a session go to the nearby Whataburger for dinner at 2 a.m. We shared a tiny one-bedroom in Meadowbrook, at the time, with nothing but our dreams and musical gear and rock star threads.

We pushed the limits of home recording with our Tascam and Fostex four-track recorders long before Pro Tools or any of software we have today. We would chill and write songs and practice our instruments all day, while working our craft. We knew that all great bands—not mediocre bands but great ones—need a great singer. Where would Queensryche have been without Geoff Tate? British metal superstars Iron Maiden dominated audiences with blistering musicianship as the background for the piercing lead vocals of Bruce Dickenson. Imagine stadium rockers Queen without Freddie Mercury? Led Zeppelin without the bluesy rant of Robert Plant? Great bands needed a great singer. In rock music, that is an absolute.

In our quest for a new vocalist, Brad and I went out to area Dallas live music venues decked out in our rock regalia with our hair spiked to the max. The Rage, a favorite Dallas hard rock venue, booked "Burlesque," a rising metal band with a great team of musicians who effortlessly played Queensryche, Judas Priest and Van Halen.

On stage, Matt Story, lead vocalist, was literally dressed in fishnet hose and tall black leather boots, with a headband and long, waist length black hair. He looked half vampire, half rock star, and he commanded the audience with moxie and attitude. He opened his mouth and out came a high pitched voice. Matt could definitely sing the highs. Back then, it was impressive when your singer could wail and hold out a scream that pierced an audience's ears.

Queensryche, a very proficient Metal band from Seattle emerged to the top, and if you could sing Queensryche then you were a singer. Matt Story could sing Queensryche; not only that, but he was very obnoxious on stage and knew how to lead the party with his David Lee Roth inspiration from early Van Halen. We needed a ballsy front man who would stir up the crowd and get the audience drinking.

We said, "Hey, Matt what do you think? We've got the light show, we've got the best sound system, and we've got the house gig with Dallas City Limits. Are you in?"

Matt replied "Yes, I am in!"

Dallas City Limits (DCL), Dallas' premier rock club was located on Northwest Highway, down the street from Baby Doll's, and Dallas Gentlemen's Club was nearby. The party zone was right there, with Dallas City Limits in the center. Dallas City Limits was a brand new club. The dancers at the gentlemen's club, wanted to party with the rock bands after work or in between shifts. Even if they just took off an hour, they would see a show, have a few drinks, party and maybe dance. It was the perfect marriage (at least, I thought so at the time).

All the big names in rock began to tour Dallas City Limits: Vince Neil from Motley Crue, Cinderella, which was multiplatinum on ATCO/ Atlantic, Faith No More and Zakk Wylde from Ozzy Osbourne. And it just so happened that we were tight with DCL Club owner Leon Maner, so Outrageous became the house band (after I talked him into it). We promised to promote, promote and promote to ensure we would get the opening slot for many of the national touring bands that came to play concerts at DCL.

Our crew helped us in any way needed and exuded professionalism. Often, only hours before the major recording artist rolled up in their bus to get a sound check, our crew was there with all hands on deck. It helped to make friends with the musicians who were "in the know," in addition to their road managers and soundmen. We had the best DFW could offer with sound man Hobie Bacus (Garth Brooks) running sound for us on a massive PA system that soon became DCL's house system. We were experimenting with effects on the drums during my drum solos, Brad's guitar solo and Matt's vocals; Hobie "dialed" in our sound. Eddie Connel's colorful lighting rig stayed in house and all the touring acts were lining up to play DCL.

We brought in a great production and played a couple of sets, except this time we played the modern music of the day from Judas Priest, The Cult, Living Colour and Queensryche, with Aerosmith and Zeppelin thrown in for good measure. We kept everybody happy, but we also did our original songs. We kept working on our originals, and Outrageous released a four-song EP with "Steal Away," "Hip Shakin' Heart Breakin'," "Shotgunn Sex" and "Alright Allnight," with producer Terrance Slemmons. Behind the scenes, we rehearsed at a music complex off I-35 and Mockingbird, where the Old Brook Mays Pro Shop used to be. We hooked up with a musician/producer who happened to have a bankroll, although we never really knew where it came from. He was generous to allow Outrageous to set up in this 20,000–plus-square foot air conditioned warehouse. We basically lived there, partied there and slept there. The craziness of it all was that this complex was right across from the fire department, and, ironically, drugs were being dealt out of there. Fortunately, we did not go down with the drugs.

Our EP attracted the attention of music mogul Kim Fowley from California. He had recently moved to Austin. Kim co-wrote "God of Thunder" with KISS, and he also wrote songs for Poison (top draw on Sunset Strip in LA), Guns N' Roses and other big names. He was a major producer. A friend of mine, Missy Veltman, who was in the music business, told me about Kim. She said, "You guys need to send your demo," so we did.

Kim heard the demo and said, "Listen, I love the music. I love the catchy songs. I love the musicianship, but the singer has to go. He is not the bluesy vocalist you need. The sound is changing." We had spent two years with Matt. We really loved Matt, and, besides, we were having so much fun doing the Miss Outrageous contests, where scantily clad ladies would compete for cash money, and our shows were always full of beautiful women. Now, all the dancers were coming and dancing to our music and winning $250 in the wet T-shirt contests. Of course all the guys flocked to wherever there were ladies and rock 'n' roll. We had a good thing. Kim, however, insisted that we get another singer if we were going to work with him, and he insisted we move to Austin.

It was a huge decision. This might be our best shot. We always kept up with what was going on in LA. We read *BAM Magazine* (Deborah Rosener was the publisher), *RIP* magazine and *Metal Edge Magazine.* I became friends with Gerri Miller from New York (Editor of *Metal Edge*), who was paying attention to what we were doing miles away in Texas. We would see all these signed famous bands in these magazines on the newsstand, and we wanted to be *those* bands.

Now it was 1990. We decided to take our chances, so the three of us—Brad, Steve and I—went down to Austin and hooked up with Missy Veltman. Wayne Nagel was a big-time music agent at the time with Pariah, Dangerous Toys and other major recording artists. We were in the middle of a hotbed of artists getting signed.

Outrageous no longer fit the bluesy direction we were heading. Brad had grown tremendously fond of Texas guitar hero "Stevie Ray Vaughn" and "Eric Johnson," along with blues legends "Eric Clapton," "Robert Johnson," "Jimi Hendrix," etc. As a lead guitarist and songwriter, Brad had drastically matured musically since 1983 in Teazer. We knew we had what it took to reach the next level. Brad was left handed and known as "The Texas Chainsaw Southpaw." Brad was also a shredder and could play Yngwie Malmsteen, Randy Rhoads and Eddie Van Halen to the "T." His guitar work would be a centerpiece of the band. We named the band Redhouse, taken from an old Jimi Hendrix classic. Our sound was in stark contrast to grunge, which originated in the Northwest through bands like Mudhoney, Nirvana and Mother Love Bone. The hair bands were still alive, but Redhouse was a little more edgy than that. We were really ahead of our time. My drumming began to meld drum loops and sequences into our songs, which was fairly uncommon in a bluesy rock band.

We found ourselves in "boot camp" with Kim Fowley. Kim was known for being hard on his artists, and he was eccentric, as we soon found out. I remember grocery shopping in Austin with Kim, and it was a trip. If I recall, Kim was dancing in the aisle of the HEB and possibly even stepping inside the diary cooler where the butter was located.

We were focused and serious. Kim was proposing we spend our days and nights rehearsing and then performing in the area Austin night clubs. We quickly searched for a new singer. The flyer read as follows:

Lead singer needed. Must have a bluesy voice.

We have a major Hollywood producer, we have backing and we're in the studio.

$100 reward.

We hoped somebody would bite, and, after a lot of really bad singers auditioned, we got a call from ex-Katt Daquiri vocalist Mike Madison. Madison played one of the clubs we had played (where Pantera built their following), Joe's Garage in Fort Worth, opening for Pantera. Mike called one day and said, "Hey, I found your singer."

I said, "No way!"

Mike said, "Yeah, I found your singer, and I want the hundred dollar reward."

I said, "Well, who is the singer?"

He said, "I'm the singer, and when I show up to audition I want you to pay me my hundred bucks."

Mike came in and just nailed it. He had that bluesy, soulful voice and a commanding stage presence. He loved the Beatles and had a great musical grounding under him. He was a perfect fit. We said, "Wow, we've got this deal done!" We never paid Mike a hundred bucks, even though he deserved it. Mike was a great vocalist, guitarist and songwriter.

Well, guess what? We found Mike too late, and Kim Fowley backed out of the deal. Our hopes with the high-level Hollywood producer crashed, and we wondered what we were going to do next.

Of course, Redhouse would carry on. In 1990, Redhouse went back to all the same clubs where we had established our name in previous bands.

By now, The Basement was up and running in Dallas, so we were headlining at Dallas City Limits, Smokin' Dave's Rock Room and The Rock Garden. Redhouse opened for many national acts, such as Faith No More, Enuff Z Nuff, Vince Neil of Motley Crue, Dirty Looks, Chris Whitley and others. Redhouse became one of the headlining acts at The Basement. We covered the Metroplex in flyers, while subsequently appearing in *Metal Edge* magazine. You could walk into any supermarket, approach the newsstand, open *Metal Edge* and Redhouse was there. Q102 KTXQ FM with Redbeard and Long Jim White loved our music and played it on "Texas Tapes." Like most DFW acts trying to make a name, we played a few of the Q102's famous "Bring in the Weekend" parties. Their slogan "anything goes" was true.

Redhouse was a band with gifted musicians and songwriters. Redhouse penned catchy, bluesy songs such as "Thrill City," "Heat," a speedy rocker "Rockin' Horse" and a beautiful ballad "Which Lie." We had great songs, and people were digging our unique original sound.

Redhouse covered AC/DC and Led Zeppelin—plus, we were doing our own music. When people came to see Redhouse, they got crazy. Mike was a partier. He was the frontman of all frontmen. He'd have them toasting until 2 in the morning.

45

Darrell, Vinnie and Rex from Pantera, who were international rock stars at this point, after *Cowboys From Hell* sold more than three million records, had been following us throughout our career, ever since we opened for them at Matley's Phase2. It was more important now, because Derek Shulman and Derek Oliver, two of the main A&R reps for ATCO Records, who had signed Pantera, were also paying attention to Redhouse.

More than ever in our seven-year history of writing and recording, our music was at another level. We were also getting solicitations by record companies and shopping our songs that we produced. Our live show was receiving acclaim from fans and top musicians; we had an immaculate production staged by our Manager Mick Panasci (Boston, Van Halen and the Rolling Stones). When you entered the front door at Dallas City Limits, with its array of lights and enormous PA system, you would see triangles hung from the lighting trusses with sheer fabric that would reflect spotlights and project holographs onto the triangles during songs like "Tripping Into Darkness" and "New Religion." Brad created a haunting bluesy slide guitar pattern for the intro as the drums of thunder entered and Mike sang razor-edged lyrics over the arrangement. People were mesmerized.

Redhouse was edging closer to a possible production deal with ATCO, and, all a sudden, after all these years pursuing my dream and leaving my family in the rear view mirror, something tragic and unexpected happened.

Prior to this, my dad and my sister Marilyn would come over once in a while and have a beer with me at The Basement. My dad would say, "Hey, you know, I want to have another stout with you." My dad just enjoyed himself, although on a few nights he had a little too much to drink. We had that kind of relationship. All my band mates called him "Pops."

After almost a decade of hard work in the music industry, thanks to my dad's support, I had realized my teenage hope of being a professional musician in a rock band. My parents' friend Rocky Shores was a drummer when I was just under 5 years old, and I recall how big his Pearl drum kit seemed and how desperately I wanted to learn how to play like him. Later on, in my pre teens, Chuck Whitby taught me "syncopation" at Christian Temple Church, enabling me to play four different rhythmic patterns with each limb.

My dad did wonderful things for me. Yes, he was hard on me at times when he would come after me in anger, but, overall, I know he loved me. I was his "little buddy." But in the midst of my rock lifestyle (playing 5–6 nights a week and going to bed at 5 a.m.), after a post-concert breakfast at Whataburger one morning I got a phone call. It was my grandparents.

My grandpa said, "Michael, your dad has passed away."

I said, "What?"

He said, "Your dad passed away in his sleep. He just woke up to get some ice water this morning, and then he went to lie back down on the bed. We came back home, and your cousin Kim had come downstairs, and discovered he was gone."

I was in disbelief—shock. All I ever wanted to do was the music. All I ever wanted to do was prove to my dad that I could be somebody. And I wanted to prove to my mom that I could still be a good person, even after running away from home and pursuing rock stardom.

After my dad passed away, I put everything on hold. During the funeral services, a Redhouse song, "Father to Son," rang true.

There's a little boy with solemn eyes and dreams no one can realize or see.

No one else can see.

But there's a man that still believes and takes his child upon his knee

And he tries to make his son a man.

And when the boy is older and grown, this man will teach him all that he knows in a world that sometimes is so cold.

But little does the boy realize that the love that comes from his father's eyes is real, and no one else can feel.

My dad's funeral was chilling. It was surreal. I had an opportunity to run to my mom and say, "Mom, forgive me for running away. I'm a prodigal. I need you, and I need my family, and I need healing." But instead I ran deeper into the music. When the funeral was over, to escape from the numbing pain of separation, I ran right back into the sex, drugs and rock 'n' roll.

The money I received from my dad's inheritance wasn't a huge sum—but the money I did get, I invested it in my dream. With a couple of thousand bucks, Redhouse wrote and recorded our songs at Dallas Sound Labs in Las Colinas. Alongside engineer Terrance Slemmons, Redhouse produced our best recordings ever. I began shopping it to major companies. Redhouse garnered interest from ATCO Records A&R reps Derek Shulman and Derek Oliver, who had signed Pantera. It was common for Vinnie, Dimebag and Rex to show up for Redhouse's last set at Dallas City Limits.

We became good friends with Pantera. One of my vivid memories with Pantera lead guitarist "Dimebag" Darrell Abbott was taking some valium, maybe quaaludes, and heavy shots of Jagermeister and going back to his place in Arlington, where we partied in the garage with a few acoustic guitars, writing a very fitting song "It's Only Rock 'n' Roll." The chorus went like this: *It's only rock 'n' roll / It's only rock 'n' roll / When it gets down into your soul / It's only rock 'n' roll.* I would describe it as very Ace Frehley-ish (KISS guitarist). I remember singing the song

47

until we both passed out.

Dimebag Darrell was a true guitar legend and a caring human being whose life was tragically taken during a December 2004 shooting spree in an Ohio night club while he was on stage with his band DamagePlan—a tragedy.

Redhouse's excitement lasted until my best friend, Brad—the guy whose house I stayed at every other day; the guy who I wrote song lyrics with and looked at our favorite records together; the guy I stood in front of his bedroom mirror with and put Aquanet in my hair until it stood straight up; the guy who was my brother all those years—this guy, the Texas Chainsaw Southpaw, was ready to call it quits.

Brad underwent a surgical procedure, which I was unaware of, requiring hospitalization for a few days. Who knows what was really going on? Brad later shared with me, "I sat there in the hospital thinking, 'What am I going to do? I have no insurance. I have no car. Do I really have a future with this rock band? Where is this thing going?'"

Brad met a wonderful young lady, Holly, and he decided he was going to start a new life and a new future, so he and Holly planned to get married. He was through with the music, leaving me without my best friend and lifelong band mate.

Brad accomplished so much musically from our small beginnings in Teazer at The Ritz to placing in the top three finalists in the guitar contests judged by Dimebag Darrell from Pantera. Anyone who has kept up with rock and metal music knows the legend that Dime left behind. Brad had gained such a reputation on the DFW music scene that Slaughter, an 80s band signed to Chrysalis Records, called and wanted him to audition. Brad was in the top three finalists with late Slaughter guitarist Tim Kelly. At the time, I hoped Slaughter needed a drummer, but they had already settled on Blas Elias from Houston. Now, our friendship and musical relationship was final. I had just lost my dad, and now my best friend. I thought, "What next?"

After all we had achieved together in Redhouse, our lives were going in different directions. Brad was going to get married, and, in 1992, I would start a new chapter in my life.

Chapter 5
Crossing Over

My new journey was not just about music; it was about learning to cope after the loss of my dad. I was now in school again, studying nutrition science in an attempt to understand why my dad passed away suddenly at age 45.

I felt numb after losing my dad. I sat in the funeral home paralyzed. I was in shock. I had a lot to learn. I had a lot of growing up to do. I ran away from home at 17 to pursue my dream of becoming a rock star, and I never was interested in my dad's idea of me going into the Air Force Academy. I was pierced to the heart. No amount of drugs, alcohol or pretty women could fill the emptiness I felt inside at 24 years of age. I ran away from God, I ran away from my family, and I wanted to crawl inside my songs and the rock 'n' roll lifestyle and never come out. I needed something bold and fresh in which to pour my life. Separation from my band mates in Redhouse and losing my dad in 1991 left a deep mark on my soul. My dream seemed as lost as a mountain climber in a snowstorm on Mount Everest.

In 1992, some profound things happened in my life. Ty Thomas, guitarist and songwriter, formed an alternative rock band "The Crossing." Ty approached me in the restroom at West Side Story, a Fort Worth nightclub, about recording with his new band.

Physically I was in good shape, because I had been playing drums on average five nights a week for a decade straight. My trademark was to take my post behind the drum kit shirtless, usually wearing leather pants or, occasionally, jeans. My hair flowed near my waistline; I had been growing it out since I was 14.

Ty's father, a.k.a, "Titanic" Thomas, was a famous gambler. Ty wore a bright white smile and had long brown hair and a beard. He often wore jeans and cowboy boots, with a flowing chiffon shirt, loop earrings and the trademark scarf. Ty was a confident band leader.

Ty partnered with an amazing bassist, vocalist and artist, Derek Lothian, from North Carolina, the son of a doctor. Derek had Jim Morrison features: strong cheekbones, dark eyes, long, flowing dark hair and a presence that would light up any jam session. Andy Timmons was a session guitarist at the time from North Texas who had transplanted from Florida who was hired to help us record.

Guitarist Andy Timmons was recruited shortly after our recordings by CBS pop metal hair band Danger Danger. Andy went on to become a great Texas legend on par with Stevie Ray Vaughn, but he is currently music director for Olivia Newton-John. Andy was a top tier guitarist, then and still is today.

My band mate in Outrageous and Redhouse, Steve Thompson, joined as The Crossing's bassist. We were a fiery rhythm section playing several sets per night since 1989. Steve had long, dark, curly hair, reminiscent of a conquistador. He was an outdoorsman and a little wild at times. He definitely had the girls chasing him. He was full of laughter. We drank our six packs on his back porch, laughing hysterically all night until early morning. We told stories and jokes and make up random words and gestures to entertain our brothers, who would follow us around. As a musician, Steve's bass parts were choice. I can still hear the fretless bass riff that he came up with for The Crossing's song "Train Religion."

We were very fortunate to have Sia on keyboards, sequencing and vocals. Sia was a signature part of The Crossing's complex sound. Sia had the short, Culture Club hair cut and was well spoken and clean shaven. Sia moonlighted as a gifted sound engineer for Studio manager Keith Rust at Crystal Clear. To this day, Keith Rust is one of the most forthright studio managers in DFW.

The Crossing had a Love-and-Rockets-meets-U2-meets-Depeche-Mode kind of vibe. Although I had never played alternative rock music before the band was so talented that it was pure joy. The Crossing stretched me as a musician who had preferred hard rock since my preteen years.

The Crossing's earliest recordings attracted the interest of Sam Paulos, owner of Crystal Clear Studios. Crystal Clear, one of the most impressive studios at the time, featured a 24-track digital recording facility. Before Pro Tools and Drumagog, engineers had to be adept back in the 90s at correctly manipulating analog two-inch reel-to-reel-tape. Crystal Clear remains one of the best studios in Dallas today.

The Crossing's sessions at Crystal Clear led to our first single, "Falling Down to Earth," which was released on KDGE 94.5 *Tales from the Edge Volume Four*, a compilation of all the top bands in Dallas. I have kept a copy to this day, and I imagine it is worth something. I envision some studio wiz compiling all my studio and live recordings into one or two CDs for my treasure of memories.

94.5 FM The Edge music director George Gimarc released our single "Falling Down to Earth," and *The Dallas Observer Music Awards* nominated The Crossing as the Best New Alternative Band in *Dallas,* which was quite a hallmark.

The Crossing headlined legendary Deep Ellum venues such as Trees,

Club Dada, Main Bar and Club Clearview. The Crossing performed shows with Interscope recording artists The Toadies, who went on to sell millions of records; Geffen recording artists Tripping Daisy, which went on to sell millions of records and later became Polyphonic Spree (they are still out there doing it today); and Course of Empire, who was signed with Rainmaker records, a local record label started by Paul Nugent. Paul Nugent was one of the founding members of For Reasons Unknown, who recorded the song "Breakfast at Tiffany's," which was number one on MTV.

Although success surrounded us, being in The Crossing was really a *crossover* for me, because I had always played heavy rock rooted in blues, and, now, I was playing alternative music with The Crossing.

The Crossing was represented by Danton Richardson, Esq., a California based attorney with connections at Warner/Chappel Music, Inc. I knew his wife Maria from working in the Victoria's Secret stockroom at the NorthPark Mall in the early 90s. This led to a dialogue with the William Morris Music Agency, a very reputable firm.

Spiritually, The Crossing were seeking New Age ideas on top of the good old-fashioned religion that had been established in our lives as kids. We were largely vegetarian, Bohemian in nature and laid back. I was seeking answers during this season as to why my father had passed away. Music is healing on many levels; just imagine life without a song as the background for milestones such as a senior prom, wedding celebrations, and even the grieving process.

The Crossing's music tapped into deep emotions and was very comforting to me. We rehearsed tirelessly in a nice older home with big bay windows and an oversized living area. Ty even had a relative he called "Uncle Buck" who had been a faithful bus driver for Led Zeppelin in the 70s.

I had been in a series of successful bands that typically lasted two to three years, and I had enjoyed a litany of pretty women that kept me feeling important. And, now, after losing my father and standing aloof from my family, I was open to finding love again. During this time, I was feeling better about myself, so I was confident that love was on its way. I inherited a small sum of money from my dad, but I was uncertain of my next move. I did confide in my grandfather (Papa) for advice, but my heart was still set on making it with my band. I reasoned with Papa that Walt Disney invested it all in his dream, so why shouldn't I? Papa understood, as he had taken his own risks in business, purchasing a foundation and drilling company from Joe Adams when he was in his late 40s for a million dollars. The signs were positive that if I invested in my music career, it would one day pay dividends. I could handle being an international rock star at age 25.

In every market The Crossing traveled to, they said we were a band that would definitely make it. I felt deep in my heart that this was probably the most talented band I had been with up to that point, simply because the music reached a vast audience. Hard rock, had an appeal for multi-platinum bands like AC/DC, Judas Priest, Motley Crue, and many more, but based on record sales alone U2, Elvis Presley, and The Beatles had superstar status. I was never motivated by compromising my musical integrity for popularity, but The Crossing just so happened to be very creative which kind of just carved a niche. The Crossing completed its best body of work, *Circus Maximus*, released by Crystal Clear Studios, with rave reviews from all of the DFW press.

"Moon Song," "The Widows," "Mrs. Robinson," "Hour of Need," "Train Religion," "2027," "Burning," "Moses Rides Again" and "Resurrection" were the best recorded songs in the alternative music genre. A sample verse from "Moon Song" is below:

Pale moon came circling down

Sky won't rain

Fire won't drown

Pale Moon came

Burning out

Sky won't rain

The fire shouts

"Resurrection" included the following apocalyptic lyrics:

No one begs for mercy

It will rise up from the Maker

Twisted operator changes the voice that sends the message

Let him come down

Let him come down

Deliver me from this destruction

Resurrection

All the signed DFW artists were calling us to open their shows, and well-to-do socialites followed us. We were *one* deal away from international stardom.

The long, arduous days in the recording studio, meticulously brooding over the songs and frequently changing musical arrangements, led to some discord within the band.

Crystal Clear's patience was waning. After *Circus Maximus* was completed, The Crossing were poised to become an international success, but, unfortunately, The Crossing changed several of the musical compositions, leading to strife in the band, and The Crossing parted ways. What was next? I found myself between "rock" and a hard place.

Chapter 6
Rock in a Hard Place

In 1992, the Crossing came to an end. As a full-time musician for 15 years, I went through many tragedies, losing my dad in 1991 and my best friend and band mate Brad to marriage, but music was always my compass—it was always my point.

When 1993 came around, I was out of a full-time gig as a musician, and I needed some part-time work in the interim. I was interested in health since my teens, and developed a desire to help others avoid disease. Emotionally void, numb and helpless, I struggled when my dad passed away of cardiovascular disease in 1991.

I believed I could help myself and others avoid devastating sickness and disease by practicing prevention and nutrition. I studied Nutrition passionately in junior college while seeking employment at Fitness Foods in Plano, Texas. I applied for a position as a vitamin clerk. I hoped to soon become an apprentice to owner Martie Whittekin, president of the National Nutritional Foods Association and a clinical nutritionist.

My rock 'n' roll image raised a few eyebrows while dealing with high profile people in Plano, such as doctors, business owners, realtors and lawyers. I tamed my hair in an orderly ponytail to make a good impression and sported a nice collar shirt.

Martie hired me, and I was on my way to discovering another passion I had developed early on at age 13. I played music full time until this opportunity came along. I had not worked a part-time job since Victoria's Secret in the stock room at NorthPark Mall in Dallas.

I was a quick study while composing my college English thesis on the Framingham heart study. At the same time, *Diet for a New America*, by John Robbins (Baskin Robbins heir), inspired me while I was on a flight to Los Angeles. Seated next to professional bass guitar tech for rock star Nikki Sixx of Motley Crue, a multi-platinum band in the hard rock genre, he turned me on to *Diet for a New America*, and its impact soon converted me to a sold-out vegetarian. The book contended that the consumption of animal protein (beef, in particular) was responsible for the demise of America's health and ecosystem. I was willing to do anything to help save lives and the planet. I enrolled in EarthSave, a foundation started by John Robbins, and distributed leaflets across the college campus and at health fairs.

Working at Fitness Foods while attending Richland College helped me keep my mind on the positive while the events of 1991 faded into the background. I studied diligently and maintained honor roll status, keeping my eyes open for my next gig—and a beautiful woman. All these changes in my life excited me again. Soon, a young Filipino beauty with golden locks, a bronze tan, a lean muscular build and radiant smile came roller blading into Fitness Foods.

Curiously peering through our selection of health and beauty products, she asked me for advice, and the chemistry between us was electric. Almost daily, she stopped by Fitness Foods. She lived just a few blocks away, and this soon developed into a friendship. We took long walks together, listened to music and practiced vegetarianism; however, spiritually we were both lost. After falling for each other, we had sexual relations and moved into a space together above a friend's home in Canyon Creek, a very nice suburban neighborhood in Richardson, Texas.

As president of the Dallas Vegetarian Society, my friend was really laid back, so it was a nice fit for us. Scrumptious potlucks every Friday night fueled our social life as we learned more about vegetarianism.

Soon, the next musical door of my professional career opened. Solinger, a popular hard rock band founded by lead singer Johnny Solinger in 1988 at the University North Texas, had decided to revamp its lineup after successfully building a following on college campuses and in Dallas premier nightclubs like the Basement and Dallas City Limits. I remembered Johnny's stage presence and vocal abilities from a battle of the bands staged earlier in his career at the Sip & Nip Club in Euless, Texas, and Johnny's charisma impressed me.

Johnny's long blond hair, athletic medium build, copious charm, and bluesy vocal grit, made him a formidable lead singer. Unknown to me, Johnny graduated from L.D. Bell High School (for you Blue Raiders).

On stage, Johnny was fearless. After my time with The Crossing playing alternative music, I was more than ready to get back to hard rock. Rhythm guitarist and songwriter John Mott approached me about auditioning for Solinger.

John Mott was a tall tan, laid back Californian. Raised Mormon, John somehow found the answers to life's pressing questions behind his songs and six strings. John, aka, "Mott," was usually the last one to wind out the night during Solinger's common after-hour parties. Mott was also known as "The Tongue" as he could perform many "interesting" tricks with his tongue similar to Gene Simmons of KISS.

Solinger had spied my drumming and songwriting abilities with Redhouse at Dallas City Limits and the Basement where they had also performed. Solinger's reputation escalated as Dallas' premier hard rock party band: booze, women, lines of cocaine and all-night parties. Guns-N-Roses' rise to superstardom fueled Solinger's success with their explosive covers of "Rocket Queen" and "Welcome to the Jungle" from GNR's *Appetite for Destruction*, which sold 10 million copies.

Southwest flight attendant and Solinger fan Doris Brazil offered me a room to rent. I moved to Mesquite, Texas, off Palos Verdes. During my stay with Doris, I met her beautiful niece, who lived in Plano. She was like a Jewish princess, and we were soon dating.

Solinger had a large following, they were headlining everywhere and they were well paid. At first, I was reluctant to join Solinger, because I had always been the band leader and businessman since Dirty Blonde at age 17, and Johnny's strong personality could potentially collide with mine. Regardless, I decided to give it a shot.

I auditioned for Solinger at the rehearsal studio in Addison, Texas. The Solinger lineup at that time was Johnny Solinger on lead vocals, John Mott on guitar and Gray Wear as bassist. Solinger also boasted a full-on lead guitarist, Tommy Hyatt, a music instructor who worked for *Buddy* magazine, as well as studio musician Andy Timmons, who, as I mentioned earlier, played with several bands around the Dallas-Fort Worth Metroplex. I could "sense" Solinger's enormous potential. Solinger's rehearsal room was

---

Let me tell you about my friend, Jamie Mclester; that's who he is to me: Jamie. James Michael McLester. We played music for many years together in the band SOLINGER, based out of Dallas, Texas.

Some of the favorite times of my life and career were while trying to build a name, career or even a following in the Dallas-Fort Worth Metroplex, where we started.

Jamie is not only a superb drummer, but he also wrote meaningful lyrics and con-tributed greatly with melodies and struc-ture to many of Solinger's tunes. Through hard work and perseverance, we achieved unprecedented success in our region, get-ting prime shows on some of the biggest stages in the state. We produced three independent albums, which also did very well. We got some national radio coverage courtesy of Madd Max Hammer of Z-Rock, which had 30 affiliates across the country at that time. All the local Dallas stations were our friends: KEGL, Q102, KZEW—and several that are either gone or I can't recall.

When I heard about his book, I insisted he allow me to tell you all what a great musi-cian he is—and an even better dude. He continues to inspire.

Good luck with all your endeavors, my friend, and God bless.

Johnny Solinger
Skid Row

decorated with rock memorabilia and, of course, top notch studio gear. In addition, the smell of crisp marijuana filled the air and the Crown Royal was handy. In spite of the party atmosphere around pursuing rock stardom, I always had my heart and mind set on the music first and foremost.

The audition was mine; they loved my playing, but felt I was a bit eccentric. Solinger bassist Gray Wear set his sights on Dave Hineman from Los Angeles, as Solinger's new lead guitarist. Solinger auditioned 60 guitar players with no winners in sight. Dave was deejaying at an LA strip joint and recording tracks for Steve Lukather from the band Toto. Dave was a very gifted guitarist and played with Joey C. Jones, members of Goo Goo Dolls and multiple Dallas bands including Terry Glaze (Pantera/Lord Tracy). While Solinger endured the painstaking wait for the "new" lead guitarist, after auditioning mostly mediocre guitarists, I worked at Vital Nutrition by day, while moonlighting at Solinger's rehearsal studio at night. This double-minded lifestyle consisted of drinking, smoking marijuana and doing cocaine to get creative and then winding up at the Dallas strip joint to promote the band. You could never have enough pretty, scantily clad women at a Solinger show. Meanwhile, as fate would have it, after a sizeable earthquake in California and having his '57 Chevy automobile stolen, guitarist Dave Hineman moved back to Texas to join Solinger. Solinger revamped with a new fire, while original guitarist Kirk Carlson and drummer Andre Avelar went on to other projects. Solinger's original lineup kicked #$@ and took names, but they wanted a change.

Dave's fiery, bluesy style was an instant fit, and Solinger reworked classics such as "If I Knew How," "Tell Sandy," "L.A. Girl," "Booze City" and "Precious Time," while cultivating new songs for the forthcoming Solinger *Electric Mountain* CD.

Solinger's professional video, "Tell Sandy," was produced by Playboy's cable show *Hot Rocks*, which aired around the world, reaching the top 10 charts on MTV Brazil. Solinger was featured in *Metal Edge* and *Rip* magazine as our national following multiplied. Solinger maintained a rigorous touring schedule and, even in the midst of touring, there were moments for our families.

Bassist Gray Wear's mother was ill, and it was a difficult time for Gray. Gray was very close to her; but never had a relationship with his father. Soon, the disease took Gray's mother's life, and, at age 27, Gray Wear dove deeper into the alcohol, drugs and painkillers to numb his pain. Gray and I were now roommates. My relationships with the Filipino girl and the Jewish princess had dissolved, and I was single. I crashed on the floor of Gray's North Dallas apartment with nowhere else to go. Shelter was only really needed after a night of partying. I just needed a corner to crash in, and Gray's floor became that corner. I saw Gray firsthand go overboard with marijuana, alcohol and Valium until it overwhelmed him.

Many of us, early in life, probably remembered having an encounter at church. Maybe we were baptized and saved, but we quickly ran after the lust of the flesh, the pride of life, and the sex, the drugs and the rock 'n' roll. We all had heard about staying sober but we refused to listen. I hoped we could somehow reach Gray, but we were all in our own personal clouds of sex, drugs and rock 'n' roll and could not see clearly ourselves.

Gray was treading on thin ice. We needed divine intervention desperately. As I expected, the news soon came that Gray had passed out in the apartment from an overload of booze and pills. Gray was out cold in a coma. The ambulance came for him, Code Blue, and sped him to Medical City hospital in Dallas for emergency lifesaving measures. Gray was in ICU, suffering from brain trauma. Alarmed, the band members and many of our Solinger fans stormed the hallways of Medical City hoping that our brother Gray would wake up. We waited and waited. Gray remained in a comatose state for 17 days. We were the "frozen chosen," numb, lost and praying to a God we really did not know any more, because we had chosen to fill our lives with sex, drugs and rock 'n' roll.

Anyone who has paced the floors of an ICU waiting room understands that there are multiple ways you attempt to cope with situations clearly above your head. Many people call a friend, some will cry, some will listen to music, or, in desperation, cry out in prayer. At the doctor's request, we found ourselves outside of Gray's room most of those dark days. We sat along the hallways of the chilled ICU unit, broken lost souls, searching for answers, hoping our brother would miraculously arise from the coma. Suddenly, the following words came to me:

Things have changed.

They came quickly

By my window/past my door

Pick up the pieces of our yesterdays

Long forgotten/nevermore

This song was for Gray and, furthermore, for everyone engaged in this tiresome battle. Solinger was on hold for now, this time for life or death. I'd never been through anything like this in my 27 years. Another verse from "Nevermore" followed:

God bless the reason.

God changed the season

For all of us at once

Nevermore

 Gray Wear passed away on August 9, 1994, and Solinger would never be the same. I grew very close to Gray as a roommate, and I was very thankful for the time we spent together. Gray always cracked jokes and at times could get obscene, but underneath that tough outer facade was a man with a smile and a heart for people. He opened his apartment to me, even when I didn't have anything to eat. We earned good money, but when you're blowing it on topless bars and drugs it didn't go very far.

We were weary. Johnny, John and David had all known Gray for years, back to Solinger's early days in Denton, Texas, where they jammed together. Unexpectedly, Gray's passing was quite a shock to everyone. We didn't know if we could carry on without our brother Gray.

After much soul-searching, Solinger decided to look for another bass player. We found a talented bassist who played with several DFW bands, but he was hooked on heavy drugs, so he wasn't a good fit for us. Next, Solinger was introduced to bassist Markus Collis. Markus was tan with long blond hair, and he had the women, so, in effect, we added more pretty women to our following. Solinger's new lineup frequently played On the Rocks, Dallas City Limits and the Basement, while crafting new songs. During his stint with Solinger, we recorded the *Electric Mountain* CD at Sumet-Burnet studios nestled near Lower Greenville, where The Rolling Stones, James Brown and several famous artists recorded.

Electric Mountain, Solinger's follow-up to the self-titled 1992 release, was a great record. I co-wrote the title track, "Electric Mountain," with The Crossing's guitarist Ty Thomas. Solinger's revamped version with heavy guitar rocked. Other songs included "The Sky is Falling," which received extensive airplay on KEGL 97.1 FM, "Years," "Funky Thing," "Another Day," "Live at Five"—all these rockers were featured on the CD. Dave's brother James designed our CD cover. His colorful illustration depicted Solinger's band members towering upon the face of skyscrapers with the Solinger triangle logo in the midst of the skyline.

We realized that musically Solinger was going in another direction and Markus exited. Solinger wasn't the same without Gray. We missed Gray's antics, onstage and offstage. We knew the "right" bassist was out there. Solinger had a date at Smokin' Dave's Rock Room in Dallas, right across from Baby Dolls. We'd play our first set and hang out at Baby Dolls for a while, then go back and play another set. We brought the girls back with us, and after our show, we would end our evening at Baby Dolls—it was a back and forth thing.

That night, at Smokin' Dave's, Jon Mann, who briefly played bass for Solinger, before Gray, happened to be playing bass in the opening band. We all watched Jon Mann just shred on the bass, and we thought, "We've got to get this guy." After the show, we talked to Jon, and, already being familiar with the other members of Solinger, he said, "Sure, I'll play." Jon Mann played brass and percussion in marching band at Michigan State and also attended the University of North Texas. Jon was really into snow skiing and outdoors, and he was funny and easy to get along with. Rhythmically, we gelled.

After Jon joined Solinger as a band, we were much tighter musically. We gained popularity in DFW through radio airplay and interviews on Z-Rock and KEGL 97.1FM. We were in with Chris Ryan, T.C. McGuire, Cindy Scull at KEGL, and Mad Max Hammer and Tracy Barnes from Z-Rock.

Solinger remained strong, and, now, with Jon Mann, we were better than before. We made one decision—to keep the band together. Jon was very proficient on bass, and he was *the man* with a great attitude, a good sense of humor and no hang-ups. Solinger kept a steady schedule of rehearsing, recording and sharpening our music skills, while shopping our music to major labels, including overseas and a distribution deal with Alfa Music Company.

Several major music labels had a growing interest in Solinger, and we kept a steady pace of playing 150-plus shows a year. We had a massive local following in the DFW area, and we played unplugged acoustic appearances on KEGL live in the studio with T.C. McGuire, as well as many local shows at the Curtain Club and Trees with Chris Ryan, Robert Miguel and Chaz from KEG 97.1 FM.

Solinger became KEGL's darling, and KEGL soon asked us to open for Geffen recording artists Tesla at the Bronco Bowl. I had always dreamed of playing the Bronco Bowl, a historical venue in the round, with a cool bowling alley, pinball machines and an amphitheater that seated 3,000 to 3,300 people.

Tesla had just released their major-label debut *Mechanical Resonance*, which climbed into Billboards Top 40. Tesla were a unique, multi-platinum band from Sacramento, California. With our connections to KEGL, we found ourselves, in 1996, doing a sold-out show with Tesla at the Bronco Bowl. Every time I had gone to see one of my favorite bands perform at a DFW arena or venue I had cried and dreamed about being on the stage. I would visualize myself sitting down on my drum throne with thousands of fans cheering in anticipation of a rock show. This best illustrates my childhood dreams.

Solinger was asked to play the Tesla after-show party at the Canyon

Club adjacent to the arena. One of my dreams came true. Everybody around town asked how Solinger landed that gig.

Walking into the empty Bronco Bowl—knowing that we would be taking the stage in front of Tesla to a packed house in a few short hours—made me feel so alive. After a good warm-up backstage, I approached the drum throne as the lights faded to black. The screams rose in frequency and anticipation as Solinger fans rose up for one heck of a show, chanting "Solinger!" Solinger fans supported us and helped us climb to this level, even after tragedy had struck just two years prior when Gray Wear passed. We took all the right steps to fortune and fame.

From the first click of my drumstick, it was game on. Solinger blistered through a set of hard rock music that rocked the crowd, opening with our song "Years." The crowd was one with us. They sensed something amazing, and in the euphoria of our set we all realized that there was something greater ahead for us. We all wanted to cherish this moment and live it night after night, city after city.

As soon as I blinked, our time was up, and we were whisked back to our dressing room as champions, but not for long. It appeared that Tesla's management decided we did not need to be backstage any longer stealing thunder from the headliner, and we were gently kicked out of our dressing room.

We entered the arena to watch Tesla put on a killer show. What a night! So many great songs: "Modern Day Cowboy," "Gettin' Better" and "Little Suzi." Solinger were local rock stars that night, and it was awesome. Our crew moved our gear across the hall to the Canyon Club, and, after Tesla, we took the stage once again in an intimate setting with 1,100 hard rock fans who wanted to keep the party rolling. We jammed Van Halen's "Mean Street," Deep Purple's "Highway Star," The Cult's "King Contrary Man" and several other hard rock tunes. Solinger shattered the attendance records and broke all bar sales.

Music manager Roger Christian, from Real Cool Marketing, began opening doors for the band. Our popularity skyrocketed. Solinger's music was constantly being played on KEGL, and we were playing the top music venues. Roger Christian's connections, coupled with Solinger's popularity, led to us being selected as the opening act for Atlantic recording artists The Scorpions and Alice Cooper at The Coca-Cola Starplex. We thought we had played the big stages with bands like Metallica (side stage) and opening up for Cinderella, Vince Neil of Motley Crue, Seven Mary Three, Blue Oyster Cult and others around town, but this was our biggest show to date. Solinger was offered main stage as local support, and we were psyched. Solinger ads plastered print and radio media while the buzz stirred.

During our set, we tossed green "Solinger" koozies to the beer drinkers in the crowd to keep them cool. There were 10,000 avid Solinger rock fans at the Coca-Cola Starplex at Fair Park in Dallas. We were local rock stars on a bigger stage and playing before rock legends The Scorpions and Alice Cooper. It was an incredible feeling, thinking about all the shows I had seen there, sitting in the audience and dreaming of someday playing on that stage. Here I was, taking the drum throne again behind my custom DW drum kit that I had purchased in '92. The kit was a sunburst fade black-to-purple-to-fuchsia. A thundering 18 x 22 kick drum, 12 x 14 rack toms on RIMS mounts, two suspended floor toms (16 x 18 and 18 x 18) and my Tama Superstar snare.

Solinger ripped through crowd favorites such as "Years," "The Sky Is Falling," "Live at Five" and Deep Purple's classic "Highway Star." Solinger had reached another status as North Texas' most prominent hard rock band, playing up to 200 shows and continuing to ride a wave of success and writing new material for our rehearsal studios in North Dallas (Plano). Johnny purchased a Roland virtual recording studio, which Dave Hineman learned to operate, and we took our live tracks from the Starplex show with The Scorpions and Alice Cooper and digitally mixed them into *Solinger Live*, released in 1996-97 to great response.

I was in a roller-coaster relationship with a beautiful brunette, whom I had met at Boozer's nightclub in Deep Ellum. She was a student at the Art Institute of Dallas, and an intern at Warner Elektra Atlantic records. My lifestyle with alcohol and drug use was out of control and led to a volatile relationship. We both had issues from our past. When we got along, it was special, but most other times it was static.

Through these dark days of my life, living with this beautiful woman before marriage, being around a drug culture and engaging in sinful behavior, I wrote songs such as "Walking through the Dark, "Low Down" and the melancholy "All in Your Head." I spent my days working in the health food store teaching others how to live right, how to eat right, how to juice, etc., while I was burning the candle at both ends during the night. After working my day job at Vital Nutrition, I would drive down Parker Road to the rehearsal studio, where we had a bar set up, and I would moonlight there after work to escape in the music.

My relationship with my girlfriend escalated to the point that I threatened to leave several times. My good friend Kenny Faulkner came to help me move my things, but she would cry and beg me not to leave. I felt sorry for her and didn't want to leave her alone. Eventually, the rollercoaster was too dangerous, and we finally parted ways. We had no foundation in God, and our relationship was just a recycled version of everything that had happened in previous relationships. Our failed relationship led me to write "Chain Link Fence," a song that represented bondage and how I felt on the inside. The emotions of the lyrics when partnered with Dave's riffs fostered a deep song.

Prior to the release of "Chain Link Fence," one of the highlights of my music career was being inducted into *Buddy Magazine's* "Texas Tornado" Hall of Fame. I was inducted with the likes of Willie Nelson, Stevie Ray Vaughn, Frank Beard from ZZ Top, Billy Gibbons from ZZ Top, Dave Abbruzzese from Pearl Jam, Vinnie Paul Abbott from Pantera and others. I thought I had arrived.

As the music began to develop, the songs "Time It Is" and "Low Down" fit squarely in with the best song ideas. John Mott contributed a heartfelt song "Crux 88," and vocalist Terrance Lee (Pantera/Lord Tracy) submitted three songs via Dave: "Step on the Gas," "If You See Me Coming" and "I Don't Mind."

Solinger focused on making its best record to date, *Chain Link Fence*, focusing entirely on the recording process, while disappearing from the local limelight. *Chain Link Fence* had a dimension the band had never explored, with the guitar and vocals going to new levels. *Chain Link Fence* received international recognition and regular airplay on KEGL. Solinger prepared to go on tour in support of *Chain Link Fence.*

Guitar player John Mott was in a relationship with Betty Jo Sylvester and not completely sold on touring. In addition, lead guitarist Dave Hineman attended DeVry while settling down with his wife Lisa to start a family. Johnny and I knew that if we were going to take the next step we had to tour to support *Chain Link Fence.* We discussed putting together a new version of Solinger ready to go on the road, since there was resistance in the band.

I'll never forget, we had a small rehearsal studio at that time in Garland, and Andre Avelar, the original Solinger drummer, had a wide network of musical connections. Andre worked with many different national bands, and traveled as a roadie. Andre's connections included Skid Row, a multiplatinum band from the early 90s from New Jersey (discovered by Jon Bon Jovi, who has sold 150 million records). Skid Row's original singer was Sebastian Bach. Skid Row were managed by Doc McGhee and signed by Atlantic Records. Skid Row's hard, edgy sound was starkly different from Poison, Motley Crue and Cinderella.

Andre heard Skid Row was looking for a new lead singer to replace Sebastian Bach, so he whispered in Johnny's ear, "Hey, did you know Skid Row is looking for a new lead singer?" The next thing I knew, Johnny was on a plane for New Jersey to meet with Rachel Bolan, Dave "The Snake" Sabo and Scotti Hill of Skid Row. Shortly thereafter, Johnny Solinger flew back to Texas with the news that he was as the new lead singer for Skid Row. You talk about a deal breaker, after five years of hard work. I found myself between "rock and a hard place," and I asked myself, "What next?"

Picture This

War and Chaos

War and chaos in Vietnam

Grandparents James M. and Arlene McLester

James Morris McLester, Jr. (Dad in Vietnam)

Mom as Haltom cheerleader

Sparkle-Tone JULY '57

Grandparents James V. and Vivian Landrum

My parents on their wedding day

"I think I can!: Nanny and me at 3333 Edith Lane.

Family portrait 1972

Second Chances

A young James Michael

My little sister, Marilyn

Cliff Diving on Coons Creek

Family summer vacation on Padre Island

My little bro, Richard

I'm With the Band

Jamie Powers, showing off

Jamie and CA Wildman

High school senior

Me at 16

Jamie Powers at The Ranch

High school sweethearts

Jamie Powers, Dirty Blonde

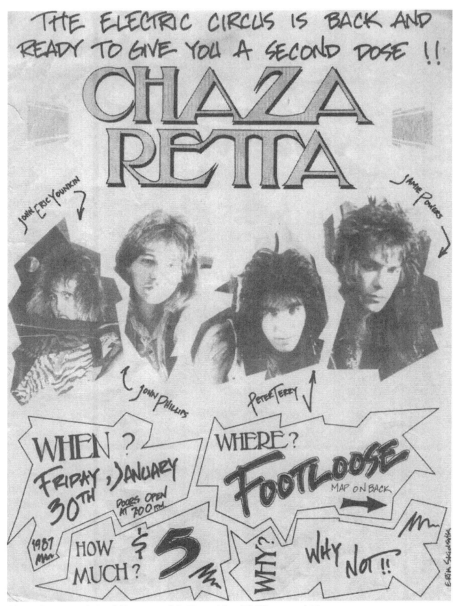

ChazaRetta original lineup with Younkin, Phillips and Nepo

ARTimes

News About the Arts in Irving   A Publication of the Irving Arts Board   June 1988

Summer is here again and to celebrate the end of school, Texas' hottest rock band, Chaza Retta, is hosting a 3-band, Texas-size concert. It will be held at the Irving Center for the Cultural Arts. Don't miss this special event – it just might be the only chance for the local youth to catch this high-energy, rock-n-roll show! Complete with their massive stage set-up and production, Chaza Retta has blown the doors off local and regional clubs as well as various concert halls. Also included on the bill will be D/FW's own Centerfold along with another surprise band from Irving. Doors open at 7 p.m. and admission is $5. You won't want to miss all the energy and excitement that will fill the ICCA, June 11!

ChazaRetta revamped

Marching to the Beat of a Different Drummer

1991 Redhouse promo pic: Brad Spalding, Mike Madison, Me, Steve Thompson

Reading *People* magazine

Brad Spalding, Texas Chainsaw Southpaw

After-show look

Visiting family during the holidays

Live at The Basement, Dallas, Texas

Crossing Over

The Crossing Live: L to R: Ty Thomas, Derek Lothain, me, Sia

Live with The Crossing and my new Drum Workshop Custom

you as a person with refined taste, a sense of adventure and pretty damn good vision. Whether seeking musical
: Volume Three." Here's another 70+ minutes of some of Texas' best new bands. There's quite a variety this
recordings that seems to spill out on my desk every week, brings no end of delight in discovering that Texas has
when they play. It's up to all of us to keep original music alive. Enjoy!

George Gimarc, October 1991

Clever Pennies — Two Stones (D. Smith-D. Smith-W. Quirk) — 3:05
This java-folk quartet moved from the confines of Dave's Art Pawn to the big rooms in town in less than a
year, due equally to Davina Smith's hypnosis-inducing vocals and the band's ability to change musical moods at
the bat of an eyelash. Sarah "Man, but I'm busy these days" Hickman produced portions of the Pennies hypnotic
debut cassette "One Big Mystery."
**Davina Smith - Lead vocals, flute. Don Lewis - Bass. Steve Garrett - Drums. Brad McLemore - Guitar. Recorded at Planet Dallas
Studios, Dallas.**

Out Of The Blue — Sad Songs (J. Brent DeShan) — 3:48
One of the most dangerous assumptions you can make about Dallas music is that it ONLY happens in Deep
Ellum. There are plenty of great bands that play elsewhere and Out Of The Blue is one of the best examples.
Frequently found at haunts like the Rhythm Room, The Library and O'Tays, this quintet has an uncanny knack for
turning a pop phrase. Every time this song came around in their sets I could have sworn it was a cover tune. It's
finely crafted and aimed at the feminine heart.
**Jonathan McVay - Lead vocals. J. Brent DeShan - Guitar, vocals. Tommy DeShan - Bass, vocals. Jonathan Lane - Drums, vocals. Darren
Mitchell - Keyboards. Recorded at Planet Dallas, Dallas.**

Judy & The Essentials — Away (Judy & The Essentials) — 3:52
In what must have seemed like the longest 10 weeks ever, these local rabble rousers had one helluva case of
bad luck. Their drummer was sidelined for months following a most heinous car crash, their bassist got splinters
under the eyelids while building speaker cabinets and Judy herself was battered and bruised after a fall down a
flight of stairs. If that wasn't enough, how about a violent allergic reaction to some markers she was using
afterwards. Don't get caught seeing this band during a lightning storm- but do catch them soon. They're hard
rocking and genuine.
Judy - Guitar, vocals. Jeff Clark - Drums. Gloria Cortez - Lead guitar. Gordy Connally - Bass. Recorded at Crystal Clear Sound, Dallas.

The Crossing — Falling Down To Earth (T. Thomas-D. Lothian) — 5:17
If you have to choose one new band to keep your eye on for 1992 this is it. The Crossing can best be
described as two parts Cult and one part Cure. They're fortunate in having attitude, a great new sound and one of
the best new vocalists in town. This is a must see band that will leave you breathless.
**Ty Thomas - Lead guitar, vocals. Derek Lothian - Lead vocals. Jamie Powers - Drums. Steve Thompson - Bass. Sio Ahmadzadeh -
Acoustic guitar, keyboards, backing vocals. Recorded at Crystal Clear Sound, Dallas**

Moon Festival — Desert City Sleeps (Salim Severés) — 4:12
A Denton band without a brass section!?! So it seems, and listening to Moon Festival the last thing to come
to mind is a tuba. They've come a long way in two years and now have their debut album "Shrine" out on Dragon
Street records. The addition of Brad Robertson on drums strengthened the bands rhythm section a year ago, and
he's almost learned all of Moon Festival's backlog of 200 original songs. Smoky, mystical and not to be missed.

Tales from the Edge Compilation CD, KDGE 94.5FM

KDGE 94.5 FM *Tales From The Edge* CD, The Crossing

Ty Thomas, Derek Lothian and me, in style

The Crossing, *Circus Maximus*

The Crossing *Circus Maximus* photo shoot. Sia, Ty, me and Derek (seated)

Rock In a Hard Place

At Solinger's studio. My love affair with Indian tobacco lasted two years.

Halloween 1996 at Boozers, Deep Ellum. with Solinger. Me as KISS's Peter Criss and Frankie Ramirez.

Solinger 1997, Rehab Lounge, with Chris Ryan, KEGL 97.1FM. L-R: Johnny, Chris, and me.

Greater Southwest Guitar Show at Fair Park, Dallas, Texas, 1998

Passion Greater Southwest Guitar Show 1997, with Solinger

Solinger live in Dallas, Texas

Garland Rollins and me backstage at Greater Southwest Guitar Show, Fair Park

My custom DW drum kit, live with Solinger

25th anniversary Dallas Guitar Show and Musicfest

Solinger, live at Boozers, Deep Ellum, 1999

Solinger Live at Q102 Bring in the Weekend party

Texas Drum Tornado. Jamie McLester. live with Solinger and Blue Oyster Cult, Arcadia Theatre, Dallas, Texas

Solinger Live at Coca-Cola Starplex with Alice Cooper and Scorpions, June 1996

Backstage at Bronco Bowl, Dallas, Texas, with Solinger and Geffen recording artist Tesla, 1996

"Never More," Solinger tribute to Gray Wear

Solinger Live from Boozers Deep Ellum, 1996

JMC tracking drums, with Eric Delegard, Chain Link Fence

SOLINGER

DATA

```
ORIGIN        : Dallas, Texas, USA
STYLE         : Hard rock
STATUS        : Dissolved
LAST UPDATE   : 2005-02-23
```

BIOGRAPHY (2005)

The American hard rock band Solinger was formed in 1990 in Dallas, Texas. The band probably split up in 1999 as frontman Johnny Solinger became the new vocalist of Skid Row. They played a show with André, Kirk, Dave, Jon, John and Johnny on February 20th, 2005.

FORMER MEMBERS

Johny Solinger	1990-1999	Vocals	See also
Dave Hineman	1994-1999	Guitars	
John Mott	1990-1999	Guitars	
Joe Mann	1994-1999	Bass	
Jamie McLester	1994-1999	Drums	
Gray Wear	1990-1994	Bass	Died in 1994.
André Avelar	1990-1994	Drums	
Kirk Carlson	1990-1992	Guitars	
Tommy Hyatt	1992-1994	Guitars	

DISCOGRAPHY

1994	Solinger	Solinger
1995	Solinger II	Solinger
1999	Chain Link Fence	Solinger

Thanks a lot to André Avelar for providing information on the band!

©2001-2005   BACK

Solinger rock history

Solinger   Page 1 of

Solinger
Formed 1989, U.S.A.

1993 Solinger EP
1995 Solinger
1999 Solinger Live
1999 Chain Link Fence

History
Hard rockers that released some great material despite lineup changes and personal tragedy. Never got any major label support, but still managed to receive praise from the local Dallas press.
   Formed in Dallas, Texas by **Johnny Solinger** (vocals), **John Mott** (guitar), **Kirk Carlson** (guitar), **Gray Wear** (bass) and **Andre Avelar** (drums). The debut EP produced a video that appeared on the *Playboy* channels *Hot Rocks* show. However by 1994 the band had revamped due in part to the August overdose of **Wear**. Unsure whether to go on, the group reorganized and soldiered ahead.
   Solinger and **Mott** recruited **Dave Hineman** (guitar), **John Mann** (bass) and **Jamie McLester** (drums). This lineup recorded the self titled debut full length as well as *Chain Link Fence* and the live album that supported it.
   But the future of the band is now in jeopardy as **Johnny Solinger** took the frontman job in the revamped version of **Skid Row**. However members have vowed to continue working together if at all possible.

Solinger biography

93

CHAN CHRISTENSEN LC

FORMERLY KNOWN AS CHAN & JODZIEWICZ LAW CORPORATION

911 WILSHIRE BOULEVARD, SUITE 2288

LOS ANGELES, CALIFORNIA 90017-3451

MAILING ADDRESS:
P.O. BOX 79159
LOS ANGELES, CALIFORNIA 90079-0159
TELEPHONE (213) 624-6560
FACSIMILE (213) 622-1154

M. DANTON RICHARDSON

July 11, 1995

Steve Harrell
Alfa Music, Inc./Brunette Label
Hashimoto Bld., 2d Floor
5-4-40 Minami-Aoyama
Minato-ku, Tokyo
Japan 107

Re: Potential Licensing Deal for "Solinger"

Dear Mr. Harrell:

You recently solicited materials from the musical group "Solinger" for consideration regarding a licensing deal in Japan. Toward that end, I have enclosed the following materials for your consideration:

(1)   A 6 song Solinger CD;

(2)   A Solinger music video featuring Playboy Playmate Susie Owens (still in rotation on the Playboy Channel's "Hot Rocks");

(3)   A cassette containing the 6 songs from the above CD plus 4 additional unreleased songs; and

(4)   A Solinger Press kit.

These materials are submitted to you solely for your evaluation and consideration for possible licensing of the rights represented thereby and contained therein, which are expressly reserved. Solinger would be interested in licensing to your company the 6 song CD. The additional songs are submitted to provide you with an idea as to other material Solinger has produced. Additionally, Solinger is currently finishing up its next CD release, which may be available for licensing at a later date.

Solinger Alfa Music, Inc./Brunette Label, Japan

HAN CHRISTENSEN LC

Steve Harrell
July 11, 1995
Page 2

      Please review these materials and contact me should you be interested in a licens
for Japan. Thank you for your time and consideration. I look forward to hearing from you soon

      Very truly yours,

      CHAN CHRISTENSEN LC

      M. Danton Richardson

MDR:cjm

Enclosures: *As Stated*

cc: Solinger

7/11/95

Jamie —

Sorry for the delay but I didn't want to send this until I got set up at my new firm. I had it ready a couple of weeks ago but could not send because the Post Office stopped taking packages over 12 oz because of the Unibomber threat. If you its on its way now — good luck + be well.

Danton.

Y:\mdr\letters\harrell

Solinger letter from Danton Richardson, Esq.

Tesla Live

BUDDY MAGAZINE'S
TEXAS TORNADO

The greatest players in Texas. Perhaps in the world.

The Buddy Texas Tornados: Vinnie Abbott, '93 • Darryl Dime Abbott, '91 • Dave Abbruzzese, '92 • Kevin Afflack, '89 • Josh Alan, '91 • Jim Alderman, '82 • Tim Alexander, '88 • Rob Alexander, '84 • Bruce Alford, '95 • James Anderson, '91 • Maurice Anderson, '90 • Terry Anglin, '84 • Miguel Antonio, '93 • Lee S. Appleman, '84 • Scott Arndt, '95 • Mike Arnold, '90 • Rocky Athas, '78 • Mark Austin, '97 • Louis Johnny Fixx Baldovin, d., '84 • Marcia Ball, '84 • Bobby Baranowski, '93 • Jeffrey Barnes, '93 • Jack Barton, '88 • Michael Bartula, '85 • Frank Beard, '82 • Marc Benno, '89 • Ray Benson, '85 • Pat Taz Bently, '93 • Steve Berg, '97 • Karl Berkebile, '84 • Gregg Bissonette, '91 • Jimmy Carl Black, '88 • Terry Blankenship, '87 • Billy Block, '82 • Little Joe Blue,d., '85 • Bobby Boatright, '95 • Ponty Bone, '85 • Lou Lazer Bovis, '83 • Roger Boykin, '85 • Roger Boykin, '87 • Doyle Bramhall, '83 • Ronnie Bramhall, '90 • Jeannette Brantley, '90 • Robin Hood Brians, '89 • Chris Broadhurst, '93 • Louis Brousard, '82 • Junior Brown, '95 • Rex Brown, '94 • Mel Brown, '86 • Charles Brown, '88 • Sarah Brown, '87 • Mike Spunky Brunone, '89 • Steven Bruton, '80 • Sumter Bruton, '80 • John Bryant, '84 • Mike Buck, '83 • Rusty Burns, '81 • Jack Calmes, '82 • Brian Hash Brown Calway, '93 • Alex Camp, '89 • Phil Campbell, '90 • Johnny d. Carroll, '83 • Johnny Case, '95 • Randy Cates, '90 • Dennis Cavalier, '83 • Matt Chamberlain, '91 • Bobby Chitwood, '85 • Freddie Cisneros, '81 • Michael Junior Clark, '82 • Dave Clark, '85 • W.C. Clark, '87 • Michael Clay, '85 • James Clay, '93 • Van Cliburn, '85 • Danny Cochran, '85 • Jim Cocke, '92 • Pat Coil, '81 • Ornette Coleman, '93 • Gene Coleman, '96 • Jim Colgrove, '83 • Sonnie Collie, '96 • Albert Collins, '84 • Aaron Comess, '93 • Johnny Copeland, '86 • Joe Coronado, '89 • d. Harbie Cowans, '88 • Chris Craig, '93 • Fred Crain, '82 • Pee Wee Clayton, '85 • Joe Cripps, '97 • Ted Cruz, '92 • Kris Cummings, '81 • Mary Cutrufello, '97 • Mike Daane, '92 • Joe Don Davidson, '82 • Kim Davis, '82 • Stevie Davis, '82 • Toby Davis, '83 • Steve Davison, '85 • Ronnie Dawson, '85 • Michael DeBaise, '82 • Milo Deering, '95 • Randy DeHart, '83 • Bobby Dennis, '87 • Ron DiIulio, '90 • George Dimitri, '94 • Randall Dollahan, '82 • Floyd Domino, '97 • Johnny Rosebud Dowdy, '84 • Randy Drake, '86 • W.R. Tony Dukes, '85 • Mike Dunn, '92 • Cornell Dupree, '85 • Ernie Durawa, '86 • Lavada Durst, '89 • Omar Dykes, '84 • Alan Emert, '95 • Paul English, '87 • Harold Evans, '89 • Keith Ferguson, '84 • Mike Fiala, '92 • Carl Finch, '88 • Wilson Fisher, '95 • John Fiveash, '96 • Donny Ray Ford, '94 • Randy Fouts, '87 • Denny Freeman, '85 • Frosty, '88 • Anson Funderburgh, '81 • Mike Gage, '87 • Mike Gallaher, '86 • Red Garland, '82 • John Garza, '97 • Mark Geary, '91 • Bobby Gentry, '82 • Billy Gibbons, '78 • Chris Gibson, '97 • Gerry Gibson, '91 • Mickey Gilley, '82 • Jay Gillian, '92 • Donnie Gillyand, '96 • Fred V. Gieber, '94 • Gene Glover, '89 • Mike Graff, '95 • Barbara Graham, '82 • Craig Green, '84 • Ricky Lynn Gregg, '92 • John Thomas Griffith, '97 • Ty Grimes, '86 • David Grissom, '96 • Lynn Groom, '83 • Buzzy Gruen, '82 • Tim Grugle, '91 • Paul Guerrero, '83 • Bud Guin, '82 • Joel Guzman, '83 • Dan Haerle, '91 • Frank Haley, '95 • Bill Ham, '90 • Frank Hames, '93 • Murray Hammond, '96 • Roy Hargrove, '93 • Joel Harlan, '87 • Hal Harris, '95 • Earl ... Ezra Charles Helpinstill, '81 • Bugs Henderson, '78 • Bubba Hernand... '97 • Matt Hillyer, '95 • Fred Hoey, '85 • Gary Hogue, '95 • Cindy Hor... John Inmon, '90 • Marchel Ivery, '93 • Rick Jackson, '83 • Ronald Shann... Matthew E. Johnson, '94 • Will Johnson, '97 • Claude Johnson, '89 • ... '83 • David Lee Joyner, '94 • Keith Karnaky, '82 • Mike Kennedy, '85 • Mi... Rick Koster, '97 • Steady Freddy Krc, '86 • Smokin' Joe Kubek, '85 • Si... Robby LeDoux, '94 • Peter Austin Lee, '93 • ... Jerry LeCroix, '86 ... '53 • Pee Wee Lynn d...

... '82 • Paul D. Matson, '84 • Rex Moon Mauney, '91 • '87 • Mike McCullough, '97 • Jamie McLester, '96 • Kelly ... • Jim Milan, '85 • David Milsap, '94 • Jason Moeller, '92 ... 1 • Alex Moore, '82 • Stan Moore, '86 • David Mora, '94 ... • Willie Nelson, '81 • Bobbie Nelson, '82 • David Fathead ...

'82 • Bill Maddox, '83 • Mitch Marine, '91 • Johnny Marshall, '87 • Rene Martinez, '84 • Ron Mason, '81 • Herman Mathews, '82 • Paul D. Matson, '84 • Rex Moon Mauney, '91 • Mouse Mayes, '87 • Leon McAuliffe, '84 • Joe McBride, '88 • Martin McCall, '92 • Sam McCall, '93 • Delbert McClinton, '87 • Mike McCullough, '97 • Jamie McLester, '96 • Kelly McNulty, '92 • Michael Medina, '90 • Brian Mendelsohn, '84 • Ray Mendias, '84 • Augie Meyers, '86 • Andy Michlin, '91 • Jim Milan, '85 • David Milsap, '94 • Jason Moeller, '92 • Jamal Mohamed, '96 • Buddy Mohmad, '92 • Terry-Groff Montgomery, '94 • Smokey Montgomery, '84 • Ian Moore, '91 • Alex Moore, '82 • Stan Moore, '86 • David Mora, '94 • Mike Morgan, '92 • Tommy Morrell, '82 • Ken Big Nardo Murray, '83 • Ernie Myers, '96 • Sam Myers, '87 • Alex Napier, '81 • Willie Nelson, '81 • Bobbie Nelson, '82 • David Fathead Newman, '93 • John Nitzinger, '78 • Dahrell Norris, '82 • Tommy Nuckols, '84 • Darrell Nulisch, '87 • Gary P. Nunn, '86 • Derek O'Brien, '89 • Newell Oler, '87 • Casey Orr, '93 • Paul Orta, '87 • Riley Osbourn, '97 • Andy Owens, '93 • Calvin Owens, '93 • Dave Palmer, '95 • Lisa Pankratz, '95 • Lee Roy Parnell, '95 • Bill Payne, '89 • Paul Pearcy, '89 • Gary Palfrey, '87 • Clay Pendergrass, '95 • James Pennybaker, '84 • Pat Peterson, '97 • Lucky Peterson, '94 • Shawn Phares, '93 • Drew Phelps, '95 • Darrell Phillips, '95 • Doug Pinnick, '97 • Brian Piper, '84 • Kim Platko, '88 • Ray Pollard, '92 • Mark Pollock, '80 • Carlton Powell, '93 • Steve Powell, '97 • Michael Price, '95 • Gary Primich, '87 • Henry Qualls, '95 • Mike Querry, '95 • Paul Quigg, '94 • Chuck Rainey, '84 • George Rains, '83 • Bobby Rambo, '95 • Bill Randolph, '97 • Terry Ranson, '84 • Mickey Raphael, '87 • Leon Rausch, '83 • Rick Casper Rawls, '87 • Jim Raycraft, '82 • Breit Reid, '94 • Johnny Reno, '93 • William Richardson, '87 • Slim Richey, '80 • Rick Rigsby, '93 • Ted Roddy, '87 • Reggie Rufier, '95 • Chad Rutter, '96 • Ruff Rufner, '90 • Joe Rugglero, '86 • Fred Rush, '96 • Patrice Rushen, '86 • Jimmy R. Rusidoff, '92 • Doug Sahm, '86 • Joe Sample, '86 • Robert Clayton Sanders, '87 • Billy Sanders, '84 • Gabriel Saucedo, '85 • Mike Scaccia, '92 • Kevin Schermerhorn, '95 • Robert Schietroma, '94 • Connie Schlig,d., '82 • Peter Schmidt, '93 • Mike Schwedler, '88 • Jeff Scroggins, '95 • John Scully, '95 • Jeff Sellers, '83 • Charlie Sexton, '83 • Tommy Shannon, '91 • Walter Shannon, '83 • Jim Shelly, '84 • Craig Simecheck, '83 • Rhandy Simmons, '87 • Wayne Six, '90 • Chris Sioles, '96 • Paul Slavens, '90 • Kevin Smith, '95 • Rollo Smith, '85 • Jimmy Don Smith, '82 • Ron Snider, '90 • Matt Snow, '96 • Steve Sonday, '91 • Ed Soph, '97 • Derek Spigener, '92 • David Stanley, '81 • Lewis W. Stephens, '83 • Jas Stephens, '83 • Kenny Stern, '96 • Ken Stock, '93 • Andy Stone, '85 • Al Stricklin, '84 • Clint Strong, '97 • Eric Stuer, '85 • Jim Suhler, '89 • Texas Slim Sullivan, '87 • Bill Swicegood, d., '88 • Robin Syler, '84 • Eric Tagg, '86 • Matt Tapp, '90 • Phil Taylor, '93 • Miss Inez Teddlie, '87 • Richard Theisen, '86 • Whitey Thomas, '82 • Ron Thompson, '82 • Bill Tillman, '93 • Andy Timmons, '91 • Keith Traquair, '94 • Al Trick, '88 • Uncle John Turner, '83 • Lisa Umbargar, '96 • Richie Vasquez, '95 • Jimmie Vaughan, '78 • Brian Wakeland, '94 • Fredde Pharoh Walden, '88 • Jimmy Wallace, '82 • Craig Wallace, '87 • Jim Jimbo Wallace, '92 • Linda Waring, '82 • Marvin E. Washington, jr, '97 • Johnny Guitar Watson, '85 • Mike Webster, '85 • Ronnie Weiss, '80 • Tim Wheeler, '84 • Scott White, '95 • Larry White, '82 • Scott Whitfield, '95 • Buddy Whittington, '90 • Van Wilks, '90 • Steve Williams, '81 • Kim Wilson, '87 • Ronnie Wilson, '93 • U.P. Wilson, '85 • Wally Wilson, '81 • Kenny Withrow, '91 • Dan Wojciechowski, '90 • Kinley Barney Wolfe, '92 • Jason Wolford, '92 • Ted Wood, '95 • Alan Wooley, '92 • Tommy Young, '92 • Red Young, '86 • Dave Zoller, '95

BUDDY

Buddy Magazine's Texas Tornados

SPOTLIGHT on PERFORMERS

Still hard rockin': *Solinger*

Solinger

WHAT DO ALICE IN CHAINS, King's X and a band called Solinger have in common? They all lost out in the final cut when the handlers of KISS were choosing an opening act for the old face-painted dudes' show on July 5 at Reunion Arena.

Who is Solinger? They're a Dallas-based group formed in 1989 by Denton's Johnny Solinger. The band has been described as a mix of Guns N' Roses and mid-'80s glam metal with a dash of UFO.

Drummer Jamie McLester, who grew up in Fort Worth, said that description doesn't quite fit. "We don't like to be compared to acts like Bon Jovi. We're definitely a harder act," he said.

"We have a straight-ahead style," said lead guitarist Dave Hineman of Denton, whose sleekness reminds one of a cross-country runner. "We're not trying to change anybody's personal tastes. We're just running with what we've got."

Solinger shows are a treat for the eye. No, we're not talking about glamboy, tight-butt jeans and leather dusters. No painted faces or fingernails, or scantily clad, busty back-up bimbo singers. Just back-to-basics guitar-driven rock. Twenty-seven

year-old screamer Johnny Solinger handles the high-volume vocals. John Mott, a tall 29 year-old from Hollywood, provides rhythm support for the group's large sound. Hineman, 27, delivers nimble and sometimes screaming leads. McLester and bassist Jon Mann, 28, from Detroit, provide the firm foundation.

In the band's original form, singer Solinger — who sports Axl Rose-ish blonde hair and energy — was backed by Mott and Grey Wear on bass. The band did the area nightclub scene before releasing an EP, which got air play on Z-Rock and Q102 in 1992. "The unexpected death of bassist Grey Wear in 1994 inspired us to write additional material for our second (self-titled) release," McLester said. Wear overdosed on Xanax after the death of his mother. "We joined together and produced heart-felt, intense music and lyrics; 'Years' and 'Nevermore' are samples of this period." Those songs speak to the band's loss with gratitude for the good times and good wishes to Wear.

The boys recently opened for the Scorpions and Alice Cooper at Dallas' Starplex, and the performance was *killer*. Unlike many bands placed in the number three slot, Solinger started the show kickin' and rockin' with lots of guitar distortion and

Johnny's screamin' lyrics. The ruckus drew fans who were drinking beer at the side plazas back to their seats. Fans awaiting Alice and the Scorps were hardly bored with Solinger as the opening act.

McLester has the chiseled facial features of a Kevin Bacon and muscular definition from years of percussion work. He got his musical training in Fort Worth, from arts to choir and band participation at North Richland Junior High and Richland High, to gigs at area rock clubs with various bands.

He found his current employment in 1994 when he met Solinger almost by happenstance at a bar and asked for an impromptu audition from the singer. Solinger belted out a tune on the spot, and McLester signed on immediately. He's enjoying the work. "Since I was very young, I have been expressive, particularly by utilizing instruments," he said. "But I now really feel at home with Solinger. I used to take things very seriously until I met Johnny. He's helped me have a lot of fun and relax a little."

Besides fun, Solinger also has attitude and heart. They seem ready to rock the house whether playing before an audience of 20 or 20,000. They offer fundamental heavy-metal stylings and energy that elude posers and wannabe alternative acts. This band is another example of the anything-but-quiet resurgence of hard rock cycling its way back into the mainstream. "Let's look at Lollapalooza for '96," singer Solinger said. "This was basically the anchor for alternative music when it first came out. Who's headlining it? Metallica and Soundgarden. So we've seen a full rotation."

Still, seven years after its formation, Solinger is struggling to win the attention of a major label. The band has played 150 live shows in the past 18 months, but they were disappointed that they were not selected to open for KISS.

"Sometimes it's the luck of the draw and who you know," McLester said about trying to get that big break. "We have been approached by one label who was working their artists heavy in Japan, but there were parts of the deal that were not appealing to us. We're going to hold out for another offer. We are working on new material for our third CD, then we will hit the show again. Now we're back to where we were, playing local clubs again. We've gone full circle."
—BRUCE CAMERON

Solinger in the spotlight

The Beat Goes On

1996 TEXAS TORNADOS

Presenting the 1996 Texas Tornados of Drums, the Lones Star State's best and foremost practioners of the Wham, the Bam, and the Holy Thump.

AUGUST 1996 **BUDDY** 17

Featured in a 1996 magazine article

"The Beat Goes On," continued

Skid Row to the Penthouse

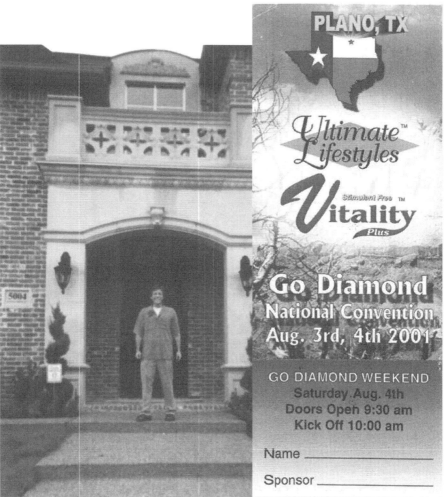

Ultimate Lifestyles dream building at
Willow Bend, Plano, Texas, 2001

Vitality Plus. Fortunes were made.

Vital Nutrition retirement party with Ultimate Lifestyles, "The Red Carpet"

Ultimate Lifestyles "Go Diamond" National Convention in Plano, Texas, August 2001

Ultimate Lifestyles retirement party, waiting for the stretch limo

Ultimate Lifestyles National convention: L to R, Mom,
Charlie "Tremendous" Jones, me and Abby

Go Diamond National Convention: Me and Diamond
Upline Alvin Glatkowski

Ultimate Lifestyles winning team, L to R: Bobbi Vitality, me, fitness
expert Reggie Bryan, Dr. Ray Nannis, DC

Ultimate Lifestyles Executive leadership team, 2001: VP Network Operations
Charlie and Sherry Smith, Presidents Mike and Sharon Norwood, Vice
President Bobbi Vitality, Vice President Cathy Parolini and me

Retirement party in the stretch limo with Gary the Aviator

All smiles at Ultimate Lifestyles retirement party

Diamond Alvin Glatkowski and James at Churchill Downs

Aim for Greatness Weekend with Marilyn St. Pierre and JMC

With VP of Network Operations Charlie and Sherry Smith, Lake Hamilton, Arkansas

In action, training the network at Ultimate Lifestyles "Aim for Greatness"

With Sherry Smith, boarding "The Belle"

Being recognized as National Marketing Director for
Ultimate Lifestyles

With "A Natural Choice"
at a Ultimate Lifestyle
conference

Sitting in on the drum kit with "Casper: on "Brick House"

Near Death

2001, stage 4 kidney failure diagnosis

Christmas 2002, pre-near-death experience. Weighed down with 30 pounds of extra fluid.

Love Sound Revival's self-titled EP, 2002

Love Sound Revival sushi party at Anzu. L to R: Michael
Madison, Ben Law, me, Steve Britt, Richard Howeth,
Mat Klabonski.

Love Sound Revival
EP
© 2002 Michael Madison

CD List price: ~~$14.95~~
CD Baby Price: $10.00   Add to cart

IN STOCK. ORDER NOW. Will ship within 24 hours!

Timeless, melodic songs in the vain of Wilco, Coldplay, & Ryan Adams. LSR is pressing the bounderies of modern popular music.

TRACKS   **NOTES**

PLAY ALL SONGS   lo-fi: dial-up
PLAY ALL SONGS   hi-fi: broadband

1. Song of Forgotten Faith
2. Flora
3. Misunderstood
4. Umbrella
5. Tranquilized

(Click a song name to hear it in lo-fi RealAudio. Need help?.)

CD Baby *Love Sound Revival* EP

Love Sound Revival 2002

IN: |All Music (except

EP
Love Sound Revival

Format: Compact Disc
(CDB0361390012)
Release Date: Jan 1, 2002
Original release year: 2002
Label: Love Sound Revival
Pieces in Set: 1

W

**Average Customer
Rating: Not Available**

Track Listings
Product Notes
Customer Reviews

Y

Audio Technical Glossary

Genre: Rock/Pop, **Sub-Genre:** Folk Roc

Track Listings:

Title

DISC 1

1. Song of Forgotten Faith

2. Flora

3. Misunderstood

4. Umbrella

5. Tranquilized

Love Sound Revival Tower Records EP

Suited up (Love Sound Revival)

"Band nerd," Love Sound Revival (photo by Michael Cox)

Love Sound Revival Open Mike Night, Club Dada, Deep Ellum, Texas

Miracles Still Happen

Miracles Still Happen, the Resurrection, 2009

Baptism Charlie Smith at the Norwoods

SuperNova Remnant
Alive in 2005

SuperNova Remnant, Alive in 2005, first promo picture

Drumming in Dallas

"In the groove," recording "The Afterglow" at Maximedia Studios

White's Chapel stained glass

"Stick it to ya"

Recording 'The Flame"

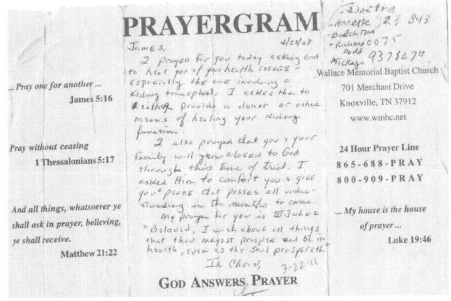

Prayer gram from an unknown prayer warrior

The Arm of the Lord is not too short to save.

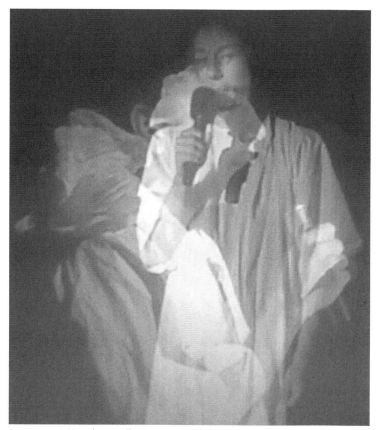

Lazarus, Miracles Still Happen 2004

Red Dress Tea, Crossroads Tabernacle, Frankie Rameriz and me

CALVIN HUNT BRIDGES

Calvin Hunt Bridges. The testimony that started it all.

At the beach, post hospitalization

Living Out Loud

Apostle youth radio, Denton, Texas

Living Out Loud with Circleslide and DJ Drue Mitchell, 89.7FM Power FM, Blake Porter

LOL benefit concert, November 2009

THE HOUSE OF BLUES
2200 N. Lamar Street
Dallas, TX 75202
(214) 978–BLUE

FROM Austin Texas HEADLINERS  Mothers Anthem

with Venture

SUPERNOVA
REMNANT

Friday 07/31/2009
Doors: 07:00 PM
Show: 08:00 PM

Prices:
$7.50 - 4-Pack Standing Only
$10.00 - General Admission
$12.00 - General Admission
Ages: all

SuperNova Remnant with Mother's Anthem, House of Blues Dallas, July 2009

SUPERNOVA
REMNANT

Photo--Frank Rameriz
supernovaremnant.net
www.myspace.com/LOLlivingoutloud

L to R: me, Robbie Gustin, James Putnam

SuperNova Remnant at The Door, Fort Worth, 2007

128

LOL ticket, The Mill, Denton, Texas, 2007

First official Living Out Loud concert, June 2006

SuperNova Remnant at 31st
Dallas International Guitar
Festival

All Access House of Blues Dallas.
SuperNova Remnant with
Mother's Anthem, 2009.

Criswell's Church, downtown Dallas

With Ches Cabler of Christian Drummers Hall of Fame

Temple of BOOM

Bearded and thoughtful

Brian "Big Bass" Gardner mixing SNR's debut "The Afterglow," 2006

Gold records in Bernie Grundman Studios, Hollywood

"Stick up" (photo Michelle Gustin)

Bassist Chris Thomas at House of Blues with SNR, 2009

Stepping out at Maximedia

Living out Loud logo

Double Bass Tama Star Classic Sparkle Fade

Robbie Gustin, Kevin and me in studio

2008 SuperNova Remnant lineup, L to R: D'Mill, me, Robbie, Perry

Is There Any Hope for Me?

SuperNova Remnant. L to R: Perry Thompson. keyboard/vocals; Daniel Miller, bassist; Temple of BOOM, JMC; Robbie Gustin, lead guitar/lead vocals.

SNR black bus, 2009, at Camp. JMC, Robbie, DW

Marty Perlman Studios

Worship & Warfare

M Northwestern Memorial® Hospital

Kovler Organ Transplantation Center

7/8/2009

James McLester
4773 Jasmine Drive
Fort Worth, TX 76137

Dear James McLester:

You have completed your pre-transplant work-up for Kidney transplantation at Northwestern Memorial Hospital. On 7/8/2009, your name was placed on the transplant waiting list at Northwestern Memorial Hospital. You will receive a telephone call whenever a Kidney becomes available, day or night.

When you are called for a transplant we want your hospitalization and post-transplant care to be as trouble-free as possible. To help give you the best possible service, **you are responsible for calling us in the event of the following:**

      INSURANCE COMPANY CHANGE
      TELEPHONE NUMBER CHANGE
      ADDRESS CHANGE
      DIALYSIS CENTER OR DOCTOR CHANGE
      YOU ARE GOING ON VACATION OR WILL BE AWAY FROM HOME
      YOU ARE ILL AND/OR HOSPITALIZED
      YOU RECEIVED BLOOD TRANSFUSIONS

It is extremely important that the Gift of Hope Organ Bank receives a blood sample from you each month. Please remind your dialysis nurse or technician of the monthly sera samples, which are due during the last week of every month. If you are not on dialysis or are a "Home" patient, a mailer containing one blood tube will be sent to you each month. You are responsible for paying the necessary postage to send the package. **Failure to send these blood samples each month will prevent you from receiving an organ transplant.** If any changes occur to your status on the wait list, you will be notified by our transplant department.

Attached is a letter from the United Network for Organ Sharing (UNOS). It describes the services and information offered to patients by UNOS and the Organ Procurement and Transplant Network.

We thank you for choosing Northwestern Memorial Hospital as your transplant center. Please call me if you have any questions or concerns.

Sincerely,

Michael M. Abecassis, M.D.
Chief, Organ Transplantation
(312) 695-0828

cc: Abdul Hafeez, MD
      FMC - Northeast Dialysis Center

Northwestern Memorial letter, 7/8/2009

Donor Consent Form Version 2.5

Northwestern University
Department of Surgery/Division of Organ Transplantation
CONSENT FORM AND AUTHORIZATION FOR RESEARCH

Title: Induction of Donor Specific Tolerance in Recipients of Living Kidney Allografts by Donor Stem Cell Infusion

Principal Investigator: Joseph Leventhal, MD, PhD

Funded by: National Foundation to Support Cell Transplant Research Inc.
Institute for Cellular Therapeutics, Louisville, KY
U.S. Department of Defense – Immunologic Testing Only

IDE: 13947: Sponsor, Suzanne T. Ildstad, M.D., Institute for Cellular Therapeutics

Stem cell study

Kovler Organ Transplantation Center

April, 27th 2009
RE: James McLester DOB 09.04.1967

To Whom It May Concern:

This letter is to provide information on James McLester. Mr.
McLester is presently in evaluation with Transplant department at
Northwestern Memorial Hospital in order to be listed for a kidney
transplant. Mr. McLester's initial evaluation occurred on March 24th,
2009.

If you have any further questions, I or my partner, Stacy Colias can be
reached at ▓▓▓▓▓▓ between the hours of 8:30a to 5:00p.

Sincerely,

Sara Miller, LCSW
Outpatient Transplant Social Worker
Kovler Organ Transplant Center
Northwestern Memorial Hospital

Northwestern waiting list, July 8, 2010

Tuesday, June 2nd, 2009

I was amazed by the hope and determination of the patients I met with today. Several patients who had
come back just to meet me! One patient sat in rush hour traffic just to come back to the clinic for the me
met today read my first book, A Promise Made- In Pursuit of the Iron Dream and told me they could rela
that they appreciated my honesty in the book. It really made my day to know that I was having this muc
continue to push myself on behalf of these patients and the patients I still have yet to meet! Tomorrow's
come Austin Texas.

NO LIMITATIONS ONLY INSPIRATION

Ironman Shad Ireland and
me, June 2009

Join us for a visit with
SHAD IRELAND

as part of his "What Inspires You" bike tour across the country!

MONDAY, JUNE 1, 2009

2:00 PM - 5:00 PM

Fresenius Medical Care Tarrant County

500 Campus Drive
Fort Worth, TX 76119
Phone: (817) 413-0330

Right Start Program Coordinator: Janice Crawford

Fresenius Medical Care is proud of our sponsorship of Shad Ireland and is supporting the "What Inspires You" tour. Along his route, Shad will speak at community events and visit Fresenius Medical Care dialysis facilities.

Shad Ireland was the first dialysis patient to compete in, and complete, the physically challenging Ironman Triathlon competition on July 25, 2004. A 26-year dialysis patient, Shad has campaigned nationwide to raise dialysis awareness while encouraging chronically ill people to take a positive, proactive approach to their challenges and achieve their life goals.

For more information on Shad Ireland, visit:
www.UltraCare-Dialysis.com/shadireland

Shad Ireland flyer, with Janice Crawford

"No Limitations, Only Inspiration," song for Iron man Shad Ireland and Special Olympics

At an old country church with Clear Camp, Mena, Arkansas, Summer 2009

Robbie in the light

Robbie on acoustic at Spin 180 Lounge, with Power FM 89.7

Bassist Jon Reed

Robbie leading worship at House of Blues

WWW.ERICYOUNKINPHOTOGRAPHY.COM

Live at Spin 180 Lounge with Dj Drue Mitchell

Slammin' It at House of Blues

DFW New Beginnings video shoot for
"DECLARATION"

Double Bass Tama Star Classic Sparkle Fade kit

Wielding the stick (photo
courtesy Marty Perlman)

SuperNova Remnant Live with Shatter Me

144

Hearts on Fire

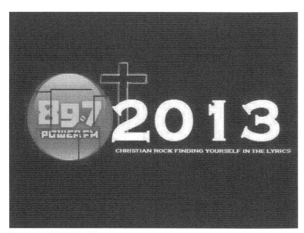

Power FM T-shirt logo submission

Hearts on Fire, at PowerFM Studios with Promotions Director Dawn Henderson

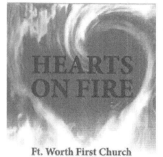

Hearts on Fire, Fort Worth First Church of the Nazarene, August 2011

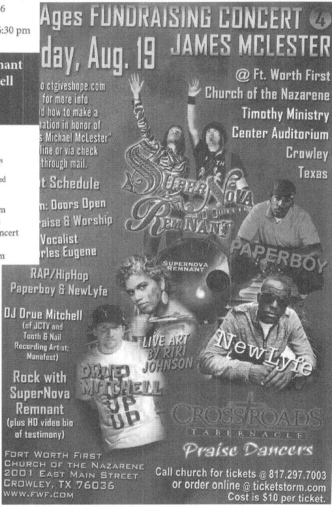

Hearts on Fire Fundraiser number two

5th Quarter @ the Cross, with SuperNova Remnant, Athena Chaney, NewLyfe and DJ Drue Mitchell

SuperNova Remnant Rockin' Worship Show, Bedford, Texas, 2010

DJ Drue and me at Hearts On Fire number one

Arms up in worship at REMEDY (photo courtesty of Jill Cross)

Twirl 4 REMEDY (photo courtesy of Jill Cross)

Stick Airborne at Remedy (photo courtesy of Jill Cross)

Robbie and me, in color, at REMEDY-(photo courtesy of Jill Cross)

With Brian Lee at Trees 2011. L to R: Me, Robbie, Brian, DW, Nepo

SuperNova Remnant at Trees with Stryper, March 16, 2011

Me in red light, at Trees with Stryper

Hearts On Fire 2. Worship
Leader Josh Boice, FWF.

Hearts On Fire 2, red light

Reaching out

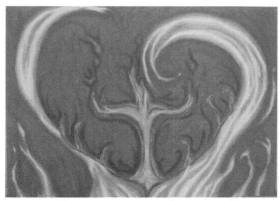

Hearts on Fire painting, by Riki Art

James Michael McLester of SuperNova Remnant

By
Billy Amendola
– August 16, 2011 **Posted in:** Drummer's Blogs, Drummers
Share |

Greetings from the Lone Star State of Texas! My heart goes out to all modern drummers, aspiring and professional. I currently am the drummer/songwriter for Christian rock band SuperNova Remnant, from Dallas/Fort Worth, Texas, as well as drummer for various Dallas/Fort Worth churches including Crossroads Tabernacle.

When I was young, I auditioned for my school's concert band, where I served as president and first-chair trombonist. I learned to sight-read and perform with an orchestra—yet I longed to play rock 'n' roll. My cousin introduced me to Journey, AC/DC, and Van Halen. I traded in my trombone for a nice Tama Brazilian kit and enrolled in private lessons from Chuck Whitby, Warren White (studio, Ice Capades), and Ron McDonald (UTA drum instructor) at Grant's Drum City in Irving, Texas.

Vinnie Paul of Pantera would frequent Grant's when the band was on the rise in our local scene. I quickly went from teen clubs to opening up for Pantera at area venues before their worldwide rise to fame. My influences include John Bonham, Stewart Copeland, Neil Peart, Terry Bozzio, Alex Van Halen, Tommy Lee, Buddy Rich, and Gene Krupa.

Drumming professionally from age seventeen led to many opportunities to record with professional artists such as the Crossing, Redhouse, Andy Timmons, and the band Solinger, featuring Johnny Solinger of Skid Row. Solinger played all over the Southwest and recorded the *Electric Mountain* CD at Sumet-Burnet Studios in Dallas, *Solinger Live* at Starplex in Dallas, where we opened for the

Modern Drummer article, part 1, August 16, 2011

154

Scorpions and Alice Cooper, and *Chain Link Fence*, which went international and became the favorite of KEGL 97.1 in Dallas/Fort Worth. This led to a sold-out performance with Geffen recording artists Tesla. I was inducted into *Buddy* magazine's "Texas Tornados" with great drummers such as Vinnie Paul, Frank Beard of ZZ Top, and Dave Abbruzzese of Pearl Jam. In Solinger's rise, Johnny auditioned for Atlantic recording artists Skid Row. Johnny flew up to New Jersey to jam with the Skids and flew back to Texas as their new lead singer.

Around this time I realized that after pouring my heart into music for fifteen years, I was burnt out. But in 2002 I reunited with Redhouse front man Michael Madison in Love Sound Revival and we recorded an EP for Tower Records. In 2003, a near death experience led to surgery on my left arm, and I was unsure what the future would hold. Drumming professionally was my life. I was discharged from the hospital after eight days. A mutual friend told Robbie I was dying. Robbie came to see me and let me know of a "change" he had in his life. He'd flat lined of a drug overdose in 2001, and he invited me to Crossroads. Soon I was playing drums at Crossroads Tabernacle.

Out of the fires of our rock 'n' roll past, God put Robbie and me together to make music for a new sound and a new generation. SuperNova Remnant was born and recorded its debut, *The Afterglow*, which was released through CD Baby, iTunes, Amazon, Rhapsody, and Best Buy. Regular airplay followed on the Christian rock station POWER FM 89.7.

SuperNova Remnant opened for Stryper at Trees, and our radio single "Glow" was released on our second CD, *Worship & Warfare*. We are now tracking our third CD, *Rockets Red Glare*.

Thanks to Max Peterson, I have three Tama Starclassic kits. I also use Zildjian cymbals, Tama hardware, LP cowbells, Evans heads, SKB road cases, and Vic Firth Natural Jack DeJohnette signature sticks.

I have been enamored by Drum Corps International drumline competitions since 2009. I want to share my passion for DCI with *Modern Drummer* readers and encourage you to develop an appreciation for this emerging art form. Please read my article on DCI Kick Off 2011 at www.jmclester.com.

Modern Drummer article, part 2, August 16, 2011

Robbie and me backstage at Rockin' Worship Roadshow at American Airlines Center with Mercy Me

The stage awaits

Bassist Chris Ivey, Worship & Warfare

SuperNova Remnant live at Trees, Deep Ellum, Dallas, with
Stryper, 2011

Hearts On Fire 2 crew

LIVE at Remedy. L to R: James
Putnam, JMC, Robbie

Robbie Gustin, warrior leading
the charge

Stryper's visual timekeeper Robert Sweet and me, pre-show

Grammy winning worship leader Chris Tomlin, backstage at
Nokia Theater

Worship in black and white

Mission SuperNova Remnant and Prologue

Bassist James "The Ox" Putnam, House of Blues Dallas

Aftershow Houston: JMC, Stryper Guitarist Oz Fox, Robbie Gustin

Backstage in H Town, L to R: Stacey Steele, Eddie "FH" Mick, Frank "CC" Rameriz

SNR live at House of Blues

Brian "Big Bass"
Gardner, mastering
"Rockets Red Glare"

Crowd, SuperNova Remnant, 2012 Tour

Robbie Gustin, singing out

SNR Chillaxin' at The Rainbow, Sunset Strip, with DJ Drue Mitchell, JCTV, 2012

Lead vocalist and SNR guitarist Robbie Gustin. Angelic voices, thunderous guitars.

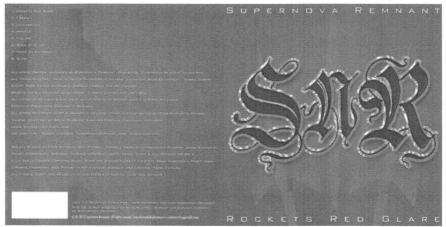

SNR Rockets Red Glare CD (Cover art by Bobby Greeson)

Ryan Bentley, Maximedia, Rockets Red Glare mix down

SNR live from above at H-Town

SNR with great fans: Karen Mc. and Dana B.

Stacey Steele, JMC, Robbie G.

In the Light

Surrounded by cymbals

SNR jammin' with Stryper in Houston

L to R: Nepo, The Ox, JMC, Robbie G.

Sound check at House of Blues, JMC with Oz Fox on Robbie's rig. FUN!

Buster's view at the soundboard

SNR and Stryper marquee at House of Blues

"It's all about the cake, Ryan." Design by PQ.

Robbie G. live (photo by HartArts)

At Starbucks ticket giveaway. L to R: Robbie G.,
Charles, Cap'n XFest, JMC

Stryper's drummer Robert Sweet, Stryper fan,
vocalist/guitarist Michael Sweet, bassist Tim Gaines

Stryper Tour 2012, Texas, view from the balcony

Stryper and SNR poster
(designed by Mitch Moore)

Thanks, Evans, for the 26' Temple of Boom head!

SNR LIVE at Rockin' Worship Lounge, Bedford, TX. Thanks, Charles!

House of Blues Aftershow meet & greet. L to R: Gary Taylor (editor), Dr. Bob, JMC, Robbie G. ,Nepo, James.

L to R: Robbie G. ,JMC, Chris (fan), Stacey, at House of Blues Houston

Robbie and me at Grace Avenue in Hollywood

SuperNova Remnant, tour 2012

Who's behind the door?

Standing and twirlin' with SNR live

Standing in yellow light, House of Blues

JMC and JEY, aftershow, Aerosmith/Cheap Trick at AAC

Black and white custom (photo by Robert Reddy)

Me as a cartoon, by Joey Spector

JMC, hanging loose

Hearts On Fire 2. Tim, I enjoyed jammin' your drum kit!

Let me hear ya!

Peter Nepo, keys, vocals, sound explosions, live with SNR; bassist James "The Ox" Putnam, low-end excitement!

Catch the Spirit.

Shout it out loud!

Peter Nepo, keys, vocals, sound explosions; bassist James "The Ox" Putnam, low-end excitement; lead vocalist, SNR guitarist Robbie Gustin, angelic voice, thunderous guitar.

L to R: Mom, JMC, DJ Drue Mitchell of JCTV

Robbie, singing out

L to R: Robbie G., DJ Drue, JMC, at Ameoba's Vinyl, Hollywood, CA

Temple of BOOM!

Standing in worship

Peter Nepo, keys, vocals, sound explosions, live with SNR

Stryper and SNR, Houston House of Blues

G.K. Rocks and Michael Sweet of Stryper

Robbie G. and Drew the Lion Heart. Good times.

Coach

At the Cross, SuperNova Remnant

Dr. Peter Jack Rockson

Team Beyond Organic at the Stockyards

Team Beyond Organic, Conscious Living

Beyond Organic Founder, Jordan Rubin, October 1, 2012, at Botanical Gardens, Fort Worth, Texas

Beyond Organic team in Kansas City

Beyond Organic, JMC and Mike B.

Dr. Josh Axe

Dr. Dan and Merily Pompa

James and "the one and only, original," Morris Duval

James and Dr. Bard, Austin State Capital, speaking out against GMOs

Warren and Rebecca Phillips

Beyond Organic flyer, Dr. Bard and me, 2012

Jordan Rubin, Beyond Organic autograph, Ephesians 3-20

PowerFM interview
with Dawn Henderson,
Tuesday, November 27,
2012

Photo courtesy Karen Overstreet

Photo credits
Exqusitie Photography, Cindy Williams
Marty Perlman Photography
Amanda Lewis, ACLEW Photography
Robert Reddy
Hartsart Photography
Brent McKinley, Photographer
Mitch Moore
Alexandria Quinn
Karen Overstreet
James Bland
Eric Younkin
Front book Cover: Chris Jones @ C Chris Jones
Back book cover: Jill Cross
Cover and interior layout & design: Gary Taylor
Web design for www.jmclester.com provided by Todd and Teresa Jungling of
WSI (www.LeadingWSIwebsolutions.com)

Chapter 7
Skid Row to the Penthouse

I had spent six long years with Solinger. I was more successful than I had ever been in my music career, but now it was over. Johnny would soon fly to New Jersey to prepare for Skid Row's tour with KISS and Ted Nugent, while I would think about what might have been if Solinger had signed a major label deal—the type of deal we had worked to position ourselves for in spite of all the tragedies over the last six years. But it was all gone. Game over. I was having an identity crisis. The music business was all I had ever known or spent the time to get to know. No university taught rock stardom, so you just followed the careers of the Beatles, the Rolling Stones, Van Halen or U2 on how to become massively successful and emulate their formula.

I did very well in college while working at Fitness Food, while making money from Solinger and Fitness Foods. I dated pretty women, and I had a lot of freedom in my life. Now, finding out that Johnny was Skid Row's new lead singer was surreal, because we had become very good friends. We lived through the tragedy of Gray Wear passing away. We lived through the victories of opening up for Tesla, the Scorpions, Alice Cooper, Vince Neil of Motley Crue, Metallica (we played side stage), Cinderella, Blue Oyster Cult—the list goes on and on. Solinger appeared in the major rock magazines. Solinger's music aired all over the radio. Solinger's reputation ushered in Johnny's next big step. We worked so hard to see ourselves out there touring 200 nights a year in different cities on a major label. Our Solinger EP, the *Electric Mountain* CD, *Solinger Live* and *Chain Link Fence* proved we had a formidable sound—and hard rock fans appreciated it. Johnny returned to our studio in Garland as I was tearing down my drums. He said, "Well, I've got something to tell you that's a little uncomfortable. I went to New Jersey and auditioned for Skid Row, and I'm their new lead singer."

In DFW, many bands covered Skid Row's songs. Skid Row penned a huge ballad, "I Remember You," which climbed into the Top Ten on *Billboard Magazine*, a high accomplishment for a new band discovered by Jon Bon Jovi. Next, they released "18 and Life" and "Youth Gone Wild." Skid Row opened up for Motley Crue and played the big stages all over the world, including Castle Donington. Johnny prepared to tour with KISS, who had built an empire over three decades since starting out in New York in 1970. Anyone who knows anything about hard rock music has heard about "the greatest rock 'n' roll band in the world." KISS had toured the world, and perfected it. Ted Nugent and Skid Row were selected as the opening acts. All of a sudden, *Chain Link Fence* was popular, and, now, Johnny was the new singer of Skid Row, preparing to tour with KISS. I was thinking, "What am I going to do now?"

I always remembered the story about the "fork in the road," and I thought to myself, "You know, I've invested all my time, but I am honestly relieved that I'm going to go on a new pathway." So I said, "Okay, Johnny, that's fine, you go on to Skid Row." I admit I was a little bit jealous. As a matter of fact, Skid Row was thinking about changing out drummers, because the original drummer, Rob Affuso, who studied at New York State, was leaving the band. I knew it was a long shot, but I put my name in the hat. The audition never came around.

I decided to retreat. I was now in management at Fitness Foods, making $30,000-plus in 2001. I was single, with no wife or kids. I ended my romantic relationship with the Filipino girl, so now it was just me. In transition, I met this pretty girl who worked at Vital Nutrition in Casa Linda. My best friend, Tom Vanderslice, managed the Casa Linda location. After a modern makeover, Fitness Foods became Vital Nutrition. Vital Nutrition opened the original store in Plano, where I worked, and a second clinic on Preston Road in Dallas. The Preston Clinic housed several doctors, including Dr. Taylor and Dr. Russell Phillips. I was their patient for a while. Owner Martie Whittiken hosted a radio show called "Healthy by Nature." Vital Nutrition opened locations on Lovers Lane in Dallas, one in Frisco and another at Casa Linda in Garland. I was promoted to head buyer for the Plano store, and Vital Nutrition had its own store brand of nutritional supplements. The 3,000-square-foot store was grossing an amazing amount of money.

I thought maybe I would just pour myself into my nutrition career and give music a break for a while. I didn't know whether I would return to music. In the meantime, I chose to support Johnny. Skid Row was playing the "sold out" Alamo Dome in San Antonio with KISS, so my friends and I got together and drove to San Antonio. As soon as I walked in, I was amazed by the immensity of the Alamo Dome. There were *masses* of people. Solinger played the Starplex in front of 18,000 people and to a crowd of 30,000 people at Festival Con Dios before I joined the band, but this was obviously a new level.

We watched Johnny take the stage with the Skids. Johnny rocked it out and sang from his heart. Skid Row fans were adapting to the new frontman. Skid Row fans developed a romance with lead screamer Sebastian Bach, a tall, lanky, blond, California-style singer from Canada with lots of charm.

That night, we all went down to the River Walk after the show. I was drunk, out of touch and inebriated. I really didn't know how to process all that was going on. I began to internalize those feelings, and the social drinking led to me drinking Crown Royal at home. At that time, I lived at 8233 Lullwater in a little two-story place right off Northwest Highway, near Casa Linda. My roommate began dating a girl from New York, who occasionally came over to the house. I would drink a fifth of Crown Royal and a six pack of imported beer from one of the liquor stores near our house. Then I would go to PT's topless bar, Baby Doll's or some other men's club and escape. I knew the deejays, the dancers and even some of the staff. It became a hiding place. This lifestyle was all I knew for a decade of my adult life.

Many nights, I would sit at the bar, and the pretty girls would come up to me, but I was never really interested at this point in taking them home and having sex with them. I just liked the music and the dark atmosphere and enjoyed talking to people about what was going on or *not* going on in my life. The evenings never seemed to end. The attention was nice. I was used to showing up at a venue at 10:30 p.m., taking the stage and performing until 2 a.m., then partying or going out to eat. Next was whatever the night had in store: sex, drugs and rock 'n' roll. During this transition, some friends introduced me to Collagen Plus. This was the new genesis of a product that we had done well with, called CalorAd, a collagen-based product consumed at night, which promised weight loss while you slept. Tom Wood, the Collagen Plus developer, brought his creation to me at Vital Nutrition. It quickly became one of the top three sellers. It helped people suffering with arthritis, fibromyalgia, diabetes and numerous other health challenges, and it increased energy. The formula was great. It was the first time I had seen anything that mixed aloe vera in a 200:1 ratio with collagen and combined it with conjugated linoleic acid, Super CitriMax, B6, B12, folic acid, Co-Q10, pyruvyl-glycine—all these buzzwords—into one product. Collagen Plus had great marketing. Sales were blooming, and I was making extra money.

Soon, this led to an appointment with a motivational speaker and salesman named Bobbi Vitality. Daily, Bobbi would drive his white Lincoln Town Car up and down Parker Road in Plano, along the corridor where I worked. I had met Bobbi earlier at Tom Woods' house where we filmed an infomercial for Tona Slim, which was the TV direct-to-consumer formula. Tona Slim was identical to Collagen Plus. Now, a network of very successful businessmen, led by entrepreneur Mike Norwood, were about to launch Collagen Plus under the label Vitality Plus.

I met Bobbi Vitality and Mike Norwood at a mansion on Swiss Avenue. Bobbi Vitality was a very successful businessman from Minnesota. Mike Norwood was extremely successful with Amway and Family of Eagles. I didn't really know what I was getting into, but God was putting another pathway together for me, now that I had laid the music down. I was living at 8233 Lullwater. I was working at Vital Nutrition during the day and visiting the topless bars at night, and, all of a sudden, this Collagen Plus/Vitality Plus thing took off, and I found myself joining a network called Ultimate

Lifestyles.

In the midst of all this, I experienced blurry vision. During this time, I was not only drinking the Crown Royal, but I was spending hours looking at pornography. I remember spending hours online and later roaming the aisles of adult bookstores looking for a thrill without the commitment of a relationship. I was really broken that things were not working out for me in a relationship, and I continued in my secrets.

I was also smoking marijuana. I had no idea at the time what my body was going through, but I could tell something was happening. Since my vision was blurry, and I couldn't see to drive, Tom agreed to drive me to my eye exam. It was an icy day, December 26, 2000. I was wearing my black leather trench coat. I went into the eye clinic, and they processed me as a new patient. I hadn't had an eye exam in years—I hadn't needed one. They took me back and did the refractor and took my blood pressure, which was 220/140. The nurse looked at me and said, "We're calling an ambulance for you. You've got to go to the hospital right away." Apparently, she saw something behind my eyes that worried her.

I was rushed to Baylor Richardson Hospital where they checked me for a heart attack and stroke. Doctors in the ER prescribed nitroglycerin to rapidly lower my severely elevated blood pressure. After my dad passed away in 1991, I began to take serious notice of my health.

The next day, I was discharged, after all my tests looked okay, to see an eye specialist, Dr. Nathan Lipton. I went to see Dr. Lipton, and he did a full-blown eye exam. He diagnosed me with hypertensive retinopathy. He instructed me to watch my diet and include lutein and antioxidants, grape seed extract and other nutrients, and referred me to Dallas Retina Specialists. I was diagnosed with mild hypertension. I also had an IVP on my kidneys, which didn't reveal anything. They found protein in my urine, but nothing revealed a diagnosis of kidney failure.

At my appointment with the retinal specialist, he examined my eyes and said," Sure enough, your diagnosis is hypertensive retinopathy." He described it as white cotton spots behind my eyes.

By now, my vision had somewhat cleared. I could see better than before, and I didn't really take these "white cotton spots" as seriously as I could have. I was inconsistent with the follow-up visits. I still had not returned to music, but I developed my network marketing business with Ultimate Lifestyles. My income was steadily growing, and my vision continued to improve. I followed up with my cardiologist, Dr. Weingarden, who admitted me to Baylor after the eye exam. He said, "James, your creatinine has crept up." It had gone from 2.2 to 3.4. He said, "I'm concerned about this. You need to see a kidney specialist."

I scheduled an appointment with Dr. Stephen Rinner of Dallas

Nephrology Associates. Dr. Rinner examined me and said, "You're in stage four renal failure." Dr. Rinner ordered the 24-hour urine collection test and suspected that I might have glomerulonephritis, or inflammation of the glomeruli, which are filtering units for the kidneys. He ordered me to keep doing the urine tests and to monitor my blood pressure.

I didn't want to prepare for dialysis, although Dr. Rinner said that I might need to do that. I decided to seek a second opinion, so I made an appointment with Dr. Jeffrey Thompson of Dallas Kidney Specialists the following year, in October 2001.

He ran a battery of tests, everything from A to Z and inflammatory markers, and diagnosed me with focal glomerulonephritis, but he didn't know the cause. He wanted to do a biopsy, but I said that if my kidneys were already failing I didn't want anybody punching a needle in them. I had some fear issues, and after all the sex, drugs and rock 'n roll, I didn't necessarily have a sober mind.

I was in a place where, even though I wasn't in the music, I still had the same lifestyle. The only difference was that I wasn't getting dressed up in the leather pants, twirling my drumsticks and playing music. I was frequenting the same places, with more money, wearing three-piece suits and hanging around millionaires.

At this point, Dr. Thompson was a little upset with me and said if I would not comply with the biopsy then he would no longer see me as a patient. I refused a biopsy and said I would seek a third opinion. I had a stool test at the Integrative Medicine Center at Vital Nutrition, which I mentioned earlier. Dr. Ken Taylor and Dr. Russell Phillips ordered a stool test from Doctors Data, to see whether it confirmed mercury toxicity.

I also had amalgams in my teeth, as I mentioned, since 1978. These toxic mercury amalgams had remained in my teeth for more than 22 years, and I knew something was wrong. They were treating me with Nutrispec (a nutrition line of different powders, minerals and electrolytes), trying to improve my blood pressure and my kidney function while purging the protein and red blood cells that were in my urine. It worked slightly.

All the while, I continued speaking and training for Ultimate Lifestyles upon stages across America. I recorded "Nature's Nectar," which became the company's top selling marketing tool. It went to doctors and other people all over the country. Just from studying nutrition and science, I guess people thought I knew what I was talking about, so I went from being the low-rung guy, running the sound system, and now, all of a sudden, I was a national marketing director. I was in Arizona with Dr. Walters, DC; I was in Joplin, Missouri, with health professionals Jane Case and Helen Kersey; I was in Washington, D.C., with Diamond Alvin Glatkowski; I was at The Kentucky Derby with Jerry and Carolyn Porter; I was in California and Kansas—

business was exploding everywhere. As a trained representative for the company, my income increased rapidly. Before Ultimate Lifestyles, I had been making a few hundred dollars a month. Now, I was earning a few thousand dollars a week—and it was climbing.

I was still employed at Vital Nutrition, and resentment was building within the store. I was dating this beautiful young lady there, and she was all into the organic foods and the same things as me. I had this great paycheck, and people around me were building me as a leader. They told me that in just a few years I would be able to retire. I said, "Really?" They assured me it was possible, and these guys were multi-millionaires, so I kept doing what I was doing. I did what I could nutritionally. I decided not to go to dialysis and not to get a biopsy.

Around 2001, my network with Ultimate Lifestyles blossomed to 8,000 individuals. Instead of wearing leather pants under spotlights and smoke machines while twirling my drumsticks, I started wearing nice, three-piece suits. I was on stage speaking and doing professional recordings as one of the top trainers in the company. My income from Ultimate Lifestyles was approximately $12,000 a month. I had more than tripled my monthly salary at Vital Nutrition. Ultimate Lifestyles' vice president challenged me, saying, "James, you should think about resigning, because if you go full time your income will grow even more."

At this point, I had a huge organization growing under Dr. Wendy Burke, MD, down in Longview, Texas, of Natural Choice. I had Chuck and C.J. at Fitness Essentials, one of the top nutrition stores in Plano, blowing and going. I had groups in key spots such as New York, California, Arizona, New Mexico, Utah—I traveled to these places and just loved the lifestyle. For the first time, I wasn't touring with a rock band, dependent on all the needs and wants of other people. I was in the driver's seat of helping other people, and it felt good.

Surprisingly, one day, My Ultimate Lifestyle team rolled out the red carpet in front of Vital Nutrition to welcome me to my official resignation from my J-O-B. At the urging of my upline, one day, suddenly, about two dozen of my team leaders from Ultimate Lifestyles greeted me with balloons and congratulated me on my retirement.

I found myself being chauffeured in a white limousine parked right in front of the store, after working in the store for seven years. The store had changed leadership after Richard Chambers purchased Vital Nutrition from Martie. Richard was a great guy to work for. I was an assistant manager and head buyer, but now I was doing better with Ultimate Lifestyles.

I was 34 years old and realizing a dream. After reading books like *Think and Grow Rich* by Napoleon Hill and *The Magic of Thinking Big* by David Schwartz, I had expanded my mind. I thought I had arrived. On the day of my resignation party, my team whisked me away to Willow Bend to walk through $340,000 mansions. I dreamed that I could soon afford one of these estates. The night of my resignation party, my family came over and celebrated with me at a steakhouse in Plano. One hundred fifty team members were there as guests. It was a celebration and a great moment. I'll never forget the way Ultimate Lifestyles treated me. I felt like royalty. I felt like my life was really making a difference, *and I wasn't sure I was ever going to go back into music.*

I stayed with Ultimate Lifestyles and continued to travel the country, but, as I exhausted myself my teammates and leaders began to look at me and say, "James, you don't look well. Are you okay?"

I would say, "I'm fine. Let's just keep making money." I wanted to keep the wheels turning.

And they would say, "No, you look ashen gray." They worked in nutrition. Some were doctors. I just wasn't listening.

Over time, my creatinine level increased to 5.7, and at this point I knew that something needed to be done, so I sought out Dr. William Cowden, MD, whom I had met at Vital Nutrition years before. He worked in several clinics around Dallas and was one of the chief contributing editors for *The Definitive Guide to Alternative Medicine*, published by Burton Goldberg.

Many of you are probably familiar with that book. It is like an encyclopedia of knowledge in a silver, hard-back form. I called Dr. Cowden and said, "I've been diagnosed with stage four kidney failure. I don't know the cause of it. Will you see me?" He had a waiting list, but he agreed to work me in. I drove over to his office, and he tested me. After giving me a lot of pamphlets on detoxification and recommendations to take chlorella, homeopathic medicines and Chinese herbs, he said, "James, have you ever considered that the dental amalgams in your teeth could be contributing to your renal failure?"

I said, "No, Dr. Cowden, I haven't." He said he could test my teeth and the toxicity levels, as well as the voltage that was coming from the amalgam fillings. No one had ever informed me that these mercury amalgam fillings could be causing my kidney function to decline. From working at Vital Nutrition I knew it was a factor for some people, but surely I was okay. Or was I?

Dr. Cowden conducted the tests and said, "Yes, the amalgams are definitely blocking the energy flow to your kidneys, and that's causing the renal insufficiency." "But," he said, "don't fear. You're going to come through this."

Spiritually, Dr. Cowden could see that there was a lot of fear around me from what I had been through. When you don't have a sober mind, and you throw your life into sex, drugs and rock 'n' roll, and a sinful lifestyle, you're estranged from God.

I was trying to find God all this time. As a matter fact, I was living in a townhome at that time in 2002, and I dropped to my knees in my bedroom one night, and I said, "Lord, I just surrender. I don't know where this pathway is going, but I am giving my life back to you. I don't know exactly the next step to take, but I am asking you for direction." That led to midnight prayer conferences with my mom on the phone. I had been estranged from my mom since the 80s when I ran away from home to become a rock star and now, through my trial with sickness, our relationship was coming full circle. My mom was a praying mom. She was a mom that loved me, and I could cry with her and tell her what was going on. She was concerned. She was trying to talk me into moving in with them in Fort Worth. I was in Flower Mound, living in a townhome with lead vocalist Michael Madison, my band mate from Redhouse.

Mike started "Love Sound Revival," a new alternative rock band, and now I had the itch to play again. I started playing music with Love Sound Revival for the first time in three years. Love Sound Revival recorded a self titled EP on Tower Records and performed weekends at Club Dada and other Deep Ellum venues, as well as at Cornerstone Church in Arlington, where Mike had attended as a youth. We were very talented. Love Sound Revival consisted of guitarist/vocalist Matt Klabonski, bassist/keyboardist Ben Law and harmonica player Steve Britt, along with lead vocalist /guitarist Michael. The band would go to the Wild Turkey saloon down off Walnut Hill and 35 for cheers and beers, but I was trying to get away from that lifestyle, so it was difficult. I took my Chinese herbs and drank my watermelon tea to improve my health as Dr. Cowden had recommended.

In spite of my efforts, my roommates still partied. I couldn't get any rest. The partiers still partied and did all the same old things that I used to do. I needed to get out.

My good friend Frankie Ramirez from Solinger showed up at my door one day and said, "Listen, you've got two choices. You're either going to the hospital now, or I'm coming and picking you up and taking you to your mom's place where you can get well." I refused both. I did not want to admit I had a problem that I could not handle. After all, my entire life was a series of "grabbing the bull by the horns" and "pulling myself up by the bootstraps when life kicked me in the face." Why should I react any differently now?

My mom eventually talked me into having her and my sister drive to Flower Mound, load up my things and move in with them. I agreed and continued seeing Dr. Cowden. During this whole time, everything that I had left in the music business had now been replaced by the financial success of Ultimate Lifestyles, but, unfortunately, a health challenge had returned. I had already received two miracles regarding my health and now a third diagnosis came to challenge my life and my faith.

God had healed me of Reiter's syndrome, which went into remission, and He had restored my vision from the blurriness and the diagnosis of hypertensive retinopathy. I now had remarkable vision. I knew that God could do it. I just didn't know how it was going to happen, or when. I moved back into my mom's house around December 2002, after living on my own for 16 years. Basically, I stayed on the couch, because, by this point, I had gained 30 pounds of fluid. My skin was so tight that when I got in the shower my legs would crack and bleed. I would bleed through my skin.

My mom became very concerned. I was ashen gray and ice cold all the time from anemia, and the last thing I wanted to do was go on dialysis. I remember playing with Love Sound Revival once at Cornerstone Church in Arlington. We were there with Mike's pastor, Brother Leon, and his mentor, Brother Tim Adams, from San Antonio. Tim happened to be Mike's youth leader early on in his career. Tim's wife was a social worker for dialysis. We went to a church potluck after the service, and his wife graciously talked to me about how I should start dialysis. I was thinking that maybe I should do this. Maybe it was a step I should take, but I never would pull the trigger, and everybody around me was asking, "James, when are you going to go to dialysis?"

I would reply, "I'm not going. I'm going to get well." Well, Dr. Cowden had ordered some blood work, at my request, around February 2003. At this point, Love Sound Revival had come to an end. There was no music at all, and my life was reduced to lying on the couch with my feet propped up on about eight pillows to keep the fluid from pouring into my lungs and causing me to drown or my heart to fail.

I will never forget the night of February 6, 2003. I was lying in my mother's bedroom under an infrared heat lamp, trying to stay warm and rocking on this thing called a chi machine that Dr. Lipton had told me about. I had tried every contraption and device you can imagine, from lasers and acupuncture and detox to wearing colored glasses, charms and pendants—everything the New Age had to offer. Everything you could imagine, I had tried it.

The next morning, Dr. Cowden called me and said, "James, based on your blood work, your creatinine has crept up to an 18, your blood urea nitrogen level is 144, and a normal level is about 6 to 19 in the BUN." A normal creatinine level is about 1.2, and mine was 18. Obviously, my levels were dangerously off the charts. My hemoglobin was a 6, and my phosphorous was an 11, so my lab values were way out of balance. Normal hemoglobin is 14–17 for a man in my age bracket.

I was 36 years old. I had pursued rock stardom. I had made money in network marketing with a group of 8,000 people, and now my body was decomposing, and I was dying.

I knew Dr. Cowden would not send me to the emergency room to start kidney dialysis unless it was life or death. He uttered these words: "*James if you want to live, you must get to the emergency room immediately,*" I felt the cold chill of fear strike my whole being. My teeth were chattering, and I was white as a ghost. My mom loaded me in the car with an overnight bag, and we sped to Presbyterian Hospital in Dallas that morning. The accolades of fame and fortune were rapidly fading as I was about to face a battle for my life.

Chapter 8
Near Death

After living 13,140 days on Planet Earth, this was perhaps one of the scariest moments in my life. As I've said throughout this book, I had longed to become a rock star since I was 15. Sickness came against me. Losing my vision came against me. My parents' divorce came against me. Losing my father when I was 23 came against me. Drugs and alcohol came against me. Immoral relationships before marriage—all these things—tried to steal the blessed life that God had for me.

Dr. Cowden examined me after Dr. Rinner and Dr. Thompson and said the mercury fillings in my teeth at 11 years old played a part in the Reiter's Syndrome, the vision loss and the recent diagnosis of end-stage renal disease. Coincidence? Dr. Cowden called me and emphatically said, "Get to the hospital if you want to live." As soon as we hung up the phone, my mom rushed me to Presbyterian Dallas.

Upon arrival, I was white as a porcelain ghost, disoriented and hallucinating. Immediately after being admitted by Dr. Syed Rizwan, from Dallas Nephrology Associates, they put me in a wheelchair and wheeled me down to the basement of the hospital, which was the dialysis unit. It was freezing cold. I entered a roomful of patients screaming, moaning and groaning, in hospital gowns, lying on beds, some in wheelchairs, watching machines filter their blood through plastic tubing. It was so surreal to me. I never even imagined that I would see something like this, especially given the environments that I had been in before. Now, knowing it was a life-or-death situation, with all the prayers within me, along with the prayers that my mom and the people around me were sending out, doctors put a femoral catheter in my leg, so I could receive emergency dialysis.

There I sat on a hospital bed, freezing cold. I couldn't get up. Lines were running into my femoral vein in my leg, and I was watching my blood go through these plastic tubes into a machine, wondering if I was going to die or if I would get a blood clot. I had no idea whether dialysis was going to fix my kidney function. I also knew that dialysis was not designed to remove mercury from the bloodstream. My creatinine measured at 18.0 (normal 1.2), my blood urea nitrogen at 144 (normal 6–19), my hemoglobin level 6.0 (normal 14.0–17.0) and my phosphorus at 11.0 (normal 3.5). My blood chemistry was completely out of whack.

Somehow, I made it through my first dialysis treatment. One guy, next to me, who I think was coming off some heavy drug like heroin, was screaming and talking to himself, and I was saying to myself, "Lord, as if it's not enough just being in this horrific place, isn't this over the top?" I know people have been in worse conditions, but at the time, for me, it was definitely the "mother lode" of misery.

My mom was a trooper; she stayed at the hospital with me. The nurses were extremely nice. They sent me up to my room and told me I needed to dialyze again the next morning. I was wondering, "When is it going to end?"

The days ran together. All I had to hang on to was the Word of faith, and I was telling God, "I don't know where I'm going from here, but I know that You are going to lead me." My mom slept in the hallway, or she slept in a chair, if that's what it took. She was always there by my side.

All my life that I invested in music, and all that time as a successful networker, I never wanted people to see my weak side. I veiled this from just about everybody. But pretty soon, the word got out that we needed prayers, and my mom began to call my family, including my Aunt Pam and Uncle Carl and my granddaddy.

Scores of people from my network marketing business showed support, including the company CEO and vice president. I thought, "I'm sure not making any sales today. I'm not the hot-shot today, but here I am lying in this bed fighting for my life, and yet my caring friends are here." These acts of kindness spoke volumes, because God said to love your neighbor as yourself. Cards and balloons poured into my hospital room, displaying the love of God evidenced through family and friends. They gathered around my bed and sang psalms over me, and prayed over me. I could *feel* the presence of the Lord. It gave me great hope.

At night, I listened to my cassette tapes and CDs with healing scriptures from John Hagee to help me believe in the Word and feed my mind positive thoughts. Before the sun surfaced at dawn, about 5 a.m., they wheeled me down to that basement again for dialysis. I thought, "Here we go again. Lord, please help me get through this."

All the dialysis staff were so nice to me, and with each passing day the trial seemed a little bit easier. As the fluid was removed day by day—taking off 5 kilos one day, about 11 pounds, and then the next day another 10 pounds, and so on— my breathing and skin tone began to improve. I received a blood transfusion, which, thankfully, brought my hemoglobin up from 6 to 10. My creatinine and blood urea nitrogen levels began to go down, and things were looking good. Well, we all know that when things are really looking good, that's when the enemy is NOT going to relent.

After seven days of fighting for my life in the hospital, I will never forget this day. Early on the seventh morning, they came to wheel me down for my dialysis treatment. I always brought my CD player when they scheduled me for a procedure or dialysis. A permacath would be placed in my neck as a temporary dialysis access until I agreed to have surgery on my left forearm for an AV Fistula as a more permanent access.

While under anesthesia, I always listened to music because I didn't want to hear what was being said in the operating room. I didn't want to hear any negativity. All I wanted to hear were the angelic voices of God, because that's what I *do*, so I went down to the basement that day with my CD player.

I was lying in the hospital bed while listening to the *Braveheart* soundtrack because that's my absolute, all-time favorite movie, especially when he talks about freedom. Like a gentle breeze, the sweet presence of the Lord just came over me, and I heard the audible voice of God. I had never heard anything like this in my life. I knew I was so close to the breakthrough of at *least* getting out of the hospital to see what kind of life I had ahead of me.

I heard the Lord say, "James you will live and not die and declare the works the Lord."

And I thought, "Well, where's that coming from? Lord, is that you?"

And He said, "Yes, you will live and not die and declare the works of the Lord." That was the first time I heard a "Rhema Word"— it was impregnated in my spirit, and no matter what came against me I was going to stand on his promise in Psalm 118:17.

After hearing the Lord speak to me, I was wheeled back up to my semi-private room. Later that night, a gentleman with pancreatic cancer was admitted to the hospital to share my room. I wondered whether I was going to get well. I began to hallucinate and became paranoid. All kinds of doubts flooded my mind. I stayed up most of that night, even though I knew I had to get up for treatment early the next morning. I was listening to a cassette tape from Paula White about faith and not giving up.

I kept listening to the word God had spoken to me, but the enemy came with an all-out assault to distract me. All through the night, the enemy tormented me, saying, "James, everybody around you in this place is dying. You're dying, and you're not getting out of here alive." This chilling night was the Valley of the Shadow of Death for me. This dark night, riddled with torment that tried to destroy me, forced me to endure and stand on the scripture God promised me on the seventh day. And the eighth day, when I arose, after my treatment that morning, Dr. Rizwan discharged me to begin outpatient dialysis. Miracles still happen.

I was going to have *some* type of life ahead of me. I was overjoyed. The orderly wheeled me down to the ground level and helped me into my mom's white Chevy Malibu classic. We drove away from Presbyterian hospital, I thought, "What next? Am I going to be able to live on my own again? Am I going to travel again? Will I play music professionally again? Do I even want to do any of these things?" I was really in a wilderness. As my cousin, Lori Hearn, penned in her chronicles of her husband Mike's battle to overcome brain cancer, it was an "unfamiliar path."

We drove back to Fort Worth, and I moved in with my family again. Now, I was no longer lying on the couch gasping for air, full of 30 pounds of waste and fluid. I was lighter and leaner, although I was still ashen gray. Nobody really knew what I had gone through except for the handful of people who came to see me in the hospital. I told my mom, "Now I'm going to begin this outpatient dialysis three times a week, and it may not be everything I had hoped for, but at least I can begin to pray and take care of myself while doctors unravel this mystery."

I started outpatient dialysis at NE Dialysis off Denton Highway clinic three times a week. At that point, I was still not driving due to the trauma of everything that I had been through. I recall getting dizzy just thinking about driving over bridges or overpasses, because my senses were so off balance. Mercury can cause anxiety, hypertension, organ failure, depression, Alzheimer's disease and a number of other chronic diseases.

My mom helped me get around from point "a" to point "b." Soon, this routine was mundane and tiring. I didn't know if there was a light at the end of the tunnel. I was looking for something else, so I kept researching, and I became interested in stem cells. I believed God said that I was going to live and not die, so I kept standing on His promise and blessed assurance.

After being holed up for almost two years, I felt the desire to go out and hear some live music again. I hadn't been to a bar in years, but I learned that a friend of mine, Nepo, was playing at a place called Bell Bottoms down on Highway 26. Nepo was the lead singer way back in ChazaRetta and I hadn't seen him in forever. I heard Nepo was playing in TOUCH with Chad Allen, who was the bass player in Dirty Blonde as well as ChazaRetta, so I decided to go.

I will never forget, I walked in, and people thought I was strange. Not only was I white as a ghost, but I kept my T-shirt pulled up over my nose to keep from breathing the smoke. It felt like a dungeon in there, with all the smoke and the people drinking. I thought, "Lord, why am I here?" And the Lord just kept reminding me, "You're here because you may have something positive to share with these guys."

They were a good band. I enjoyed myself. After a set break, I went up and talked to Chad and Nepo. They said, "Wow, it's good to see you," but what happened to you? Chad, concerned, after seeing me that night, called a friend of mine, Robbie Gustin.

I met Robbie during junior high. When I would get drunk and pass out, Robbie would take the keys to my truck and make sure I got home safely. Or, if I was lost somewhere, Robbie would have my back. Robbie auditioned for my band early on in the game around high school, and we stayed in touch throughout the years. While I toured and aspired to become a rock star, Robbie was cutting his teeth at The Brook Mays Pro Shop in Dallas and Guitar Center, servicing some of the country's most talented musicians. Anytime I had a big show happening with Solinger, I would drive by Guitar Center to make sure Robbie knew about it, but other than a few after show parties for the major concerts, we did not hang much.

Robbie suddenly came back into the picture because Chad and Robbie worked together at Guitar Center. Chad went to Robbie and said, "Hey, have you seen Jimmy McLester?" Everybody called me "Jimmy" back in the day.

And Robbie said, "No, why? What's going on?"

Chad said, "Robbie, he's dying." Robbie was alarmed. Robbie had been through similar things, except he flat lined and bled internally from a drug overdose at the NAMM show in California. Robbie flew back home to his wife to tell her he was doing drugs and "come clean" to get his wife and kids back. But when he returned home all he found were his amplifiers and guitars thrown out on the lawn. His wife and kids were gone. Robbie had nothing to come home to. For a long time, his parents and family prayed for him, and, finally, he came to a place called Crossroads Tabernacle in Fort Worth, Texas.

Robbie was very resistant, but in 2001, on New Year's Eve, he attended a special service at Crossroads and heard Calvin Hunt's testimony. Calvin was a successful vocalist for years. Calvin's wife, Miriam, was saved at Christ Tabernacle in New York during one of their prayer meetings. After her new birth in Christ, she cried out for Calvin as he had become estranged from his family. He was smoking crack in a doghouse—not even living at home. His wife Miriam continued to cry out for Calvin at this prayer meeting, and Calvin went home that night in a stupor after hearing voices in his head, saying, "You need to go *immediately* to Christ Tabernacle."

Calvin stopped everything, got on the subway and went across to town to Christ Tabernacle. He entered the massive building in Queens, New York, and went upstairs to ask where his wife was. They were praying for him, and that night Calvin Hunt gave his life to Christ. Soon, our Pastors Corey and Beth Ann Jones were touched by Calvin's story on CBN 700 club. As a result, they felt God calling them to plant a church in a rundown neighborhood of Meadowbrook, instead of the upper class neighborhood of Southlake, TX.

After Calvin received his salvation, he journeyed to Crossroads Tabernacle on New Year's Eve 2001, testifying to what God had done for him. Robbie heard Calvin's testimony with his arms folded against the back of the wall, but, eventually, as a result of that moment of Calvin's obedience, Robbie was saved. Robbie recalls driving home that evening, saying to himself, "Calvin sure is a good speaker."

Robbie's new salvation led him to study the book of *Ephesians* in his Bible. Mental counselors attempted to convince him he was crazy. *Ephesians* became Robbie's 12-step program to overcome addictions to cigarettes, alcohol and drugs, including ice (methamphetamine). Unemployed, Robbie frequented Starbucks looking for men to fellowship with who better understood God. Robbie stayed faithful for two years, so the minute he heard from Chad that I was dying, Robbie called me and, in an instant, made a beeline to my door. Robbie wanted to find out what was going on with me. He said, "I am coming to your house!" And, little did I know, that moment would change our fate forever.

Chapter 9
The Knock and Miracles Still Happen

Once I was finally discharged from the hospital, music took a backseat to survival and getting well. I still loved music, as I had all my life, but I wondered, "How much do I love it?" In 2002, I was still writing songs, performing and recording with Love Sound Revival with lead vocalist/guitarist/songwriter Michael from Red House—yet it seemed so distant. I thought maybe I was laying my music down for good. There were no tours, no recording sessions, just the sound of worship music resounding through my headphones. But God had other plans.

All of a sudden, at the modest beige brick home nestled at 4773 Jasmine Drive, I heard a knock at the door. My mom went to the door and said, "It's your friend, Robbie."

I said, "Robbie…Robbie Gustin?" I hadn't talked to Robbie in four years. Well, Robbie came with one mission in mind: If I *were* dying, he wanted to make sure I was saved and had a relationship with the Lord. Robbie sat down in our living room and looked across at my ashen gray frame lying horizontal on the couch, and I told him, "Look, people around me think I'm going to die any day, but I know what the Lord said to me." Even today, Robbie tells me that when he was looking at me that day—with my colorless face and the catheter in my neck, for some reason, he heard in my voice that I was *not* going to die. Robbie was overjoyed to hear that the Lord spoke to me in the hospital, and he was ecstatic that I gave my life over to the Lord. He understood how that single moment of surrender brought me freedom.

I was searching for a church. I knew I needed to get back to living, as I had been holed up in my apartment before and after my near death experience. My mom and I were visiting Northwood Baptist Church, where my aunt Linda attended. It was the first time I had ever seen anyone incorporate the classic rock sounds of Jimi Hendrix into a church service and effectively merge it into worship music and the sermon. For a musician who knew nothing about worship, I thought it was cool. I didn't understand

God's word much more than John 3:16 and the Ten Commandments, but I could discern that the music was good. The Lord knew we were looking for a church, and Robbie said, "Hey, let me tell you what happened to me." He was talking about Crossroads Tabernacle. Robbie said, "I'm not asking you to join the Navy. I'm really not asking you to do anything except come to a Tuesday night prayer service. I can't put it in words; I just know if you come you'll be blessed."

I said, "Sure. I have nothing else going on." So Robbie, wounded, but hopeful from his divorce, brought me to Crossroads Tabernacle for the first time that night. I walked into the humble foyer of Crossroads and glanced at two foundational scriptures framed and boldly displayed upon the stucco walls: Matthew 22:37 and Jeremiah 6:16. I really felt the love of God there. I was a man who once carried suitcases of shame from my past experiences, but was hopeful that my Savior could carry the shame far away from me. My old nature was to roam the aisles of adult "fine arts" stores looking for thrills at 3 a.m. and having topless dancers sitting in my lap in the dark of gentlemen's clubs. It would trip your wires, the things I saw in those two decades, but when I walked into Crossroads, I felt the love of God. I felt something different. The people didn't seem to be pretentious.

All my life, I had abandonment, rejection and trust issues, so I assumed that the problem was with everyone around me. The enemy used the lie that everyone in church was a 'hypocrite" to keep me from learning and abiding in the truth. I am amused how many people use this excuse not to seek a church home. My reply to them is, "Name one baseball game, concert, golf tournament or charity event where there is not at least one hypocrite in the audience?" They realize that everywhere we go there are people pretending. Yet, at least in a body of true believers where the Holy Spirit is welcome, the light penetrates the hearts of the congregation and brings about real, lasting transformation. Sure, I was okay going one-on-one to a New Age counselor who never really dealt with sin or deliverance just self- reflection. I was okay spending time in an upper class neighborhood on a fine designer leather couch. I did not hesitate to spend $125 an hour airing out my life issues in private, but church would require me to learn to serve and submit.

I have since realized that our flesh fights us at every turn to resist the alien nature of submitting and serving. I was beginning to see things for the first time, as I realized my mountain had become so overwhelming that no one on the holistic side or allopathic side could repair it. I needed a supernatural faith and belief that in the midst of chaos God *alone* would perform the miracle in my life and fulfill the promise He made to me in the basement of Presbyterian on the seventh dawn of fighting for my life.

There is power in the prayer of agreement, so a lone ranger, who once laid pent up in his room hiding a formidable diagnosis of chronic kidney failure at age 34, was realizing that keeping a heart full of bitterness, anger and victimization inside was a bitter pill. I had swallowed this bitter pill all my life for "convenience" and not to burden anyone else. The sensual allure of sex, drugs and alcohol were my escape from the pain of not feeling loved or accepted, whether real or imagined. These vices only buried and magnified inner turmoil, with no lasting resolution. I remember John 3:16, and the scripture "God is Love," and reasoned that my broken, dry heart needed mending, and love and acceptance were the new medicines God prescribed. Perfect love casts out all fear and I had a myriad of fear closets. I sensed a presence as the greeters at Crossroads welcomed my broken heart with compassion and unconditional love that only God can provide, flowing from a servant's heart.

Life is not about a fancy building. Crossroads Tabernacle was planted on the corner of Meadowbrook in a semi-ghetto—there is nothing comely or modern or outwardly attractive about it. It's just a brick church with white trim and a pointed steeple, much like a Christmas tree ornament that pierces the sky.

The long-term members tell me Crossroads Tabernacle has come a long way since the days of Meadowbrook's old school paneling and shag carpet, but I never knew it that way. In every stretch of my imagination God does trade beauty for ashes. I was thankful that someone like my schoolmate Robbie was obedient to the urging of the Spirit, as he reached out to me.

Robbie could have invited me to a concert, a cook out, or "Ghengis Grill" (we like to eat there) but he invited me to join Crossroads' Tuesday night prayer meeting and enjoy a real meal where people learn to cry out to God for the desires of their heart. For a rebel without a cause who spent his life pulling himself up by his bootstraps, grabbing the bull by the horns and marching to the beat of his own drum, the idea of kneeling at an altar made of wood and talking to a God who seemed distant and angry was foreign to me. As a child, I certainly learned that "grace" was said before a meal and on special occasions such as Thanksgiving and Christmas, but I was not accustomed to praying on a Tuesday night for two hours with a congregation of people you had just met. I was tormented during my battles with mercury toxicity and the diagnosis of end stage renal disease that somehow if God really loved me I would not have become ill—would I? This is a major question in the church today that millions of people struggle with: "Why, Lord? Why me?" For the record, if you read the same Bible that I read (King James), you will find it replete with scriptures for healing. Healing is God's divine nature.

John 2, Acts 10:38, Jeremiah 30:17 and 1 Thessalonians 5:23 are a few gems that will work healing in your spirit, soul and body—only if you believe. We must destroy the stronghold of unbelief. The enemy works tirelessly in the minds of believers that it is not God's will to heal all from sickness and disease.

True, God allows trials and tribulations that can be a result of sin or a spiritual issue, but God can turn any situation for His good if we allow Him; however, most of us, even in the Church, have been handed down dangerous traditions of men that the Lord warned us about, and we bought the lie that it is not God's will to heal. Read the book of Job and study his life to learn how the Lord allowed Satan to afflict Job with sickness. Read the *entire* book of JOB, and you will see the restoration that God granted Job.

God allowed Satan to afflict Job, but because Job did not curse God and instead repented, Job realized that the power of life and death were solely in the hands of his Maker. As a result the Lord r*estored double* to the wealthiest man in the East. Job is one of the oldest books in the Bible, written long before Christ died on Calvary where he fulfilled the atonement that paid the price for mankind's healing by his precious, unstained, sinless blood. Imagine if God "Yahweh" was able to restore double to Job even *before* the atonement, how much more in the New Covenant?

I felt the love of God at Crossroads. After the wooing of the Holy Spirit through the heartfelt message of Pastor Corey Jones, I knelt down to the altar that night, and I'll never forget how the Lord met me there. I traded the ash heap of my broken, tattered past for the beauty and newness of life offered in Christ. Robbie invited me to come back on Sunday, and I gladly accepted. At this point, my mom was going to church elsewhere—we were just visiting places—so I went back to Crossroads on Sunday, expecting more.

At Crossroads I found a church home. I went another Sunday and another Tuesday, and another Sunday and another Tuesday. In between, Robbie and I listened to music, driving around the neighborhood and talking about our past and the battles the Lord had brought us through while looking to the future.

We were reading the book of Ephesians and learning to stand in faith and put on the full armor of God to withstand the enemy's bombardment of fiery darts. We eventually started a men's midnight prayer hour at Crossroads on Saturday nights. We cried out in prayer for new wives, new jobs, cars, good health, whatever was on our hearts. My relationship with Robbie and the men of Crossroads began to deepen. I was now attending Crossroads regularly. I missed writing and recording music, so as an usher during the praise and worship at Crossroads, I longed to play drums again. I wanted to pour out my passion through my gift for my Lord, who had rescued me. I asked Him to humble me and show me how to serve. This change of heart opened the door to serve as an usher at Crossroads.

I have learned as soon as you make a commitment to do something for the Lord, the enemy is there to test your will. Pride began to rise up in me, and I could hear its voice: "Why are you not in the band?" I was the "Texas Tornado" Hall of Fame drummer who always had a professional gig. Surely they want me up there playing drums. Well, that's not the way it works. The Bible says that "pride comes before a fall," so, with this evident pride in my life, of being puffed up and looking out for number one, I was suddenly humbled. I *wanted* to be in band. I wanted to feel like I belonged, but it wasn't time.

I joyfully served as an usher, seating people and handing out prayer cards. It was a different perspective. Standing by the main door to the sanctuary watching Robbie, who was actually a guitar player and singer, play drums in the praise band was eye opening. Crossroads praise band didn't have a drummer at the time as Robbie's brother Troy played prior to that. So Robbie was up there playing the drums, and I would be standing against the lobby door ushering the congregation there and thinking, "What's wrong with this picture? Surely they want me up there." But I kept serving faithfully.

In time, my mom visited Crossroads and she really liked it. Soon, she was involved. My Mom had been in the church since she was 9 years old, and there was no sign of her ever stopping. It was not long before the opportunity for me to play drums on the praise team presented itself. Robbie moved to playing guitar, and now the church could see that my walk was faithful and true. It was not anything that I did, of course, but through the righteousness of Christ and His love for me.

So I joined the worship team and began to play, and it was awesome. Learning how to worship God without trying to be a show-off by playing as many licks as I could was refreshing. No smoke machines and no lights. And, you know what else was cool? I was playing at 10 a.m. in the morning and done at noon, versus playing until 2 a.m., eating lunch at 3 a.m. and going to bed at 4 or 5 a.m. that morning. It was a far different lifestyle, and I really enjoyed it.

Through my connection to the worship team at Crossroads, I learned about an event called *Miracles Still Happen*. During this drama, literally hundreds of people would pour in over the course of three nights—Friday, Saturday and Sunday on Resurrection weekend—to see this drama, which was like *The Passion of the Christ*.

In 2003, Robbie portrayed the paralytic man mentioned in the book of Luke, who was lowered down through the thatched roof. In the account, the man's friends were so desperate to get him to Jesus, that they were willing to do anything. Crossroads bassist, and long-time member, Paul played Christ. I watched the *Miracles Still Happen* DVD and it moved me to tears. Then, 2004 came around, and Pastor Corey said, "James, you're involved in the church now, and we're doing this drama called *Miracles Still Happen*. Would you share your testimony?" Now, I had shared my testimony with a few people in person, but the idea of getting up in front of over a thousand people and baring my soul, was different. I feared I would be nervous and naked with nothing to hide behind.

Even though I had performed for hundreds of audiences, now it was just me sharing the sharpest wounds of my soul with strangers. I prayed about it, and I heard the Lord saying, "Yeah, do it."

Pastor Corey asked me if I would play Lazarus in the drama. And I thought, "That ought to be pretty easy, playing a dead man. I can relate to that." I literally had no lines in the drama, other than my testimony. I was wrapped in a mummy costume and hidden in a cave. Then Jesus said "Lazarus, come forth!" All I had to do was walk out of the tomb. I should have easily won an Oscar. Jesus unraveled me, and I reluctantly walked to the front of the stage and gave my testimony. The Lord moved by his Spirit and touched *so* many people through *Miracles Still Happen*. To this day, we have people in our body at Crossroads who testify that they were saved and baptized based on my testimony which all began on New Year's Eve 2001 with Calvin Hunt's testimony, which pierced Robbie's heart. The prophet Isaiah spoke of trading beauty for ashes, and it was happening before my eyes, as the altars were flooded with God's children seeking beauty for ashes.

Miracles Still Happen was based on Pastor's Corey's witness of a drama conducted by a local church and his youngest son Luke's testimony. Luke was diagnosed with leukemia at 3 years of age, and doctors expected Luke to die. I watched the video of Pastor Corey and Beth Ann holding Luke up for the congregation to see and saying, "Luke will live and not die and declare the works of the Lord."

I thought, "Wow! Can you believe this is the *exact same* scripture that God spoke to me on the seventh day in the basement dialysis unit of Presbyterian hospital the day before I was miraculously discharged?" Not only was it the same scripture that God gave Luke during the time he went through the chemo treatment, but Luke today is in remission and is completely healthy. Luke is active in sports with a high profile little league baseball team and is an honor student.

During the filming of Luke's testimony, Luke looked like the Michelin Man. His little body was puffed up from all the drugs. Luke also endured routine lumbar punctures to receive the chemo. Pastor Corey and Beth Ann knew firsthand when they were at Cook Children's Hospital recording these painful procedures that Luke would be healed. Luke bowed his head in prayer into his mother's bosom as the doctor prepared a needle at least 4—6 inches in length. Luke became known as "Luke the Mighty Warrior" because of the enduring grace provided by God to help him withstand the pain. Pastor Corey and Beth Ann faced a very unfamiliar path when Luke was diagnosed. But after seeking the Lord, and praying and fasting, Luke was discharged from Cook's Children to "live and not die and declare the works of the Lord." Yes, miracles still happen.

I was diving a little deeper into my walk with my Lord. Robbie and I initiated private prayer meetings for men where we fervently cried out to God for Crossroads, salvations, Godly wives, children, jobs—you name it. We met at midnight on Saturday and prayed Crossroads Tabernacle down. Prayer was our lifestyle, in contrast to our old lifestyle of sex, drugs and rock 'n' roll. Robbie and I began to write in our journals about all the wonderful things the Lord was doing in our lives. We would soon transform our journals into songs for our fledgling music ministry.

We needed a name for our new band. Robbie suggested "The Remnant," but our due diligence uncovered several bands named "The Remnant." We knew that a name was very important in establishing something for God. The Bible is replete with examples of great men and women whom God used to build the kingdom and who changed their names at key junctures in their lives. We launched an online search for "The Remnant," which led us to NASA's website. We were fascinated with space and galaxies, so NASA's high-resolution, colorful website grabbed our attention.

Amidst dozens of space images, we saw the header "The Vela Supernova Remnant." We looked at each other in amazement. We pondered it and felt the name was too long to be catchy. We were on a mission to reach the world through our music, and we needed a name that rocked. After brainstorming and exchanging ideas, we settled on the band name: We heard the Lord say, "You will call the band SuperNova Remnant." We played music in the church from Hillsong, Chris Tomlin and Israel Haughton, but now we were going to journey out on our own, and it looked like I was going to be writing and recording original music again. Glory to God! SuperNova Remnant was my twelfth professional band; however, the mission was drastically different from every other band in my career.

While SuperNova Remnant prepared for blast off in Texas, I shifted my focus to school. I enrolled in junior college. Previously, I had studied nutrition science and was keenly interested in becoming a dietitian after my dad passed away. At that time, surely no one diagnosed a "broken heart" as the cause of a heart attack. I reasoned that my dad's consumption of peanut butter, bologna, drinking copious amounts of coffee and alcohol and smoking cigarettes were to blame for his early death, so I set sail to discover why.

Through a life changing experience on my way to Los Angeles, as I wrote earlier in chapter five, I discovered vegetarianism in the book *Diet for a New America*, by Baskin Robbins heir John Robbins. He postulated that we could transform our planet if we simply abstained from meat and dairy products. I bought the idea 'hook, line and sinker." I hoped to improve my health and longevity. I believe all mankind was endowed with a free will, and I do not condemn those who practice vegetarianism or veganism or any other diet. Today, I personally choose to follow the scriptural outline for diet and hygiene, after learning Biblical wisdom.

In 1994, as a newly converted vegan, I scolded waiters and waitresses for a sliver of cheese on my plate at a restaurant—with the same mouth that drank imported beer and smoked weed to quench the emotional fires of my heart. How is that for a healthy lifestyle? Surely, none of the issues were of the spiritual heart, were they? In my quest for answers, as many men do, I returned to education.

At TCC, I enrolled full time and selected classes in anatomy, physiology, biology and chemistry. Science had fascinated me as a tyke full of wonder. I vividly remember creating some volcanic eruptions in my Mom's kitchen with my first chemistry set. Science seeks to explain the "who, what, when, where and why" of people, places and things. It's interesting how many of today's scientists prove their theories in test tubes that did not magically appear; rather, they forged these test tubes from elements they discovered but did not create. Without test tubes, where would science be today? Mankind travels to the ends of the earth and beyond to study all of the *known* elements on the periodic table in a test tube. Scientific experiments must be conducted in a controlled atmosphere, such as a laboratory, outside of the natural elements where the elements they seek to understand were collected to begin with. Doesn't it require faith when scientists act on a "hunch" and spend countless hours in a lab to verify its truth? Somehow, intellectualism and post modern relativism have replaced two of science's greatest contributors, who were also believers. Einstein and Edison are two of my favorite scientists because they recognized the splendor and grandeur of an awesome Creator. They beheld and acknowledged the Glory of God reflected in the universe and mankind.

At TCC, through my concentrated effort, I made the dean's list. I decided to go on the fast track to school and do music on the side, while the vision of Supernova Remnant came to pass. Between 2004 and 2005, I served in the church and played drums on the worship team. Pastor Corey came to me and said, "Listen, Paul is going to be leaving Crossroads, and we need someone to play the role of Jesus in *Miracles Still Happen*. Will you do it?"

I was thinking, "Well, Lord, I'm not worthy to do that. I'm not a professional actor. Look at all the sin I have in my life." I reasoned that I could come up with a plethora of excuses to talk myself out of it. But I prayed about it again, and I felt the Lord was saying, "Look, I gave everything for you. Would you do this for me?" I almost felt guilty in a way—all those nights that I poured myself into Vampire Lounge, Miss Outrageous wet T-shirt contests and untold hours in gentlemen's clubs with all my energy. I was thinking, "God, if I could only do something now to help other people—to help the drug addict, the guy addicted to pornography, the guy cheating on his wife or his girlfriend." I told Pastor Corey, "Yeah, I'll do it."

I learned all the lines, and it was an amazing experience to see other people with real-life testimonies act out real-life miracles from the Bible. The choreography, costumes and staging were amazing. The production was first class on a shoestring budget. I grew a beard for the first time in my life. We witnessed several people out of the 1,500 in attendance get saved. Lives were changed. It was worth every bit of it.

Robbie and I began crafting songs from our worn, tattered journals—the battle scars of our hearts leapt on to the pages of our journals, which were now filled with praise. In 2005, we prepared to play at Texas Motor Speedway. We loved our name the Lord gave us. SuperNova Remnant represented the worn fabric from our past lives of sin and iniquity. A remnant chosen by God is a recurrent theme throughout the Bible.

SuperNova Remnant demoed a couple of our early songs, and an acquaintance of Robbie's, Mike Pisterzi, owner of Maximedia, offered us recording time at Maximedia Studios in Dallas. Pop music icon Justin Timberlake, Clay Aiken, Ruben Stoddard and Kelly Clarkson—all of these top American Idols recorded hit singles and records at Maximedia. Our recordings at Maximedia with Michael Havens became our first CD *The Afterglow*. Soon, SuperNova Remnant's music was aired on Power FM 89.7, the Christian rock station. My crazy nights hanging out in the topless bars, transformed into prayer walks at youth camps and church camps.

During the process of recording and releasing our CD, I faithfully kept my dialysis treatments, but things hadn't changed much in my kidneys. My blood work changed somewhat, but the actual filtering units of the kidneys, the nephrons, were not yet repaired.

One major change in my health was that I no longer had a mouthful of toxic mercury. At least Dr. Cowden and Dr. Sprinkle had successfully devised a plan to remove the mercury to stop the exacerbation of symptoms and instruct me how to cautiously detoxify. In 2004 and 2005, I had gone through 11 extractions of the mercury, and now, finally, after 25 years of deception, the mercury was all out of my teeth.

Dr. Allen Sprinkle, a biological dentist recommended by Dr. Cowden, removed all the mercury from my mouth. It was an agonizing process for months, but my brother Robbie was there to get me to my appointments, as it was not safe for me to drive.

Thanks to Dr. Sprinkle's specialized expertise in mercury amalgam removal, I did begin to improve. In the meantime, I was semi-interested in a kidney transplant, but I hesitated considering the cost of medicines and their numerous side effects. I talked with Harris Hospital in 2005 about doing a transplant, but I never pulled the trigger. This sets the backdrop of where I was in 2006.

That same year, I was asked to perform in *Miracles Still Happen* again, and this was a major outreach at Crossroads. While working to memorize pages of my lines, I experienced brain fog. I didn't know whether this was caused by the mercury detox or from something else. I was still in school, so I decided to take some time off because it was too much to handle with a full-time load. Maybe I would get a transplant, get completely well and then finish school, but I needed a break.

I withdrew from school, and Robbie and I continued to work on our songs that became *The Afterglow*, which we released in 2006. Churches, Power FM 89.7 FM and Christian Internet radio stations began to play our songs. We knew we had a calling ahead of us.

Everything was going great at Crossroads. My mom and I were restored, and I was beginning to see restoration in my sister Marilyn's life, as well as in my niece Abby's life. We were praying for my brother Richard, and I reconnected with a woman I had dated five years earlier, after she came to the *Miracles Still Happen* drama. In the years ahead, we would be exclusively involved in a serious relationship, which, for the first time in my life, would hopefully lead to marriage.

These remarkable victories in my life ushered in 2007, as I continued my new walk.

Chapter 10
Living Out Loud

N̲ow, after this unfamiliar journey through my life, I was born again, and that's all that really mattered. I had overcome all these things from my past that had tried to take me down. I won these battles simply because of what God spoke to me in his Word—and nothing that I had done in my own flesh. It was really just a matter, as Jesus said, of being able to "only believe." All that the Lord required was that I mix my faith with what He had already said.

For eons of years, whether you're an evolutionist or believe in intelligent design, somewhere in space and time there is a Creator. Whether it's been 6,000 years or a billion years since human life first formed, it doesn't really change the fact that we can *choose* whether to have a relationship with the One who created us. We are free moral agents on Planet Earth. I love the lyrics from the Canadian rock trio Rush in their wildly popular song "Freewill": "*If you choose not to decide, you still have made a choice.*" Could any lyricist say it better?

So, all my life I had run with the things of the world, but now I caught a glimpse of my heavenly Father. In 2002, on my knees in my modest bedroom, all alone, I willingly traded my scarred, broken heart from past hurts and failures for a clean heart found in the Father's will for my life. The fork in the road that emerged in 2000, which spawned my decision to lay down music as my first love, merged into a yield sign to God's will for my life. As I let go of the reigns, I learned that he loved me, and I learned what he was willing and able to perform in my life.

God sustained my life. Robbie and I were a team now at Crossroads, and I attended church with my mom, my sister and my niece. No longer was I spending time with my family only at Thanksgiving or Christmas, showing up high or drunk with a pretty girl on my arm, but I was with them daily. We prayed together, laughed at one another and enjoyed each other as families should.

Now, sober almost seven years, I reflected on the goodness of God: "Yeah, God, You really brought me through the Valley of the Shadow of Death. You delivered me out of the basement dialysis unit at Presbyterian Hospital. You brought me through the surgeries and blood transfusions. You brought me through all the dental surgeries, Thank you, Lord, for helping me through everything."

God proved that he is faithful, and I just knew He was going to do something amazing. We met DJ Drue Mitchell at a loft office building located at I-35 West in Carrollton, and, as he talked about his love of Solinger's music in 1996 while at KEGL 97.1 FM, I thought, "Lord, have things come full circle a decade later for a mightier purpose?" Drue once deejayed at KEGL 97.1 FM The Eagle and played bass guitar in a local band, which had competed with my band Solinger on the DFW music scene. But after his "awakening" and new found sobriety, Drue was now on the airwaves at Power FM 89.7, "the Christian rock station."

Drue frequently played Solinger's "The Sky Is Falling" on KEGL 97.1 FM and talked about how much he liked us. Now, all of a sudden, he was at Power FM 89.7, playing SuperNova Remnant's song "The Flame." Drue loved "The Flame." He loved our fire, and he agreed to spin our Indie song. He appreciated that we did things "old school," which meant that we went out and hit the streets with our message, just like Motley Crue, Poison and others who were successful on LA's Sunset Strip. "Boots on the ground" marketing developed in the 80s, long before the days of social media. We hit it off with Drue, our music aired frequently on Power FM, and, as a result, we booked several key local gigs. We played youth events, Texas Motor Speedway (side stage) and the Ridglea Theatre while we prepared for SuperNova Remnant's future.

In 2006, something special was born. I kept seeing the phrase "LOL," so I asked my friends what it meant. They told me it was Internet chat or texting shorthand for "lots of love" or "laughing out loud." I heard the Lord say, "It means 'Living Out Loud.'" I built a Myspace page and shared my vision with Robbie and Drue, and we approached Maxi-Media studio owner Mike Pisterzi about hosting the first official LOL on The Maxi-Media soundstage. Mike agreed. We recruited volunteers and sponsors to resource LOL and, thankfully, many giving individuals and businesses answered the call. With resources and production secured, we selected LOL's first official lineup. LOL featured various Christian artists from different musical genres and emphasized unity in the Spirit with diversity of sound.

In June 2006, LOL sold about 400 tickets to musicians, churches, unbelievers, grandmas—just people from all walks of life that loved music and desired to live life "out loud." The anticipation, even before the opening chord, was electric. The atmosphere was charged. Several artists, bands and pastors lent their gifts for building the Kingdom of God: Poor Rich Folk, Crimson Fall, Ephesus, Five Talents More, Patrick Ryan Clark, evangelist Blake Porter, Luke Huch and SuperNova Remnant. I was very grateful that the seed God planted was fruitful, as LOL attendees were touched by the music and the message. New salvations for Christ and rededications flowed to the altar. The momentum between LOL and Power FM 89.7 airing "The Flame" carried SuperNova Remnant into 2007.

During 2007, I was enduring the battle with my health. I was standing firm on key scriptures like 1 Thessalonians 5:23, Psalm 118:17, James 1:12 and Romans 4:17-22. One of many symptoms afflicting my body was anemia. With hemodialysis, my blood gets filtered every other day, so it's very important that I receive a medication called EPO if my blood exhibits anemia. Epogen stimulates erythropoietin, a hormone that's made in your kidneys. I never even thought about it until I *had* to think about it.

Dr. Melinda Morris, who worked at the Fem Centre, treated me for anemia, and, thankfully, she introduced me to humates. Being around nutrition all my life, this was like a gold nugget because I was looking for anything to holistically improve the anemia. Dr. Skiba, DO, my hematologist, prescribed the strongest medication, Procrit, 40,000 units, with 10,000 units of Epogen. I had to sign a waiver at the Center for Blood Disorders, saying that I could die if I took this shot from the side effects. I didn't like that. I didn't like it at all, so Dr. Morris said that I could try Humus4All, and I replied, "Why not? I might as well." I began taking one capsule daily in 2007. When Dr. Skiba checked my blood a few months later, she stated that my red blood cell levels and hgb (hemoglobin) were text book—just from taking Humus4All.

While engaged at Crossroads Tabernacle, I investigated the transplant program at Harris Hospital. I had heard that with a transplant I wouldn't have to go to dialysis, and I would have a better quality of life; yet, when I met some transplant recipients, I realized that their life was not all that rosy. My social worker invited me to a transplant seminar, so I filled out an application and had blood drawn. During the seminar, they talked about anti-rejection medications, which are required post transplant. Dr. Podder, M.D., Ph.D., was nice and very knowledgeable, but something during the presentation made me uncomfortable. Several people there were already on cyclosporine, or some kind of steroid, and when they spoke it sounded like they had just sucked the air out of a helium balloon, and their faces were swollen. A male kidney transplant recipient told me in the Harris parking lot that his heart was racing and his blood pressure was 200 over something, and I said to myself, "I don't know if a kidney transplant is the way at this point."

As a person who errs on the side of caution, I thoroughly researched the side effects and costs of the anti-rejection medications. If you conduct your own online research of reputable sources, you would probably be surprised to discover the sheer number of deaths and medical mishaps just from prescription drugs. I am not contending that all prescription medications are bad, but I believe an informed patient/doctor relationship is essential. When we ignore our spiritual health and enter a doctors' office for a 15-minute visit, unwilling to make lifestyle changes on our own, what outcome in our healthcare can we expect? My girlfriend at the time was very supportive, and I told her, "I just don't know if I need to do this," so I put it on hold.

In 2007, I was still performing *Miracles Still Happen* at Crossroads, while SuperNova Remnant realized the idea God had given me for "Living Out Loud." LOL staged a concert at Denton Bible Church (Denton Bible was nearly impossible to book unless you attended there). We were initially told that LOL would be staged at the Denton fairgrounds with Ed and Shelia Tucker, founders of Apostle Radio. They were committed to spreading our message. So, while I contemplated the prospect of receiving a kidney transplant, I was performing music and sharing my testimony.

The Lord showed me a compelling vision: What if we went out into the streets on semi-trailers, equipped with generators, and featured multi genre music from techno, DJ, rap, hip hop, rock and worship—just go to the neighborhoods and really proclaim the Good News? The goal was to uplift the masses through a message of hope, faith and love. So we selected Circleslide, a signed band on Centricity Records. Circleslide worked in Nashville and appeared on Daystar's television show *Sound Check*, featuring up and coming artists. We booked DJ Drue Mitchell, worship leader and solo artists Jordan Critz, and Frank Hart from Houston. LOL had an official lineup.

Although Circleslide and SuperNova Remnant were confirmed, LOL had no venue, because the fairgrounds had canceled. We printed a thousand tickets by faith, and on a hot summer quest, driving all over Denton in search of an available venue for LOL, we were led to this place called The Mill, which was part of Denton Bible. Week after week, we met with pastor after pastor. After the tickets were all printed with The Mill as our venue, I was thinking, "God, I sure hope The Mill allows it." We took a giant leap of faith by printing and distributing the LOL tickets. Denton Bible's youth leader, Joe Batluck, presented it to the church committee over several weeks, and, finally, they called and said yes.

This was our first official Living Out Loud concert in Denton, and it was noteworthy because hundreds of people bought tickets and signed on as LOL sponsors. Apostle Radio, Habitat for Humanity and Sircle of Safety for battered women set up tables and booths for community awareness; it was very altruistic. We arranged for an appearance by Power FM 89.7 and Christian Clothing Vendors to display their rock fashions. I realized a dream and a vision. Years prior, I thought maybe I wouldn't even perform music anymore, but here we were with these national artists producing LOL. I confessed, "Wow, God, you really are a restorer."

Soon, James Putnam, our bassist at the time (formerly of By the Tree, who were nominated for a Dove Award, a Christian music award similar to a Grammy in secular music), departed the band after a divorce. We had some great shows with James and continued recording and writing songs as we moved closer to 2008.

Chapter 11
Is There Any Hope for Me?

I still hadn't received a kidney transplant, and I began to think about stem cells and organ regeneration. I learned that researchers had successfully restored hearts, eyeballs and pancreases with stem cells, but regenerating kidneys and liver function seemed to be more perplexing.

Despite the slow progress of science in solving the stem cell mystery, I decided that I would begin to investigative it. I stayed in touch with Dr. Cowden via email, even though I was no longer his patient. I had already spent thousands of dollars on homeopathy, acupuncture, laser acupuncture, detoxification, flower therapies, colon therapies, the hothouse machine and the Chi machine. I tried these gadgets, treatments and therapies with moderate success. But I was still looking for something, and I knew from my anatomy and physiology courses that kidneys needed stem cells to regenerate nephrons, so I scoured the Internet, and the globe, for stem cell scientists who could help me.

One day, while using Google, I typed in "stem cell/kidney transplant," just to see what came up. At that time, you could go to China, or somewhere else overseas, and it would cost at least $30,000! The cost was reasonable, but I couldn't afford it. Unfortunately, adult stem cell therapy was not FDA approved.

I wanted to clearly hear the Lord; after all, it had been five years since my near death experience, and the Lord had faithfully sustained me and brought me through numerous battles at dialysis, with alarms clanking, machine malfunctions and access problems, and He helped me overcome waves of fear through his Word and the prayers of saints and angels. I know that when we *feel* out of control, and we seem vulnerable, the Lord is only a prayer away to rescue us.

My online search results on stem cells yielded a couple of trial studies: The University of Pittsburgh was working with stem cells and transplant recipients, as was John Hopkins University, but Northwestern Memorial Hospital in Chicago was actually conducting a study by Dr. Joshua Miller, M.D., Ph. D. The study focused on identical twins who were "six of six" HLA (human leukocyte antigen). If you're an exact match, it's much less likely that you will reject a donated kidney. In addition, you would likely require less anti-rejection medicine. The study's goal was to take identical twins, and then have one of the twins donate a living kidney and then condition the recipient's immune system by administering chemotherapy and total body radiation. The doctors explained that they must reduce the recipient's immune system to make room for the new stem cells that would be injected into their blood, post-transplant. It was foreign to me, but after the seminar on all the anti-rejection medications, and the cost and side effects, I was hopeful that this might be a better way.

With a successful kidney/stem cell transplant, instead of having to take anti-rejection medications for life, they would give the medicines minimally for perhaps a year. After a period of time, the donor's kidney would achieve harmony, or "chimerism," with the recipient's immune system. This was a groundbreaking concept. The National Institutes of Health was funding the study, and there was some preliminary research on which to build. It sounded good to me, so I pursued communications with Anne Rosen, RN/BSN, the clinical coordinator of the Northwestern Memorial study.

I soon found out that unless I had a sibling who was an identical twin, I wouldn't qualify. But I wasn't one to lose hope. I thought, "There has to be a pathway to healing," so I began to learn to ask a very important question. I said to Ms. Rosen, "Anne, I know you don't know me, but is there any hope for me?" I had learned that this was a valuable question, because you never really know what is behind the door until you "knock."

She paused for a moment and said, "You know what? Dr. Leventhal is going to be doing a study a few months out, and in his study he's going to be looking for people that are only a three of six HLA match. If you and your sister are a three of six HLA match, you would qualify."

And I said, "Thank you, Lord. There is hope for me." I stayed in touch with Anne and kept her informed about my labs and dialysis and how my music was going. We built a relationship throughout the screening process.

Meanwhile, in April 2008, SuperNova Remnant was sent to the GMAs (Gospel Musical Awards). We were fortunate to see multi-platinum artists like Third Day at a music showcase at The Wild Horse Saloon, which was just amazing. We also went to the Rocket Town Showcase, where we talked to Tooth and Nail Records and met some of their new artists like Children 18:3. I was tripped out by a video I watched in the artists' lounge prior to their live show. Children 18:3's lead singer, David, struck me as a skinnier, modern-day Alice Cooper. I was a little shocked. I had been backstage with Alice Cooper when Solinger opened in 1996 at the Starplex, and it felt surreal.

Little did we know we would be performing with Children 18:3 in Deep Ellum at The Door in the near future. After James Putnam's departure in 2007, we recruited worship leader/keyboardist Perry Thompson and his bassist friend Daniel Miller from Louisiana. We took promo pictures with Marty Perlman (*Rolling Stone* magazine) and recorded "Spirit Fall on Me," written by our friend Derek Horne, along with our original song "GLOW" from *Worship & Warfare.*

We journeyed to the GMAs to shop our music to the industry. We offered more of a unique, yet commercial sound, and we made key contacts at the GMAs, including Pastor Samme Palmero of Heirchex, who owns a digital music website for DJs all over America to easily find new songs by categories.

The kidney/stem cell transplant study was getting closer, and I asked what I needed to do. They said that I needed to get tested. If I already had some of the labs from Harris Methodist transplant they could use them, and my sister would need to get tested as my living donor. We went through the process and now, all of a sudden, my opportunity to trade hemodialysis three times weekly for the previous five years was here, assuming that I received a successful kidney transplant.

The year 2009 arrived, and Northwestern Hospital called and said they needed me and my sister to come to Northwestern Memorial in Chicago, in March. My loving family and a dear business man from Crossroads helped us pay for our airline tickets and hotel room.

I was thrilled that we had the opportunity to go meet with their highly ranked transplant team. My sister and I flew to Chicago on March 25, 2009. We met with Dr. Leventhal and Anne Rosen and her team. They said, "Here's what's involved. You sister will get worked up. You'll get worked up. You're a three of six match, and you have a lot of the antibodies that are helpful in preventing rejection. If you decide to participate, we'll get you in the queue for the study. You'll go through the study. You'll have a little conditioning. You might have a little chemo to reduce your immune system during the process—"

I said, "Wait a minute…chemo?"

And they said, "Yeah but it will be a mild dose."

I said, "Okay, maybe we can work through that." Of course, history tells us that some people improve with chemo and others do not. What is the difference? I believe it is the cell membrane's ability to heal. Nourishing your cells with organic, non-GMO, chemical-free foods and proper detoxification make a huge difference biologically.

The Northwestern transplant team also said that I needed to meet with Dr. Hayes, the radiologist, and that I would have to return to Northwestern Memorial in July 2009 for a separate appointment, because Dr. Hayes would need to set up a Total Body Irradiation. And I said, "Now, wait a minute— total body irradiation?"

They told me, "Yes, we're talking nuclear medicine. You lie in the plastic chamber, and he will make a mold for your body to try to absorb the radiation as much it can."

The radiation is going to go through your body and burn all of your immune system down to zero."

I said, "That doesn't sound very good." And I thought, "I'll pray about this." So I returned to Texas, and I prayed about it.

Meanwhile, getting back to the music, I had been involved in Clear Camp since joining forces with Perry Thompson and Daniel Miller in 2008. Clear Camp is a Baptist organization that sends people out all over the world to minister music and deliver the Gospel message to young people. We went to Clear Camp, and we were blessed. We made a lot of new friends and sold all of SuperNova Remnant's merchandise— a tremendous blessing for SuperNova Remnant. I had a band of prayer warriors standing with me for healing. I still at this point had not manifested the full miracle that I knew God had promised.

In May 2009, I heard the Lord speak to me. I was familiar with Dr. Don Colbert, M.D., author of several books, including *The Seven Pillars of Health*, as well as books about detoxification. I frequently watched him teach *Nutrition and Foundations of Biblical Health* on Evangelist John Hagee's program on TBN (Trinity Broadcasting Network). I thought, "You know, Lord, I need to go to someone who really knows you and possesses revelation knowledge. Not someone with just head knowledge, but someone who can really look at me, top to bottom, and say, 'James, this is why you should or should not get a kidney transplant.'"

I made up my mind that, even though I was listed at Northwestern, I was going to go to Florida and see Dr. Colbert. I asked my Aunt Pam if she had a flight pass, and she said, "Yes." I asked my friend Mick Panasci (who once managed my band Redhouse and worked for Van Halen, The Rolling Stones and Boston) if I could stay at his apartment, and he said, "Yes." TBN had a Holy Land experience based on the terrain of Israel where our Lord walked, and I planned to see the pageantry firsthand. I had it all planned out if my mind.

Once I secured the resources to fly to Orlando, I called Dr. Colbert's office. I shared my medical history with his nurse and spoke to a nutritionist. They said they would run my medical history by Dr. Colbert to see if he would accept me as a patient. It would be $2,500 for a six-hour appointment, top to bottom, not including the supplements they recommended. I was thinking, "Lord, where am I going to get the money to do this?" I was getting ready to travel to Orlando, and Dr. Colbert's office called, and said, "Listen, James, Dr. Colbert's feels that in light of all the money you have already spent and your possible kidney/stem cell transplant in the coming months, you are best suited not starting treatment in his clinic."

I thought, "How could Dr. Colbert turn me away? Wow, now what, Lord?" Bewildered, I returned to my original question I had asked Anne

Rosen. While on the phone with Dr. Colbert's nutritionist, I paused, and said, "Is there any hope for me?"

She said, "You know what? As a matter of fact, James, I attended a seminar this weekend in Florida, and I met Matthew Jacobs, who works with a science called QRA, quantum reflex analysis, and he believes he can help people with kidney failure get well."

I said, "Please give me his phone number." She agreed, and I called Matt immediately. A few minutes into our conversation, he said, "James, I've got some good news and bad news. Yes, I can treat you, and I know what's going on, but the better news is that the man who trained me is Dr. Bob Marshall, from Premier Labs in Austin, Texas. Wouldn't you be a lot better off just going to Austin?"

I said, "I would. Thank you, Matt," and I jotted the phone number down on a piece of scrap paper in excitement and called Premier immediately. At this time, I still wasn't driving myself everywhere, and they instructed me that if I went for these treatments in Austin, I would need a driver because of a heavy detox, called "mudding," and one of the prominent detox symptoms was "blackout." To remove, or "chelate," mercury from my blood and tissues, they would use an ancient technique of strategically placing mud packs all over my body. Chelating mercury would help me get well. After six years of hemodialysis, three days a week, the mercury was still a burden to my health. I thought, "I had all my fillings removed in 2004 and 2005, and yet mercury is still a burden?"

Please see Dr. Haley's account of this on YouTube. Also visit my biological dentist Dr. Allen Sprinkle DDS at www.drsprinkle.com for mercury-free dentistry. Traditional dentists are not properly trained on how to safely and effectively remove mercury amalgam fillings. Do not proceed with mercury amalgam removal until you absolutely have screened a competent biological dentist or you can jeopardize your health.

The USA's own Department of Health and Human Services lists mercury as the second most toxic element on the known periodic table, next to plutonium. Yes, it is astounding that the United States Secretary of Health and the FDA allow the ADA (American Dental Association) to continue using a dangerous alloy, mercury amalgam, in dental fillings. In addition, many people are exposed through environmental pollution, cremation, hazardous wastes from dental offices, and food and water. Vaccinations containing a mercury derivative thimerosal are also an area of concern for many today, as more and more immunizations are required. Visit www.smokingteeth.com for info on the dangers of mercury amalgam fillings. Visit my website, www.jmclester.com, for more links.

One of my best friends, Frankie, whom I first met during my Solinger days, agreed to drive me down to Austin. I made an appointment with Dr.

Harrison Moore at the Premier Clinic. Dr. Moore had studied under Dr. Marshall. Dr. Moore was an MD with an interest in toxicology, who almost died of lead toxicity himself. His lovely wife also suffered immensely from heavy metal toxicity and almost became a casualty of war from heavy metal toxicity. Dr. Moore went on a quest during his medical disability to discover holistic therapies that would effectively chelate dangerous heavy metals out of the blood.

Before I settled on Dr. Moore, I asked around town in Austin, "Who is the man of God that practices QRA?"

Those I spoke with replied, "Dr. Moore." I had confirmation. God had also answered my prayers, as Dr. Moore was filled with the Holy Spirit and had overcome debilitating illness. He received his medical training at the University of Alabama.

Frankie and I arranged to travel to Austin in June 2009, between my dialysis treatments. We traversed Interstate 35 North in my 1998 BMW 528i and laughed while rocking out all the way. I have found that laughter is the greatest medicine next to prayer, especially when you are going through something difficult.

We pulled up to a giant, well groomed marble structure. When we entered the tall glass double doors, I was stunned at the architecture: It was modern but also very spacious. I was hopeful that I would find an adequate detox protocol behind those doors, which would subsequently lead to my total healing. A large winding marble staircase led upstairs to Dr. Moore's office. I checked in at the receptionist desk and was soon called back to see the doctor. I carried a satchel of vitamins and herbs that I was currently taking, trying to get well. You would think I was going on an expedition with Indiana Jones.

I entered Dr. Moore's office and was greeted by a warm, hospitable smile and southern accent. Dr. Moore was a tall man in his late fifties, who appeared to be very smart but also down to earth. Doctorates in medicine and certifications from the University of Alabama lined his modest office. Dr. Moore examined me and, without looking at any blood work, just using energetic testing, he said exactly what Dr. Cowden had said: "Your kidney energy is blocked. Your meridians are blocked, because you have mercury in your blood."

I said, "Well, I've heard this for years now. I've had all the amalgams removed. I've done chelation. I've done everything I know to do. Tell me, "What do you recommend I do?"

He said, "Listen, you're going to need about $700 worth of supplements. Many are liquids and are easier for you to digest, so you can use more of your energy to detox and heal. Premier uses nanotechnology, which makes the particle size smaller, so you can absorb it easier. I need you to take these liquid supplements daily, along with these mudding packs, and, if you can, use a technique called remediation to make your environment less toxic."

I thought, "Okay, this is a lot of money that I don't have." But I pleaded with two brothers in the Lord to donate the resources. One of them gave me $1,000, and the other one gave me $700 to purchase the supplements and do the treatments.

Dr. Moore said, "James, I recommend, based on what I've seen, that you not get a kidney transplant any time soon, until all this mercury is out of your body. Your new transplanted kidney will likely be the victim of another shutdown because of the mercury."

And I was thinking, "God, is there not an easier answer?" Frankie drove me down for the first treatment, and I had a lot to consider on our way home.

I booked a follow-up appointment with Dr. Moore in June 2009. When I returned home, I was scheduled to go to church camp with CLEAR in June/ July 2009. After a sleep study conducted by neurologist Dr. Rabia Kahn, MD, revealed a diagnosis of sleep apnea, I was prescribed a CPAP machine to assist my breathing at night. I had a tote full of supplements being shipped to Mena, Arkansas, where I was hired to play drums with Clear Camp. Try sleeping with a CPAP machine in a dorm full of pastors and young guys. It was really awkward and cumbersome, but it was what the doctor ordered. The supplements arrived at camp, and I looked like a mad scientist there in the dorm room, mixing these liquid potions every morning. My roommates wanted to know what I was doing. I hadn't even started the mudding yet, but I consumed the liquid supplements daily.

In spite of battling to remove mercury and detox to regain my natural kidney function, those three weeks of camp were glorious. The scenery was breathtaking atop Mena Mountain in the Ouachita Mountains. Of course, "Rabbit's" van broke down on our way down the mountain, testing our ability to withstand the humidity while waiting for the ranger to escort us back to town. The streams and brooks, foliage and trees were refreshing. The prayer, Bible studies and late night worship services were so invigorating to my life.

Watching the young kids grow in love and God's word was very healing. I remember one young boy from camp, who was diagnosed with a serious illness, required his mother to bring him some lifesaving medication to prevent a serious episode. My heart went out for him. I developed a special bond with him that week. I had many new drum students during recess learning drum rudiments and twirling drum sticks. Before I actually left for camp, I met Shad Ireland at Campus Dialysis.

This was a divine appointment recommended by Fresenius social worker Janice Crawford. I was feeling a little down that morning during dialysis, and Janice came by my chair to cheer me up and suggested that I meet Shad.

I drove over one hot June afternoon to Campus Dialysis in Southwest

Fort Worth to show support for Shad's new bike tour across America. The tour was designed to keep him in top shape and also to educate dialysis patients about good health and exercise. When I arrived at Campus Dialysis, several dialysis patients had gathered to celebrate Shad's milestone of cycling hundreds of miles daily across the United States to touch lives and inspire miracles. A nice cake and decorations adorned the lobby at Campus dialysis. I introduced myself and also met Shad's film producer, Randy. I explained that I was a songwriter/musician and that I would like to submit a song for Shad's upcoming finale of *A Promise Made*. They said, "Great".

After reading Shad's book *A Promise Made*, I was inspired to write a song called "No Limitations, Only Inspiration." I was enduring severe hypertension, depression and brain fog at the time. I cried out, "Lord, I just want this to change." When I met Shad, he gave me hope. Shad was diagnosed with chronic kidney disease at an early age and actually had a death wish because he had been told by many doctors he would not live to see 25. Shad started dialysis early on and also received a few kidney transplants, which his immune system rejected. Shad had endured many battles as a champion but was still standing. One day after his quest to meet an early death thanks to wild, reckless living, he saw a television program about the IRONMAN Triathlon and resolved that this was his goal—to compete in and complete the IRONMAN. After training rigorously against all odds and a newfound faith in Jesus Christ, Shad baffled doctors and did the impossible. He qualified to compete in the IRONMAN, and he became the first dialysis patient in history to complete the IRONMAN. Shad's book, his ministry and foundation harmoniously helped dialysis patients get better.

I took the hope that Shad's story infused in me, and I ventured to Mena, Arkansas, with Clear Camp. I wrote the song "No Limitations, Only Inspiration" in the dialysis clinic with my new friend, Phillip Cole (Clear Camp worship leader), on the acoustic guitar. The people from camp would drive me to treatment in town and bring me back. We'd sing for them during my dialysis, and it was an awesome summer. Even though I was going through dialysis and praying for a miracle, I still stood on the promises the Lord gave me for total restoration. As we led them in song, Joy was displayed on many of the dialysis patients faces I could now call friends. Once I returned home from Clear Camp in July 2009, I was prepared to go back to Chicago to see Dr. Hayes.

Total Body Radiation was required for the stem cell/kidney transplant research study I had inquired about in 2008. But two serious events transpired. Dr. Moore, who was helping me get well, went on sabbatical. So, after finally being led to Dr. Moore, who could help me, I discovered he was not available.

Now what? What was I going to do next? Dr. Colbert had turned me down and, now, this door to Dr. Moore was shut. I thought, "Lord, certainly there has to be somebody they can refer me to." Dr. Moore's office said there was another doctor that practiced at Premier, but I didn't have a good vibe about it. Premier's receptionist referred me to Dr. Chalmers, DC, who practiced QRA in Frisco, Texas.

In August 2009, I made an appointment with Dr. Chalmers. This was convenient, because his office was so much closer. He was only 45 minutes from home, not three hours away.

In the meantime, Northwestern called and said they were postponing the kidney/stem cell study indefinitely. I asked why, and they said the research study had some kinks to be resolved. Incidentally, the problem was a conflict between The University of Kentucky and Northwestern Memorial Hospital over some of the study guidelines. At least now I wasn't going to have to go through the Total Body Radiation. I found myself waiting again upon the Lord.

I purchased a used copy of *The Book of Miracles* from Half Price Books and was captured by a particular story. Yahweh (Hebrew name for God) made the sun stand still for Joshua, Son of Nun, when he was fighting his enemies so Joshua would have adequate time battling around the clock to defeat his enemies. I felt the Holy Spirit speaking to my heart that Yahweh was making time stand still and allowing me time to defeat the enemies of sickness and granting me the patience to wait for the Lord's best plan.

Back to my music career, SuperNova Remnant was asked to play at House of Blues Dallas, Texas, with Mother's Anthem, a red-hot hard rock band from Austin. I was reunited with Dawn Van Breeman, a friend from the early eighties at Savvy's nightclub. I contacted Dawn (who had a degree in Communications from the University of Texas in Austin) to see if she would consider becoming my fundraising manager. She agreed to meet me at House of Blues. We reminisced over old times and we agreed to get together and talk about the NFT fundraising campaign. She called and invited me to her home in Carrollton, Texas, to meet her husband, Mike Wilkes, and Michael Marco. Both were professional filmmakers. I arrived hopeful and open to whatever the Lord would do. After eating and drinking at the table, the discussion turned to my story. For an hour I bared my heart and soul to Mike and Michael in sordid detail about my story and all God had done to restore me. They were moved to tears with compassion and asked what they could do to help me.

I explained that I needed to raise funds for stem cell therapy and/or a possible kidney transplant. They arranged to stage a video shoot, which would convey my story in under three minutes to engage the audience and implore them to give to my cause. We set up a professional video shoot at a Dallas Studio (donated for the cause) with my mom, Robbie Gustin, me and a $30,000 camera. Dawn drafted the script, another dear friend, Kathy Cogar, composed the music, while Richard, and others volunteered their talents.

The team produced a riveting 2:42-second video of my story and the dangers of mercury. The video was edited over the next few months for a release to coordinate with an LOL fundraiser concert in November 2009.

Frankie drove me to see Dr. Chalmers in August 2009. We zipped across the North Dallas Tollway to Frisco and drove up to an impressive cottage style brick building. I walked into the corridor and was greeted by receptionist Liza Dela Cruz with a warm, friendly smile. After a brief wait, I was called back and, again, very hopeful that this was the therapy that would allow me to regain my health and natural kidney function. As I met Bill and Ann Chalmers (Dr. Matt's parents), I had a good feeling about being at Chalmer's Wellness. I was led back to be examined and learned that Dr. Chalmers, a stout, well built man in his thirties, had overcome his own near-death illness from a spinal and brain injury that almost took his life; however, God had different plans. It was this near-death experience that led him into his clinical neurology specialty.

I handed Dr. Chalmers my medical history in a clasped manila file folder. He could not see what was inside. He didn't know what Dr. Moore or Dr. Cowden had diagnosed, going back to 2003, and he didn't know about the dental work Dr. Sprinkle had done. He tested me with QRA.

Dr. Chalmers was a firm believer in miracles. He was a certified clinical neurologist, as well as a chiropractor. He tested me and said, "James, you have a burden of mercury. You really don't need to do anything until you completely detox from the mercury. Mercury is your obstacle to healing. We're going to do the mudding pack on you. We're going to do the remediation, and we're going to test these supplements." He wrapped an apron full of glass vials of Premier supplements around my waist, checking various energetic points on my meridians (energetic pathways in Traditional Eastern Medicine) and I thought, "Is this saga with mercury ever going to end?"

I continued seeing Dr. Chalmers as often as I could afford it when I had a ride to his clinic, because "blackout" was one of the many symptoms of "mudding" and detoxification. I would take my "Talit" (Jewish prayer shawl), which my missionary friends Laura and Guil Mecham brought me from the Holy Land, to my dialysis and mudding treatments. Matt's father, Bill Chalmers, would prepare a mixture of specialized clay, water, chlorophyll and minerals and apply it topically to various weak points on my body. We would be in an area of the clinic that was "remediated" to remove any interference from the environment. It was just Bill and me in a ten-by-ten room, and I would pray before he applied the healing clay. I would then witness to Bill, and we would talk about the miracles God performed and was still performing today. We spoke of Jerusalem and the way the city was built and the wisdom God gave the Hebrews in designing the temple, the Ark of the Covenant, the tabernacle, the mercy seat—all were inspired by divine revelation and were built on principals of remediation. Once the mud was applied, Bill would leave the room and I would pray in the Holy Spirit while covered in my Talit.

In August 2009, I received a call from my friend, Rita Hinkle, who at one time was Dr. Cowden's nurse. We had met in 2005 at "A More Excellent Way," a deliverance ministry founded by Pastor Henry Wright. "A More Excellent Way" exposed the spiritual connection between sin, iniquity and sickness. Dr. Cowden actually referred me back in 2002, after he sensed that there were some unresolved fear issues in my life. I also received the book *A More Excellent Way* from a dear friend, Georgia Bessett, during my hospitalization in 2003.

When Dr. Cowden referred me to the ministry, I wrote down the name of a local minister who had been delivered of several demons, such as drugs, alcohol and pornography. I scribbled the name "John Aldridge" on a tattered piece of paper and kept his name in my wallet. I attended "A More Excellent Way," at The Holiday Inn off Highway 360 in Arlington, Texas, where I met John. I did not pursue attending Son Rise Church until one day I was given John's name by another believer. I opened my wallet and there was the confirmation. I spent five years attending Son Rise every Saturday morning, learning the foundations of deliverance. I would crawl out of bed and rise up in desperation for the Lord to touch me and receive prayer and ministry.

I needed the Lord to renew my mind through His wisdom and understanding and undo the mental strongholds that were holding me captive. I never knew what sin and iniquity really were outside the Ten Commandments, and I certainly did not have a well developed understanding. To this date, I have learned that the most important characteristic a believer can possess is to have a teachable, humble spirit. While attending Son Rise Church, I tried countless holistic remedies and therapies, in addition to the thrice weekly dialysis treatments, taking minimal medication for anemia and high blood pressure.

In the fall of 2009, I was contacted by Rita Hinkle. Things were coming back in a cycle as the Hebrew thought teaches. I learned that the Greeks thought in linear terms and evolutions of dispensations of time, while the Hebrew thought teaches that there is "nothing new under the sun," as evidenced in King Solomon's writings in Ecclesiastes. Almost six years after working with Rita and Dr. Cowden, the Lord had put Rita back in my life.

Rita called to see how I was doing and asked if I received a kidney transplant, and I replied, "Not yet."

She said, "James, you must try our new rice product called PXP." She continued, "Dr. Dan Clark of Florida is working with PXP, as well as doctors and hospitals around the world, to help patients diagnosed with chronic kidney failure, and some are regaining kidney function."

I said, "What's PXP made of?"

She replied, "100% Non GMO, organic rice from Thailand's Siam Valley, and it is very concentrated and undergoes a special milling process so that you absorb it easily." She said, "Just trust me, and talk to Dr. Clark. He knows all about it. It will help you. Some people have come off dialysis, and others have reduced their dialysis. You need to try it."

I said, "How much is it?"

She said, "A hundred bucks."

I said, "I'll be there right away." I went to Rita's house and bought my first bottle of PXP. I took PXP as directed for ten days. Now, mind you, I'd been doing all the other stuff, and I had improved a little with my mercury amalgams removed, but I still wasn't out of the woods. At that time, we didn't even know what kind of mercury it was or how much it was, because I wasn't making urine, and they couldn't obtain an accurate urine sample. Dr. Thompson questioned the stool test and data from October 2001, and notated his doubts about chelation therapy, so there was no way to know where the mercury was or what type of mercury it was. We can be exposed to several types of mercury.

I began taking PXP under Dr. Clark's supervision. Ten days later, I attended church at Son Rise in Addison. I rose up every Saturday morning and stood on the Word of God and his promises and prayed. I kept moving forward, even though the whole right side of my body would be burning and my face would tingle—symptoms that I hardly spoke of because it didn't make sense to talk about. I just believed God was going to do what he promised me He would do. In ten days, I felt an awareness in my body that I had never felt before. I knew that I had a new type of energy, a new kind of calmness and, with all I had been through, this was a welcome feeling. I said, "Lord, I need to see if this is really PXP," so I quit taking the other stuff. I said, "I'm going to take this for 40 days and nothing else." During that time, my relationship with Dr. Chalmers and Dr. Clark developed. Both doctors implored me over the phone to take more of this rice, and I said, "Okay, I'll keep taking the rice."

After 40 days on PXP, I went to my scheduled dialysis treatment and afterwards, when I was most dehydrated, I drove from dialysis to competitive bodybuilder Blake Miller's house, and we did a live blood cell analysis. Blood is much thicker when it's dehydrated. I looked at my clumped blood on a high-definition screen under the microscope, moving very slowly across the screen. I mixed one five-gram scoop of PXP in four ounces of warm water and drank it on an empty stomach.

Five minutes later, Blake took my blood again, and my blood was shimmering across the screen with energy, and glowing. The erythrocytes (circular red blood cells) were perfectly circular. Blake said, "That's definitely a testament to what's happened in your blood the last few minutes." I was hopeful.

I shared PXP with other people I knew who were struggling with various health challenges and were tired of medications or being sick. I met Laura and Guil Mecham at McDonald's on Esters Road in Irving, Texas, to share PXP with Guil, who had been having seizures and taking medications for years. Laura agreed to begin taking PXP and to give it to Guil. At that meeting, Morris Duval, whom I had met at Son Rise Church, was also present.

Morris listened to what I had to share about PXP, and soon he could see a physical difference in my skin color. He testified that where once my skin looked like "etched glass" or "ashen gray," I was beginning to look much healthier as a result of PXP. Dialysis is only designed to filter excess fluids and a few toxins that accumulate in the blood when the kidneys are not properly filtering, but dialysis is not designed to nourish your blood.

I encouraged Morris, Laura, Guil and our mutual friend, Ladell, to have their blood tested by live cell blood analysis, take a scoop of PXP just as I did, and then have their blood checked five minutes later. Each of them improved dramatically, just as I had. We were convinced that PXP was not a typical vitamin, mineral, herb, juice, etc., but a specialized whole food that had great potential. Fortunately, I had already learned some dos and don'ts of networking from my success at Ultimate Lifestyle, and we began sharing PXP with our network and using doctors who had clinical experience working with PXP as credible witnesses. This transition to PXP and helping others again was a positive blessing in my life and only occurred because Rita Hinkle took time to share with me.

In November 2009, I was still awaiting word from Northwestern. I knew I would need to raise money if I was going to have a kidney transplant, so I contacted the National Foundation for Transplants. I received some material by mail to educate and inform me about the process, and they succinctly laid out a plan for me to attract volunteers.

With a little help from my band, along with my family and friends, we held a fundraiser at Crossroads Tabernacle. The video I mentioned that we scripted and produced in July 2009 was now released. Michael Marco uploaded the video on You Tube and within days it shot to the top three videos, drawing more than 50,000 hits in a single day. I thought the video would be a huge success, and it was, as far as awareness goes; however, once people watched the video and wanted to pledge a donation, the PayPal account was not set up, so people were discouraged from giving. I did not have the resources to apply for a nonprofit charity, and it takes several months to process, so I wasn't able to proceed.

Yes, I had a video that was successful in reaching viewers, but not in raising donations. I was still encouraged and hopeful that the LOL concert would help raise funds. I had shelled out more than $70,000 out of my pocket at this point, trying to get well.

Our LOL lineup included deejay Drue Mitchell, New Lyfe, Planning Yesterday and SuperNova Remnant. It was great. We filled the Tabernacle, and raised a couple of thousand dollars to help me with my ongoing medical bills. I was spending about $1,000 a month just on out-of-pocket care.

In December 2009, I learned about the "MELISA" test (Memory Lymphocyte Immunostimulation Assay), developed by pharmaceutical manufacturer Astra-Zeneca. MELISA was designed to provide scientists with a good idea of what type of heavy metals you're reacting to. It tests for lead, iron, mercury, phenylmercury, methylmercury, ethylmercury—all these types of mercury I was vaguely familiar with from chemistry. The MELISA test was now available in the United States. I met the rep, Shellie King, who sent me the test that Dr. Chalmers administered, and guess what? Now we knew, after nine years of mystery, on the cusp of 2010, that the phenylmercury levels in my blood were elevated to 6.8. Anything above 3.0 was positive, so now I knew for certain that I was reacting to phenylmercury. I didn't know if it was still from amalgams, or where it came from, but we knew we needed to deal with it, and it proved what Dr. Cowden, Dr. Moore and Dr. Chalmers had said. Revelation had finally come on the heels of uncertainty after almost a decade of feeling like I was crazy when I spoke to traditional doctors about mercury.

Because I had done so well with PXP, on January 10, 2010, God gave me the scripture John 10:10, "The thief comes but to kill, steal and destroy, but I have come that you might have life and have it to the fullest," as a sign to join Enzacta, and many people followed suit. They had their blood tested and they witnessed exactly what I had seen: Their blood improved drastically within five minutes after consuming PXP. They felt better, and their hemoglobin A-1C (a measure of how well you are controlling your blood sugar over time) improved. I'm not saying PXP is a cure. PXP or any other food or supplement is not intended to treat, cure or diagnose an illness, according to FDA guidelines, but whole foods and supplements may provide nutritional support and value in your daily diet.

Now that I had joined Enzacta, Northwestern Memorial Hospital was getting ready to ramp up their study again. I wasn't on any other kidney transplant lists, but I was thinking that maybe I would go back to Harris Hospital if it didn't work out

I continued to see Dr. Chalmers while consuming PXP and Humus4ALL, doing everything I knew to do and standing on the Word of God. Crossroads Tabernacle had blossomed from *Miracles Still Happen* to hosting major prayer conferences with 250 pastors from all around the country. In many ways, my life was getting better, but I was still waiting and praying for a creative miracle.

Chapter 12
No Limitations, Only Inspiration and Hearts on Fire

In 2010, the song I wrote and recorded for Shad Ireland, "No Limitations," was made into a video. I needed something else to help me raise funds, so I asked Mark, Nepo's friend and owner of Still Crowes Studios, if he could help. Thankfully, Mark said, "Yes."

I recorded "No Limitations" at Still Crowes Studios. Nepo, who had sung and played keys in my other bands, agreed to help me with keyboard arrangements and backing vocals. Sound engineer Ron Lord played rhythm and lead guitar and helped with the song structure. Robbie Gustin played rhythm guitar. Chris Thomas (ex SuperNova Remnant bassist) played bass, Mark from Still Crowes sang backing vocals and Athena Chaney sang lead vocals. I was truly blessed to be surrounded by such talented friends. I really anticipated the release of "No Limitations, Only Inspiration" and was looking forward to sharing the song with Shad Ireland.

In the meantime, in August 2010, Dr. Chalmers retested my blood using the MELISA test, and, after eight months on the PXP, along with Humus4All, the phenylmercury reaction in my blood had dropped by 75 percent, from 6.8 to 1.2. Now we knew clinically, on paper, that my immune system was not overreacting to any heavy metals, which meant that I might be closer to a transplant or healing.

On New Year's Eve 2010, SuperNova Remnant played at Crossroads Tabernacle to a full house with our brother Benjamin Lang, who jammed some Holy Spirit infused reggae, as well as hip hop and rap delivered by Paperboy and New Lyfe. We had an awesome time playing music again for the Lord. The Crossroads worship team continued to improve musically and spiritually. God brought people from my past back into my life for me to make music with and witness to. I am so thankful for Mike Wilkes and Michael Marco and their dedicated team who produced and directed the short video testimony to help get the message out about the dangers of mercury toxicity. They intended to help me raise money to proceed with my mission. I am also thankful for Mike's wife, Dawn Van Breemen, who once watched my band Chazaretta from behind the chain-link fence when I was 17 years old. More recently, I reunited with her at a SuperNova Remnant show at House of Blues Dallas. God used all these divine appointments to prepare SuperNova Remnant for a new mission in 2011.

God birthed a vision through me in 2011. I was first introduced to the Christian Rock band Stryper in my late teens. Brad Spalding and I would sit in his living room and spin their vinyl record *Soldiers under Command* while listening to *Too Fast for Love,* the debut album from shock rockers Motley Crue. Stryper's hard edged sound, with loud guitars and drums and soaring lead vocals, sounded amazing. As musicians they rocked, but we really weren't into the message at that time. Stryper reached number one on MTV with their video "Honestly," a power ballad that rose above their hard rock counterparts Motley Crue, Ratt and Bon Jovi.

Based on their incredible success on MTV and platinum record sales, Stryper toured the world, traveling to many countries. Even at 18 years old, I loved the sound of their music. Back then, I didn't get them throwing Bibles out into the audience or dressing in yellow and black spandex, but I realize now, of course, that Stryper aimed to accomplish important things for the Kingdom of God. Little did I know that after 18 years in pursuit of rock stardom, and the sordid lifestyle that went with it, I would soon be opening for Stryper at a major Dallas venue.

After playing every Tuesday, Saturday and Sunday at Crossroads Tabernacle, with SuperNova Remnant gigs in between, we received an important offer from a mutual friend who plays in Dallas-based hard rock band Downlo and for eighties rap sensation Vanilla Ice. Dallas musician and live music venue owner Clint Barlow of Trees in Deep Ellum, asked SuperNova Remnant to open up for Stryper at Trees on March 16, 2011. Trees is a legendary Deep Ellum venue, and the tickets sold out quickly. Avid SuperNova Remnant and Stryper fans formed a line around the building at Trees as the anticipation built.

We were ready to prove to the world that the newfound life we had found in Christ was something real. From the opening guitar riff of "The Flame," our first single off *The Afterglow,* rock fans were awestruck. SuperNova Remnant reunited with Nepo on keyboards and backing vocals for this landmark show, and hundreds of our friends and fans piled into Trees. The intensity grew as we rocked through our 30-minute set, which included crowd favorites like "You Are," "Miracle," and "Hand on My Heart." Trees' capacity crowd of 800 rock fans jammed the stage, and at the end of our set, when we played our song "Glow," the audience seemed to be frozen in time, mesmerized by the Spirit of the Lord falling upon Trees, as they had never experienced anything like it before.

After a hard rock band that was party driven played the middle slot, Stryper took the stage in yellow and black and proceeded to *rock*. Stryper mixed up songs from their previous platinum albums *To Hell with the Devil*, *Soldiers under Command* and their most recent album *The Covering*, which featured Stryper's version of rock classics such as Deep Purple's "Highway Star" and Black Sabbath's "Heaven and Hell." Dozens of friend that Robbie and I hadn't seen in years came out to the show and stayed late on a Wednesday night to watch Stryper. At the end of Stryper's set, there was total silence while lead vocalist/guitarist Michael Sweet prayed for the victims of Japan's Fukushima earthquake.

In the summer of 2011, I traveled to Camp Arrowhead for family camp, like I had every year prior, but this year there were more pastors praying and deeply seeking God. I also had the opportunity to share my vision for Living out Loud and "No Limitations," and several churches at the camp were buying my CD single that I wrote and recorded for Shad Ireland.

It was at Camp Arrowhead in the backwoods of Glen Rose, Texas, where God inspired me to create a new concert called Hearts on Fire. I created Hearts on Fire to convey compassion through various music and artistic forums, combining rap, hip-hop, rock, gospel, praise and worship, spoken word, visual arts, and blending it into one unified purpose of bringing glory to God and touching lives.

After networking, I received support from KLTY 94.9, the largest Christian music station in the Dallas-Fort Worth Metroplex, through the community show *DFW Perspectives*, hosted by on-air personality Starlene Stringer.

While listening to KLTY one Saturday morning, I heard Starlene on the radio broadcasting from Brookshire's Grocers in Fort Worth. Prompted by the Holy Spirit, I hopped in my BMW 528i, peeled the sunroof back and drove straightway to meet her. Starlene cordially agreed to interview me on June 3, 2011, to promote Hearts on Fire. I communicated the message God had given me and testified to the miraculous saving and healing power of the Lord, who had raised me from death to life.

During our interview, Starlene asked me a question to which I responded, "Do you want the *Reader's Digest* version?" Starlene chuckled, because I can be longwinded if you wind my motor up, but she let me continue. I replied, "Starlene, if you want the long answer you'll have to read the book!"

Starlene prophesied during our conversation that maybe a book deal would be forthcoming. At the time, I did not take her words seriously, but I soon remembered Mrs. Lacroix's words in third grade that I was a gifted writer and that one day I would be writing. Of course, I had written songs for over two decades at this point, but the thought of doing a bona fide book had not crossed my mind.

While promoting Hearts on Fire to raise awareness and funding for stem cell therapy and/or a kidney transplant, I was blessed to be interviewed by Power FM, 89.7 FM on-air personality and Promotions Director, Dawn Henderson. Dawn is a very kind, lighthearted radio voice who dripped with compassion over the airwaves while sincerely questioning me about Hearts on Fire.

My former boss Martie Whittiken, CCN, and host of the *Healthy by Nature* radio show on WORD 100.7 FM, agreed to have me on as a guest to talk about Hearts on Fire. Martie also generously displayed a flyer on her website, which allowed her audience to donate to my cause. Martie's brother and computer expert Jim Russell designed a web page that would help me receive donations and to reach others.

These open doors greatly helped promote Hearts on Fire. After eight weeks of planning, suddenly we didn't have a venue for Hearts on Fire, due to an unexpected major issue, but thankfully Charles Schechner offered The Rock and Worship Lounge in Bedford, Texas. On Friday, June 3, 2011, Hearts on Fire became a vision realized.

Ladonna Paulson, a friend from high school, organized the volunteers and sponsors and worked tirelessly to help. Ladonna's mother, a kidney dialysis patient, had gone to be with the Lord, so Ladonna wanted to help get our message of prevention to the community.

We proposed that patients be screened to help stave off chronic diseases, such as heart disease, diabetes and renal failure. Although screening for chronic disease has greatly advanced in the last generation with X-rays, CT scans and MRIs, which reveal structural damage, medicine had not explored the cause and effect of heavy metals in the blood when diagnosing many of today's chronic diseases. Hearts on Fire brought a new awareness to the screening process, because of what I had lived through firsthand, after living 25 years with toxic mercury in my blood from dental "silver" fillings. Truthfully, dental amalgam fillings are 50 percent mercury and do not belong in anybody's mouth. I wanted others to be aware of the dangers of mercury and heavy metals in dental work, vaccinations and the environment. Mercury is dangerous at any level inside our blood and belongs only in thermometers or ballasts.

Many people donated their talents to Hearts on Fire. Chris Jones designed a brilliant color poster, Curry Printing offered amazing prices on promo cards, and caring individuals donated quality merchandise for our raffle. Brad Vanderburg and Buster Clark helped with production. Our faithful crew of Joe Norris, Frank Rameriz, Troy, Gerald and Sheila Gustin ensured a great show. Eddie Alcaraz, Power FM's station manager, showed up to support the show, and a generous couple, who remain anonymous, paid for all the tickets to be printed.

The Crossroads worship team, led by Chad and Martie Jones, Athena Chaney, Gina Hartson and Angela O'Neal, all agreed to come and lead the worship, accompanied by Robbie Gustin on guitar, Chris Lim on bass guitar, and Jeremy Harris on acoustic guitar.

Crossroads youth leader and gifted artist Riki Atkins painted during the concert and led the Crossroads Praise Dancers through an intense dance that signified "breaking chains" in our lives. The Crossroads Tabernacle Youth Band, led by Tim Adams on keyboards, Josiah Hunter on Guitar and Addison Fraustro on drums, played "Jump Around," and the praise singers engaged the feisty crowd.

My dear friend, Charles Eugene, whom I met at NE dialysis, had sung with various talented musical groups, including "Ardiche'" of New Orleans. He also once sang on the bus and backstage in Baton Rouge for the Commodores. What is riveting about Charles' story is that in 2005, in an attempt to escape Hurricane Katrina, which demolished the Gulf Coast of New Orleans, Charles heard the Lord clearly command him to immediately load up his family and flee to escape the impending danger. Charles drove his family to Houston until doors in Fort Worth opened and he could settle down. The sheer emotion that Charles felt deep in his heart for all God had done for him, culminated with a tear jerking version of "To God Be the Glory," which brought the audience to its knees.

The concert continued with The Gustins singing a beautiful acoustic version of "Wild Horses" that sent chills through the audience. Next, New Lyfe and Paperboy pumped up the crowd with blistering raps and hip hop jams while professing Christ. Both young men have been delivered of street life and a lust for materialism that drove them in their early teens.

Deejay Drue Mitchell, from JCTV, flew in to spin his eccentric blend of music and jams to a crowd of kids from 3-year-olds to 80-year-old grandmothers. Drue always rocks the crowd and is known for his "secret change-up" in every set of music.

The stage was set for SuperNova Remnant, and we blew the roof off The Rockin' Worship lounge with an over-the-top sound system and a combination of original songs and worship songs.

We raised about $2,000 that helped me pay some mounting medical bills. Although it was much less than our target, it was a start. Hearts on Fire touched hearts serving its higher purpose.

Meanwhile, I went back to Northwestern Memorial Hospital to find out firsthand about the stem cell/kidney transplant research study that I discovered in 2008. I had to make a decision about participating in the study. Some close friends helped with my plane ticket, and I arrived in anticipation of meeting Dr. Leventhal and study coordinator Laura Coleman. I felt very confident in their abilities after conversing with them since 2008 and researching the various transplant programs offered in the United States. After discussing the requirements of the research study, I finally said, "Please escort me to the Nuclear Medicine department. I'd like to see it with my own eyes."

After a long walk down the hospital corridor, the first thing I noticed was a gigantic Star Trek-looking door. The door, a few feet thick, said one thing: GRAVE DANGER. And I thought, "I don't know if this is a door that I want to walk through." However, timidly, I did walk through it though and was greeted by a friendly staff. They showed me a plastic box that looked like a coffin, without a cover, where I would be required to lie still against the wall adjacent to a radiation lamp. They said the radiation lamp was to administer radiation to condition my immune system in order to receive my sister's stem cells that they would transplant into my bone marrow, post kidney transplant.

I thought, "Lord, I'm not sure this is a door I want to go through. Maybe I want to receive a traditional kidney transplant, after all." Of course, in hindsight I am glad I went to Northwestern Memorial in person so I knew what was actually required to participate in the research study.

I left Chicago and prayed for God to sustain me, as he had the past eight years, and to open a new door. I was clear that the chemotherapy and radiation required for the study were not ideal for me. Perhaps Hearts on Fire could raise enough money for me to try the stem cell therapy and see if it would help regenerate my natural kidney function. This was a more organic option to me.

In July 2011, SuperNova Remnant was invited by Jesse Money to play his new music venue Remedy, in Rockwall, Texas. Jesse is an executive with Verizon who also started Four Flames, an indie record label. SuperNova Remnant blew the power breakers at Remedy with our massive guitar amps and big drums during our stellar rock show. We gained fans everywhere we played.

Earlier in 2011, the editor of *Modern Drummer* magazine, Billy Amendola, asked me to draft a blog, which was finally published in the online version of *Modern Drummer* magazine on August 16. Great things were happening and, at the same time, Hearts on Fire was planning a follow-up concert in September.

After speaking to several medical clinics around that world that specialized in stem cell therapy, I learned that I needed to raise $30,000 to start. I contacted my friend, Pastor C.B. Glidden, of Fort Worth First (FWF) Nazarene, and he graciously offered me the Timothy Ministry Center for Hearts on Fire 2. FWF has a giant facility. I prayed about the artists and sponsors of the event. I knew from Hearts on Fire in June that we had a formidable goal ahead, $30,000, but all things are possible with God. Crossroads Tabernacle, Power FM 89.7 FM, WORD 100.7 FM and KLTY 94.9 FM all offered to help.

I selected Fort Worth First Praise Team to lead worship, Riki Atkins to paint during the concert, Deejay Drue Mitchell from JCTV, Adrian Hummel as emcee from Power FM, vocalist Terrance Reed, Jana Bell (Kirk Franklin/Martha Munuzzi) and SuperNova Remnant. Ladonna was in a limited role for Hearts on Fire 2, so many of the details were left to me and it was exhausting. Brad Vanderburg offered his massive sound system, and Buster Clark agreed to mix the artists. Lee and Cyndi Cobb, my dear friends, offered to load equipment and sell Hearts on Fire t-shirts. Sherry Waters, who designed t-shirts for Larry Hagman (a.k.a., JR on *Dallas*, the successful television drama) created a fiery, colorful shirt. Several of the youth at FWF offered to help load equipment and work in the concession stand.

FWF youth pastor Josh Boice went beyond the call to help coordinate the event. He played in the worship team, along with drummer Tim Tharp, guitarist Sam Tharp, bassist Tony Jacobs and singer Hannah Walton. Josh also hosted a pizza party upstairs for the youth, contacted area businesses for donations and constantly prayed for Hearts on Fire, while leading his youth by example.

Hundreds of people attended Hearts on Fire, but the majority were young people. Young people are on fixed incomes and want money for cokes, and candy, etc. We offered the tickets for $10 and sold a few hundred, thankfully, but, again, fell way short of our goal of $30,000.

The audience was rocking and dancing, kids were break dancing, singing, flipping—they were doing all kinds of stuff—and God orchestrated all of this. Kids were touched and moved. I stood and told the audience, "I need your prayers for healing and resources for upcoming expenses." I did not feel led to take an offering from a young audience, so I offered my "No Limitations" CD and Hearts on Fire T-shirts for donations. Hearts were on fire as we witnessed all the Lord was doing.

All this led up to finding out that I wasn't quite sure whether I was going to be able to get the stem cell procedure, because we didn't raise the money. I had been praying on what to do next since I decided against the Total Body Irradiation required for the stem cell/kidney transplant research study. I was still listed at Northwestern, but as I talked to Keith, Dr. Leventhal's nurse, he said, "You should get listed in Texas." So I called Texas Transplant Institute, after one of the dialysis nurses asked me if I had thought about going to San Antonio. She said they had the best program and that she had worked with them. I had heard this once or twice before, but you don't always listen on the first call.

I traveled to San Antonio and met with Dr. Bingaman, MD. They are the highest ranked transplant program in Texas. Dana, the transplant nurse, was knowledgeable and caring.

Texas Transplant Institute would require me to take anti-rejection meds, but at least there was no issue with me taking supplements, as there had been with the Harris transplant. Dr. Bingaman said, "I won't have a problem if you want to take fish oil or coenzyme Q10." After six years of searching for a transplant program that best harmonized with me, I had found it: no chemo, no radiation, minimal anti-rejection meds and the liberty to take proven nutritional supplements.

I have witnessed many malnourished dialysis patients in the past nine years, because they are on a renal diet. They're not eating good, wholesome, organic foods. I have an online farmers market that gives people all over the world access to these foods and beverages (see www. JMC.mybeyondorganic.com).

I had prayed for a decade for my miracle to manifest, yet it remained in my heart and was reflected out of mouth by faith in God's word. I have learned that when I wait for God's best he always blesses me better. Even all those episodes, where the door shut with Dr. Colbert, Dr. Clark, Dr. Chalmers and Dr. Moore—all these things that happened—happened for a reason. Read Romans 8:28.

One day, while reading through a used book *Book of Miracles* I bought at Half Price Books, God reminded me of the story in Joshua, when Joshua was commissioned to go out and fight his enemies. God said, "I'm going to turn the dial of the sun. I'm literally going to suspend time, so you have more time to defeat your enemies." And in the spirit, that's what God showed me while I waited upon his best. I can honestly say my patience has been refined by fire the last 11 years.

You know, all the damage the enemy meant for my harm was (and is) being restored by God. My brother, who was on drugs, is now happily married and working on his Engineering degree in College while seeking the Lord. My niece is studying to be a paralegal and growing up in God. My sister has overcome many challenges and is still growing today.

God performed all these wonderful things in my life, while I have continued to stay focused on the promise. And when I returned from my trip to San Antonio, not only did we have a successful Hearts on Fire, but we also enjoyed being a part of the worship team at a prayer conference with Pastors Maria and Michael Durso at Crossroads, in October 2011, which was amazing.

The Dursos prayed for fellow New Yorker Calvin Hunt from Queens, New York, to get delivered from a severe crack cocaine addiction that estranged him from his loving family, his job and his music. Crossroads Tabernacle developed a long lasting relationship with Christ Tabernacle after Pastor Corey Jones (senior pastor) traveled to New York at Calvin's urging to not faint after the congregation at Crossroads was falling apart.

Robbie first heard Calvin testify on New Year's Eve 2001. In turn, Robbie was saved, and then I was saved. God used all these miracles full circle. During the prayer conference at Arlington First Church, there were 600 people, and 400 of them were from 20 different states, seeking God. The Glory of God fell so strongly. It was amazing to be a part of it. God has given birth to more opportunities for SuperNova Remnant, who is currently recording *Rockets Red Glare*, our new CD that's slated for a summer 2012 launch. We tracked 23 songs at Wes Putnam Studios. We are also working with Mike Pisterzi and Michael Havens from Maxi-Media. This will be our best project yet.

Rockets Red Glare is about what's going on in the world. Syria is warring in the Middle East. Palestine and Israel continue quarrelling since the days of Abraham over the land, and America appears to favor a new regime that rules Egypt and the Middle East. God revealed how the famous lyric "and the rockets' red glare" from "The Star Spangled Banner" (America's song of independence), would really speak of the forthcoming liberty that all nations will enjoy under the rule of His Kingdom.

Our songs are full of hope. They're full of faith. They're full of love. They were written straight from our hearts. God has used the fires of our past to glorify himself through our music. I was inducted into the Christian Drummers Hall of Fame; this and the accolades from *Modern Drummer* were awesome hallmarks.

God has restored all these things back to me, which I am so thankful for. Today, I am still listed at the Texas Transplant Institute in San Antonio, and I am looking for outreach to raise funds for stem cell treatments at the Weisman Institute in Tel Aviv, Israel, which I believe could help my kidneys regenerate and help my biology. I continue to take PXP and Humus4All, and I am vice president in a new venture with Jordan Rubin from Beyond Organic. My partner, Dr. Bob Bard OD, who offered to publish my book, works to educate the nation with healthy foods and beverages the way the Bible mandates it.

The opportunities ahead of me are exhilarating. I am trusting God each and every day by faith that whether it be a transplant or stem cells or an awakening or quickening in the middle of the night, His Word is what has genuinely healed me. First Thessalonians 5:23, one of the greatest scriptures, declares, "I pray the God of peace will sanctify you wholly in spirit, soul and body and preserve you blameless unto the coming of our Lord Jesus Christ." And the reason that's such a beautiful prayer is that we don't just stop at getting a beautiful body, as a bodybuilder or a supermodel does. We don't stop marching to victory by going through the things that have wrecked our past. But we go on, renewed in the Spirit, where we're born again and believe we can overcome.

God has brought me through multiple close calls of drinking and driving, blown out of my mind on drugs, sleeping in places I had no business being, and even acting like Superman on top of buildings high on ecstasy. I never wanted to kill myself; I always wanted to live to be 120 years old, like Jiminy Cricket said on the black-and-white projector during homeroom in first grade. We as believers must "believe" what the Word of God says for it to come to life.

I want to encourage kids, youth, young adults, and parents and grandparents that nothing is impossible with God. I am certain that the prayers of my mom and family and intercessors had everything to do with this prodigal returning home to dine at The King's banquet table that the Lord has prepared for all of us.

That leads me to the conclusion of the matter. You know, all the years, all the tears, all the heartaches, all the victories—it really comes down to one thing: that our lives can be used as an example to shine a light into somebody else's life, into their darkness. From that pit in 1999, when I was singing about a "Chain Link Fence," or "Dirty Lowdown" or "Walking through the Dark"—now SuperNova Remnant is singing about "Miracles," about being "FREE" and how the Lord "Glows" in our lives. And SNR is doing it all for the glory of God.

MISSION SUPERNOVA REMNANT

Rockets Red Glare

I felt the fire burning inside to share with you a "behind the scenes" glimpse of the writing, recording and producing of *Rockets Red Glare*. The last two weeks in Maximedia Studios have been a brilliant blur, punctuated by 3–5 hours of sleep each time the late moon wanes. The cultivation of *Rockets Red Glare* began in early 2010, shortly after SNR released *Worship & Warfare*, featuring the radio singles "GLOW" and "Spirit Fall on Me." Following are many of the key events that led up to the final completion of *Rockets*

247

Red Glare in May 2012.

We met Heirchex owner Pastor Samme Palmero at the 2008 Gospel Music Awards convention and played *Worship & Warfare* for him, and he loved it. Samme sent emails to deejays across the United States for album oriented rock (AOR) and contemporary Christian rock radio formats, and deejays around the country began downloading and adding SNR's songs for airplay. "GLOW" was among the most requested singles, at seven minutes long, on Indie Christian Rock Station Power FM 89.7. Power FM has supported SNR's music since "The Flame" debuted on Power FM 89.7, thanks to our dear brothers Eddie Alcaraz (Power FM 89.7) and Deejay Drue Mitchell (JCTV). Along my journey, Promotions Director Dawn Henderson and Deejay Adrian Hummel at Power FM 89.7 have been kind and generous with SNR interviews. We were writing new songs for *Rockets Red Glare* in late 2009 with plans to travel to Virginia Beach and record with Grammy-award winning producer Michael "Elvis" Baskette (AlterBridge, Chevelle, Ratt); however, the resources for his services did not manifest and SNR had to shelve our plans and cancel.

We were a bit deflated but stood firm in faith, believing. I also learned that my long, 24-month wait for a stem cell kidney transplant at Northwestern Memorial Hospital in Chicago would continue, as the research study by Dr. Joseph Leventhal was postponed. Also, Dr. Harrison Moore advised me to wait on pursuing a kidney transplant until I had sufficiently detoxed from mercury. Disappointed, but not defeated, the Lord led me to the book of Joshua and instructed me with a Word. The Lord made the *sun stand still* for Joshua until he conquered all his enemies, and He also promised to do so for me.

The arrival of 2010 found SNR, and me, waiting on the Lord. SNR continued writing songs in preproduction for *Rockets Red Glare* in hopes for an indie record deal, which would provide SNR the financing to hire producer Michael Baskette.

Power FM 89.7 continued playing "GLOW" during their all-request hour, while inviting SNR to perform concerts for the SPIN 180 Indie Lounge. Despite SNR's growing popularity from airplay, radio interviews, concerts in secular and church venues, and social media outlets, *Rockets Red Glare* was not complete, nor did we secure an indie record deal. Opposition reared its ugly head, but SNR kept praying and hoping the Lord would soon open the right door.

Also in 2010, my four-year relationship with my girlfriend ended for unresolved reasons. I was heartbroken. I really made a concerted effort to walk as the Lord instructs a man. I walked in a relationship in the manner that leads to marriage, according to His plan, and it failed. Not because of the Lord's design for relationships, but because the enemy works to deceive, divide and conquer. Instantly, "just like that," my best friend was long gone.

I cried at the altar during each church service, praying that the Lord would draw her back to Crossroads Tabernacle by His Spirit. Lonely, I held on to an empty promise, in hopes she'd return. She never did. I longed for us to be "one" and also for my music career with SNR to take flight.

SNR performed a wonderful New Year's Eve concert at Crossroads Tabernacle with rapper New Lyfe, hip-hopster PaperBoy and evangelist Dan Bohi, and soon 2011 was upon us. SNR was ready for another chance to launch out.

I received word from Dr. Leventhal that Northwestern Memorial's stem cell /kidney transplant research study was about to resume if I would like to participate. I flew to Chicago in March 2011 to meet the transplant team. I had been told that the research study required patients to undergo chemo and Total Body Irradiation (TBI); therefore, I wanted to meet with the Nuclear Medicine department and see what was required of me. Would chemo and TBI be a better option than a traditional kidney transplant requiring a lifelong commitment to anti-rejection medications? Medications can be expensive and impose potential side effects such as diabetes, unhealthy cholesterol levels and cancer. I had been dialyzing three times weekly for eight years. I had stood in faith while praying and believing for a total breakthrough and recovery. What I needed most was wisdom—Godly wisdom. God had been faithful to sustain me.

Upon my arrival in Chicago, I enjoyed meeting Keith, Laura, Dr. Leventhal and the transplant team at Northwestern. I believed Northwestern had one of the top tier transplant programs in the country; however, once we trekked down to the Nuclear Medicine department, I was greeted by a Star Trek type door decorated by the yellow-and-black universal radiation warning symbol that read "GRAVE DANGER. ENTER AT YOUR OWN RISK." Once inside the capsule, I was shown a cutting-edge radiation lamp that could outshine the sun. I don't even like microwave ovens and would not want to sit inside one for an hour. After praying and seeking Godly wisdom, I chose not to participate in the stem cell/kidney transplant or subsequent TBI. On the flight back home to Texas, the nuclear disaster in Japan was all over the news, warning of the impending dangers of radiation, and I believe the Lord confirmed my decision to wait on him.

Meanwhile, in the face of disappointment, I hoped that SNR's new music would finally be recorded so we could release something fresh and bold and go on tour. Robbie was chomping at the bit, but there were obstacles in our way, so we resolved to pray through them. We prayed night after night, waiting for a breakthrough.

Once I returned from Chicago, SNR caught a big break later in March, and Trees nightclub owner Clint Barlow in Deep Ellum invited us to open for multiplatinum Christian rock band Stryper. Stryper's fan base continued to flourish more than two decades after they climbed to #23 on *Billboard*

Magazine's Top 100 with their hit single "Honestly" in 1987. They had four top 10 videos on MTV, they enjoyed an international fan base and they had sold ten million CDs. They were touring in support of their 2011 CD *The Covering*—a collection of hard rock classics by such rock super groups as Deep Purple, Van Halen, Ozzy Osbourne and Judas Priest, to name a few. Christian rock was SNR's genre, and who better to play with Stryper than SNR?

Stryper was a pivotal influence in our ministry. SNR and Stryper sold out with a line around the building. SNR ripped through new music from *Rockets Red Glare* and fans wanted more. SNR amassed many new fans that night. SNR rocked Trees capacity crowd to a crescendo after a blistering "All Things Rock" set. SNR's original song "The Flame" shook the rafters, as Robbie's signature guitar riff was accented by Nepo's keyboard explosions and a rock-solid groove from the low-end excitement and "Temple of Boom." SNR ripped through new songs featured on *Rockets Red Glare*, such as "You Are, "I Remain" and "Declaration." "GLOW," our most requested single, mesmerized the audience with its piercing militant drum cadence and razor-sharp guitar riff. This wave of success carried SNR into the summer, along with the departure of bassist Donny Wills. Our recording and preproduction stopped cold. We were not giving up, but we could not just hire any bassist. It was important to SNR, above all, to be equally yoked in our genre of music.

Power FM 89.7, who has supported SNR's music since debuting "The Flame" in 2006, supported SNR's by playing our seven-minute epic "GLOW" frequently on their all-request hour. We knew God had bigger visions for SNR to fulfill, so we kept our eyes on the dream, despite the financial distractions, physical distractions and relationship distractions. In August 2011, I hosted a "Hearts on Fire" concert at Fort Worth First Nazarene with Paperboy, New Lyfe, Riki Atkins, Terrance Reed, Jana Bell and the FWF Worship team, along with JCTV music director Drue Mitchell. It was a glorious night of worship for the 300 hundred-plus that gathered to witness and worship, but from a fundraising standpoint, when $30,000 was needed, we raised much less, and it only covered the production costs. I remember after all the work poured in not feeling right about taking an offering from the teenagers who were largely present. I was handed the money at the end of the night, and it was about $300 short of covering expenses for production, so the fund raiser was *not* a fundraiser. I knew as I counted the money the right thing to do was pay everyone involved, although I knew I could use the money. But God told me, "Trust me," and pay everyone what they agreed upon and, "I will bless you." The Lord did meet my needs, and I was glad I could help the others. I was unsure what to do next after having done two fundraisers, with the first one in 2009, helping to pay a few minor medical bills but way short of the $30,000 needed. I had spent $75,000-plus on holistic therapies and detoxing from mercury, and I did not have any savings left. I decided to move forward but not arrange any more fundraisers unless someone felt led to come to me and organize it. I was really burned out from the effort to raise funds and nothing returning. I just rested. I also was a little disappointed that the YouTube video received 60,000 hits but generated *zero* donations. There are many worthy causes, and God is concerned about all of His children. I know there are foundations and charities out there that can help me, but I have not found them yet.

That evening at Fort Worth First, Dr. Bob Bard was in the audience and suggested I write a book. We both agreed that many people from all walks of life could read and glean from my testimony. I remembered in an interview to promote the vision of Hearts On Fire, Starlene Stringer (KLTY 94.9 FM) suggested I write a book during our conversation. I knew this was my next step, because unlike concerts, which require people and production, I could simply write my story and share it with others.

My take is pure and simple: my story for God's glory. So, in the fall of 2011, I began interviewing with Dr. Bard and sharing my story in 10 chapters of what was becoming this book, *Wannabee Rock Star Who Finally Found the Rock*. I continued writing this book into 2012, even though initially I hoped to release it by Christmas 2011. My editor had a heavy workload, and I learned to be more patient and wait for God's best. The year 2011 passed without too much excitement, as Robbie was getting acclimated to marriage, and I was waiting for the next door to open for me regarding a kidney transplant or stem cell therapy. SNR had written some of our best songs to date and continued to worship in church at Crossroads Tabernacle on Saturdays, Sundays and Tuesdays for prayer meetings.

Robbie and I kept writing songs, and God revealed the perfect album title to me for the times: *Rockets Red Glare*. *Rockets Red Glare* reflected the prophetic, forthcoming activity in the Middle East and is much more than a lyric from America's *Star Spangled Banner*. From childhood, we are taught to proudly sing "The Star Spangled Banner" at any festival, sporting event or historical gathering. We feel the anthem's climax when the line "And the rockets' red glare / The bombs bursting in air / Gave proof through the night that our flag was still there." Through *Rockets Red Glare*, I wanted to illustrate how our true independence is only found in God's kingdom and not in a nation alone. I am very thankful to be an American and live in this great nation; however, spiritually, I realize that without God in the center of America, we are destined for decimation.

We both *knew* we had to record *Rockets Red Glare*. We meticulously created songs in a home studio and played a few key shows on the strength of "GLOW" and "The Flame" on Power FM 89.7 We did a benefit concert to help raise money for what I thought would be a kidney transplant fund, yet the funds only covered production costs. We reached out to several people around us for help SNR with the ministry but nothing was clicking.

We searched for a new bassist as we continued writing. SNR hoped we would find a permanent member to finish *Rockets Red Glare* and go on tour. Nothing was gelling. Robbie and I began tracking about 20 songs at WP studios with Michael Havens to start the process. It seemed scattered as we could only work in three- to four-hour increments on Sundays, according to everyone's schedule. Some Sundays after church, Michael would be so worn from working all night during the week and rising early on Sundays, I am surprised he did not pass out at the mixing console.

In 2012, we continued pre production on *Rockets Red Glare*, and with the help of a few friends we started recording at WP studios in the Mid Cities. We endured multiple spiritual battles, such as my waiting period for a kidney transplant, family issues and Robbie's life. Even our studio arrangement with a dear friend in Texas fell apart midstream after our engineer, Michael Havens, was forced to move and all of the studio tracks on the hard drives were scattered about. The whole recording process was so out of order that I was sometimes unsure that we even kept the right drum take. Everyone knows the drums are the foundation of any recording. There were a few recording sessions where we found our "groove" and knocked out multiple songs, followed by weeks of cancellations and no activity. There were times where our engineer fell asleep because of battle fatigue and working round the clock. There were times that physical heaviness set in my body and made it difficult to lift my arms. Often, on Sundays, after eating and drinking from Friday morning through Sunday, many toxins and fluids can build up in my blood and trigger a burning sensation in my body. Robbie fought to overcome the normal migraines and upper respiratory and sinus infections that plagued him. Money was scarce and everything we did was on a wing and a prayer. We anchored our faith in God's promise and believed our tour would follow completing and releasing *Rockets Red Glare*. SNR knocked on many doors searching for a donor to send us to Los Angeles to master Rockets Red Glare.

Our journey to the City of Angels in May 2012 reminded me of the first time I braved the Texas Giant rollercoaster at Six Flags over Texas. Seated in our time capsule, we climbed up the rickety wooden tracks, story by story, as we elevated hundreds of feet high above Interstate 30 in Arlington, Texas. In great excitement and anticipation, we approached the apex, only to freefall with pure adrenalin coursing through our veins. Exhilaration is an understatement, as SuperNova Remnant paid a great price the two years prior to our journey to Los Angeles to master *Rockets Red Glare* with Bryan "Big Bass" Gardner. Before the trip, Robbie was in his element at the Greater Southwest Guitar show and pressed for time. Meanwhile, we both networked to find investors to help us finance our trip to LA, and complete *Rockets Red Glare* but we only ran into walls. After reaching out to everyone we could imagine would help us, I contacted a local indie label and arranged a meeting on a Sunday afternoon after church; however, Robbie was at the guitar show and could not attend.

I met for almost two hours with this record company with the implicit request of $5,000 to complete *Rockets Red Glare*. I simply asked for a loan that would be paid back on CD sales. Any long-term agreements to sign as artists with the label were not on the table. We were down to the wire, and I hoped they would step in. After the discussion, they agreed to help us get to LA, finish mixing the CD and get the CD packaged. I left the meeting expecting that we had the funds secured to proceed. Robbie and I discussed the terms of the loan, and agreed we would sign a simple document saying we would repay the $5,000 based on CD sales of *Rockets Red Glare*—nothing more.

Our flights were booked, and we were convinced we had the funding we would need to pay Bernie Grundman's mastering once we arrived in LA. We packed our bags and took flight with no money in our pockets, going on faith. We boarded the plane weary from the late night mixing sessions at Maximedia Studios with engineer Ryan (thanks to Russell Whitaker, who blessed us with the opportunity). Battle fatigued, we chilled on the flight, as anticipation built that we were realizing our two-year dream. Countless others tried to convince us to master *Rockets Red Glare* in Dallas for less money, but we stuck to our instincts.

We hardly talked on the plane, and once we landed at LAX we had no arrangements or money for a rental car to get to our hotel near the studio. We camped in the Starbucks at LAX and prayed for an open door. After four hours we finally found a shuttle that would take us to our hotel. Our first goal was to get to the hotel room and catch up on some much needed rest before meeting Drue Mitchell in Orange County, but when we arrived at tour hotel we were told our investors had not paid for the room and there was a late check-in time. Once again, we were waiting in the hotel lobby with our bags, restless and praying that something would give. We were told that the room was not paid for, and we could not reach the investors. We networked on the lobby computer and attempted to call and email the investors, but there was no answer. We had decided to sit in the cafe and have a bite to eat, when I received an email with what I thought would be the "simple" repayment agreement for the loan; however, what I saw was completely different. They were asking for 50 percent of Supernova Remnant's merchandise rights, copyrights and publishing rights. I was unsure how to break the news to Robbie. Once I did, Robbie called a lawyer friend. Robbie returned to the lobby, and we asked the hotel clerk if we could check into our room to catch a nap before meeting Drue. We were still unable to get in the room, as it had not been paid for, and I also received an email from the investor about withholding the funds to pay Bernie Grundman if we did not sign the agreement. We stood firm and refused to sign anything. We knew the next day when our session started with Brian "Big Bass" Gardner that Bernie Grundman would ask for the $1,700 in mastering fees that we did not have. We would have never boarded that airplane to LA knowing we had no money to pay the studio. What a quandary! We prayed that the Lord would see us through. After all, in the past eight years, He had delivered us from many battles.

Finally, the hotel clerk said that they had received payment for the room, and we climbed the Hollywood Hills staircase to our room for a nap. We asked Drue to come pick us up around 6:30 p.m. so we could grab a bite at The Rainbow Bar and Grill on Sunset Strip and catch a local band afterwards. Drue was cool with our plan and arrived in his jeep about 6:30. We met him in the lobby and walked over to Amoeba, LA's famous vinyl record shop.

After perusing a wonderland of classic vinyl, and taking time for a few photo ops, we decided to dine at The Rainbow. It had been a while since I last stumbled out of The Rainbow wasted, but now it was different. I could see the "old man" was gone and now I had a new perspective. We talked with Drue about SNR's strategy for *Rockets Red Glare*, including the meltdown with the investors. This conversation turned from good to bad quickly and initiated a war of words between Robbie and me. Here we were on the verge of something potentially great and we were fighting.

Yes, *Rockets Red Glare* could have featured more SNR songs but we did not have ample time to develop more of them due to our May 15 deadline. We had hoped to release the CD by our tour with Stryper. We have written some great songs that will be forthcoming. We have been SNR from the start and agreed that we would be 50/50 partners. We work better as a team, and after going to the investors to make something happen, we resented the way things turned for the worse. Bands do fight. We hardly ever do, but this night we were at a boiling point. Everything we had fought for was in jeopardy. After a cool-down from Drue, we chilled and enjoyed our food and the atmosphere. We bolted the Rainbow and just walked down the Sunset Strip looking for a band worth seeing. After an empty search, we stumbled into another underground record shop. As Drue talked with a good friend, I thumbed through collectors' vinyl by all kinds of dark metal bands. I was bored, but the autobiographies of Steven Tyler from Aerosmith, Ozzy Osbourne and Nikki Sixx from Motley Crue captured my attention. I wanted to read the tone of their books, as I was finishing mine. We wrapped it up and Drue dropped us off at the hotel so we could sleep and be refreshed for our session at Bernie Grundman's.

Our wakeup call boldly opened our eyes, and we scurried downstairs to catch the shuttle to Bernie Grundman's studio. When we arrived, we were greeted by Brian's very cordial assistant, Marie, who offered us coffee, tea, etc. Brian was running a little late, so we took some pictures in the studio and toured the facility. Platinum albums from Elton John, Linkn Park, Michael Jackson, Prince and other artists lined the posh studio walls. After speaking with Marie, we learned that the investor back in Texas had called and instructed her to send the masters of *Rockets Red Glare* exclusively to their offices. Why were we surprised? We pleaded with Marie to allow us to complete our mission in the studio, for which we had waited two years, although we could not pay for the time. She agreed that we were Bernie Grundman's client and that they would bill SNR. Thank God, at least we had bought some time and would return to Texas soil with *Rockets Red Glare* in hand. We planned to deliver the masters to Jim at Crystal Clear Studios in Dallas so that he could press 300 limited edition copies for us to offer at House of Blues.

We situated ourselves in Brian's studio, which is very simple but boasts some of the world's finest mastering equipment. Mastering is what takes the sound recording to the next level, preparing your songs for radio airplay. Brian "Big Bass" Gardner had worked with Grammy award winning artists No Doubt, Van Halen, Foo Fighters and RUSH.

We arrived, after a bout with traffic, and Brian immediately turned to us and said, "Thank you for your prayers and patience." Brian had some family issues to resolve, which required us to reschedule our initial studio date. It worked out for both parties, as it gave us extra time with Ryan at Maximedia to tweak our mixes.

Robbie and I were seated on the couch, surrounded by platinum records (Linkn Park, Foo Fighters, Rush, Eminem, Michael Jackson, Van Halen) from the past two decades, while Brian began turning the knobs. We had worked together with Brian on SNR's debut *The Afterglow* in 2006 and again on *Worship & Warfare* in 2009, so we knew what to expect.

From the opening song *"Rockets Red Glare,"* we could sense that Brian really liked our work. We were just as excited, because everything was fresh out of the studio. As Brian dialed in our sound, he moved through track two, "I Remain," which prompted him to turn around from the mixing console and intently look at us and pay SNR a great compliment: "I am hearing some flavors of RUSH." Now, that is cool when the mastering engineer, who just mastered RUSH's new CD, turns to you and says he hears some RUSH influences in your music. Thank you, Brian. We are both three-piece bands that rock, but RUSH is from Canada and SNR is from the United States.

Brain continued mastering, as we relaxed, confident, knowing *Rockets Red Glare* was about to launch as soon as we returned to Texas. By the time Brian heard "Declaration" he was all in. He loved the new SNR sound and songs we had worked hard to cultivate. Our excitement grew as he mixed "Miracle," "You Are" and "Sons of Glory," followed by SNR classics "Hand on My Heart" and "GLOW." Time flies when you are having fun. We truthfully wished the other 15 songs on which we tracked drums and some guitars were finished and ready for Brian, but we would have to wait. Our Texas tour with Stryper was on the horizon, and we were thankful to know we would return to Texas with an EP to offer at our concerts.

We talked about the plans God had for SNR and told Brian he would

255

continue to be in our prayers and assured him what a blessing he was to us. Marie, Brian's assistant, shared that her husband was in artist relations and suggested we contact an indie record label in Austin, with whom her husband worked. Every plan the enemy had to trip us up had been trumped. Marie said she would allow us to depart with the masters, even though payment had not been received. Again, the Lord provided. We were broke, so we planned to walk back to our hotel—we had no money for cab fare or the shuttle. As we joyfully walked the streets of Hollywood Hills, we were shining like the LA sun with gladness that our dreams were being realized after the two-year battle to complete *Rockets Red Glare*. As we traversed the sidewalk up the rising terrain to our hotel, I spotted a unique street sign that towered twice as high as the street signs we see in Texas. It was appropriately named "Grace." I yelled at an Asian female jogger to please stop and take a picture of us under the "Grace" sign. If a picture paints a thousand words, this picture said it all. Everything we endured up to this point, including the difficulty with our masters, the mix-up with our investors and being penniless in LA, led to SNR arising from the ashes victorious. After we kindly thanked the young lady for helping us, we found our way to the hotel and soon were in a cab arranged for us to catch our departing flight. We were psyched to know that all the battles were well worth the realization of our new CD *Rockets Red Glare*. When we started SNR in 2004, it was just some scribbles in our journals and a heart to reach lost, broken souls, as we once were before the Lord gave us our "second chance."

Back in Texas, we began dialing for dollars so we could settle our debt with Bernie Grundman Studios. On a Sunday afternoon, battle fatigued from the trip, Robbie called a dear friend to pray with him. After the prayer, Robbie's friend asked "What can I do to help you?" Robbie shared our dilemma in LA with the investors and our pressing need to pay Bernie Grundman. We needed to pay them, or else we would not be able to press *Rockets Red Glare* in time for our Texas tour with Stryper in a few short weeks. Robbie's friend, without hesitation, agreed to foot the bill to Bernie Grundman. What a blessing. God was ahead of us the entire time, preparing the way. It was beautiful knowing there are people out there who genuinely want to help.

With the payment secured, Bernie Grundman studios expedited our *Rockets Red Glare* masters, and I delivered them to Jim at Crystal Clear Studios to press the limited edition EP of *Rockets Red Glare*. What a feeling! SNR was prepared for the tour by rehearsing and networking to sell out the House of Blues. Believe me when I say, it was nothing short of a miracle to get to Los Angeles to complete *Rockets Red Glare*.

After recording and refining our songs from January through May 2012, our first big show of the year came with House of Blues calling us to provide main support for Stryper in Dallas on May 17. Soon, there was a new buzz at

Power FM 89.7 FM and other markets over the launch of *Rockets Red Glare* and subsequent live shows. SuperNova Remnant matured as a band, and as believers, and we knew God was setting the stage for a new season. Music can reach so many people from all walks of life, and whether you play bluegrass or metal is irrelevant to the Lord if your heart is set on reaching others for Him and His kingdom. As the House of Blues gig approached after returning from Los Angeles to master *Rockets Red Glare* with Brian "Big Bass" Gardner, we were on a local promotional circuit and went to see John Waite (Bad English/ Babys), and on the return home I was in a car accident. My car was totaled. I stood bewildered in the streets of downtown Dallas. I do not want to harm anyone. In the aftermath of the accident, I was trying to rest on a Tuesday afternoon when my cell phone rang. I thought it was Allstate's insurance adjuster regarding the auto injury, because it was a 713 area code. Turns out, it was Dolores Lorenzo at Live Nation, a booking agent for House of Blues, who said Houston House of Blues wanted SuperNova Remnant to provide main support for Stryper at their Houston show. Now we were set for back-to-back concerts with Stryper, *and* our new CD was ready. We agreed to travel to Houston, not knowing whether our bassist James Putnam would be able to go, as he had a prior commitment to Robert Gotcher. We asked 14 bassists to sit in with SNR, but nothing gelled.

Robbie and I had resolved to play to the show in Houston as a two-piece, if needed. During our midnight sessions at Maximedia Studios, prior to going to Los Angeles, we left the studio one night to go promote our House of Blues show at Trees, where we played with Stryper in March 2011. I ran into Randy St. John (drummer with Ty Tabor of Kings X and Mind Body Soul). It was The Basement reunion at Trees, and we saw hundreds of musicians and fans that we had not seen in 15 years. Randy encouraged us to stay until midnight for their set. We were reluctant because we needed to return to the studio, but we agreed. I opened for Randy St. John many times as a teenager when he was in DFW's top drawing Hard Rock band Sweet Savage as I was learning about the Dallas music scene. Because of that encounter at Trees, I stayed in touch with Randy via Facebook and then met his bass player in Mind Body Soul, Stacey Steele.

I messaged Stacey on Facebook and invited him to come see us with Stryper, and he said he planned to come. At this point it did not occur to me to ask if he could play bass for SNR. After no one seemed to be available to us two days before the show at House of Blues Houston, I asked Stacey if he played bass. He said, "Yes," so I invited him to sit in for SuperNova Remnant while we were in Houston. He agreed, we emailed Stacey the songs and he learned them.

After a quick five hours sleep from the Dallas House of Blues show, we loaded the luxury SUV our friend Chip Street rented for us and we were bound for H-Town. The trip down 45 South was quick, punctuated by "Hair

Nation" on XM satellite radio and our trivia game "Who's this band?" was created to pass the time and educate our twenty-two-year-old sound man Buster Clark a little about 80s metal. While truck driver Eddie Mick and Scott Davis braved the road in our box equipment truck at 60 mph, Frankie (stage hand/video), Sheila (Robbie's wife/bassist) and Buster (theology student/ sound man) cruised with Robbie, me and Chip. We were full of excitement from the fully engaged crowd in Dallas, in anticipation of our debut in Houston, having never played there before.

We arrived in Houston around 2:30 p.m. and checked on our rooms at the Hyatt Regency downtown. A good friend of ours, Michelle Wood, arranged for us to upgrade our rooms from another hotel and saved us big bucks (thanks, Michelle).

Once settled in, within an hour we were at the House of Blues, which was located within five minutes of our hotel. I entered the venue, not knowing where to go, and found myself in the middle of Stryper's personal sound check. It was just me leaning against the back wall and listening to Michael kindly ask the sound engineers to tweak the vocal monitors while the band found the right levels. During sound check, Stryper played one of my all-time favorite songs, "Calling on You," and I lifted my hands in worship along the back wall. It was a great moment.

Once Stryper finished sound check, I approached the stage, and as I walked up I encountered Stryper vocalist Michael Sweet, and I asked, "Michael, do you have a minute? I would like to ask you something." Many questions flooded my mind, but I decided to ask Michael how he enjoyed working with guitarist Tom Scholz, an MIT graduate from legendary rock band Boston.

Michael said, "It was a great experience and, as you know, Tom is so gifted, but many times the arrangements of the songs would change." Michael has been used by the Lord as front man for Stryper, as a soloist, and with mega-platinum classic rock superstars like the band Boston.

Once Michael exited the stage, I met our bassist for the night, Stacey Steele, at sound check. We proceeded to fine tune our gear, once our crew had staged it, and ripped through "The Flame," "Miracle" and other songs, allowing Buster to dial in our sound. House of Blues production crew in H-Town were so laid back and very accommodating to us. We sounded phenomenal, and our adrenalin level was peaking. We were led back to our green room, stocked with Perrier, bottled water, and fruit and veggie trays, and we had a chance to visit with Stacey.

Stacey shared something very meaningful with us. Stryper made an impact on him and he wrote the band asking for prayer. The letter was dated May 1989, almost 23 years to the day, and Stryper replied to encourage him. He showed us the yellow letterhead with Stryper's signature and an encouraging note at the bottom. To see Stacey, whom we just met that night at House of Blues Houston, along with Stryper, praying over us and also signing his "yellow and black" letter from 1989, was surreal. We were on a high from such a great performance in front of our hometown crowd at House of Blues Dallas. *Rockets Red Glare* was finally out, and we were excited about what God would do next.

Stryper wanted to pray with us before we played. SNR prayed together in our dressing room, and then we were led down the backstage corridor where we gathered with Stryper's lead guitarist Oz Fox, his good friends and Michael Sweet's wife, Lisa. Afterwards, our road manager led us to the House of Blues stage to take our post while our intro rolled. SNR sounded amazing, thanks to Buster Clark, our professional sound man. The crowd was a bit sterile, but later we learned that they were really intent on the music. We ripped through our 30-minute set, sharing brief testimony in between. Once finished, we received resounding applause. We immediately headed over to our merchandise table where we offered SuperNova Remnant CDs and t-shirts and, literally, there were 10 rows deep and 10 rows wide of people flooding our table. We signed *Rockets Red Glare* CDs with Bible verses, we autographed drumsticks and guitar picks and we prayed and made hundreds of new fans. After our meet-and-greet with SNR fans at our merchandise table, we headed upstairs to the balcony to watch Stryper. Being upstairs with the fans in the balcony at House of Blues was a great experience.

On the way to the elevator to go downstairs, I noticed a paralytic man who had served in the U.S. Army. I went over to see about him and met his attendant, who had been healed of Hepatitis B and C—impossible for man but not for God. We talked a few moments and agreed to meet downstairs before they left to take time for pictures. It was meaningful to encounter people from all walks of life worshipping God through music at House of Blues. When Stryper finished their two-hour rocking set, we returned to our merchandise table to meet dozens of new SuperNova Remnant fans. I received a call from a top music journalist in Houston, who was there and wanted to cover SuperNova Remnant in a story for a few magazines when we return. We made our way to the hotel and had fellowship and pizza until the wee hours of the morning. The hotel lobby was filled with laughter, as we were delirious from the 48-hour joyride.

Sunday morning, we arose and received an offer from Michelle's friend to perform at her wedding on a 100-acre ranch. We discussed the details for about an hour, as our crew became anxious to leave Houston. We journeyed back to Dallas/Fort Worth, and on the way home gave our young sound man Buster a "school of rock" education, walking him through the history of RUSH, Led Zeppelin, Van Halen and Stryper, of course. We were amazed at all the lives we touched through our music and our testimonies and how their lives also ministered to us.

Robbie and I were excited to return to worship at Crossroads Tabernacle after rehearsing for three weeks prior to our Texas Tour with Stryper. We missed our family at Crossroads Tabernacle. We felt their prayers and were humbled to return. Many of our congregation came to House of Blues Dallas on May 17, 2012, to support SuperNova Remnant. Our single, "Declaration," was played and requested on Power FM 89.7 with plans to add the song to an HD station, NGEN, out of Houston. We are setting up logistics for future tour dates in support of *Rockets Red* Glare and want to also continue working on our new crop of SuperNova Remnant songs, adding drum tracks, adding the wall of guitars and bass and vocals and mixing and mastering them for release. Since our tour of Texas with Stryper SNR has been on a rollercoaster.

SNR envisioned building on the huge momentum we generated from the tour and carrying on through the summer, as it is the best time to tour and perform festivals. The Lord said differently. Soon after we settled back in DFW, Robbie created a myriad of stunning SNR posters. I am certain he has spent the last 180 days on his face in prayer and in scripture. We all continue to pray for Robbie's speedy recovery from his recent accident.

Meanwhile, I have felt like I am in a cave waiting for a "SHIFT" and a glimmer of hope. I have decided not to launch out with another artist but continue to seek the Lord for direction and enter his rest. Even though I totaled my car in May, a dear friend recently blessed me with a nice used car. Even so, I cannot remember feeling this stuck in a long while. I have been homeless and fallen on tough times in the past, yet this feels different. After chiseling away for two years to complete *Rockets Red Glare* and tour in support of it, we finally had the CD complete after our trip to LA and we had a tour lined up—only to see it fade in the midst of another setback. SNR has been approached with several offers since our Texas tour, and it has been challenging for us to decline, but we are hopeful the Lord has something "exceedingly, abundantly, above all we can think, ask or imagine, according to his power working within us." (Ephesians 3:20, one of my favorite scriptures.)

Prologue

Another life event that just occurred was the passing away of my beloved friend Dr. Peter Jack Rockson from All Nations Charismatic Church in Dallas. One sunny afternoon in late-spring 2011, while I was at Barnes & Noble presenting the Enzacta (Global Nutrition Network) opportunity to Jose Perez, I noticed a peculiar man eavesdropping on our business conversation. He was dressed very nicely in black slacks, checkered shirt and expensive snakeskin boots. At the time, he did not speak. He soon left the store, but I could not help but feel I was supposed to meet him. As I continued sharing Enzacta's business model with Jose, I noticed the "peculiar" gentleman had returned with a sack of nutrition products from Vitamin World. This time he sat on the opposite side, eager to know more about our business model. He peered in as a giraffe in the jungle and asked in an African accent, "What are you talking about?"

My first thought was, "Thank you, Lord," as I had been praying the Lord would lead the right people into my path. I had searched the aisles and altars of many churches and healing conferences the previous five years, until The Lord said, "No more," just rest in Him. So, after a season of rest, the Lord had sent a genuine prophet to me. Initially, I thought Dr. Peter would be a great business prospect. Little did I know he would become a formidable influence in my spiritual growth over the ensuing year.

Dr. Peter invited me to join him at church, and something deep inside compelled me to begin driving to Dallas on Friday evenings to study the Word and worship with All Nations for Christ Charismatic Church. I reasoned that surely I wasn't seeking a conference or responding to a colorful postcard invitation, but rather the call of the Lord. Dr. Peter had circled the globe conducting miraculous crusades in New Zealand, Australia and Fiji, after his humble beginnings as a school teacher in Ghana led him to preach to the nations.

I soon learned from YouTube videos that Dr. Peter did flow in the gifts of the Spirit, as I witnessed him lay hands on the sick and they were healed. Blind eyes were opened, the lame walked, and the deaf could hear. As one who had received the miracle of being delivered from Reiter's syndrome at age 13, and recovering my vision at age 33, in addition to my experience with

Miracles Still Happen at Crossroads Tabernacle 2005-2010 I had seen these miracles with my very own eyes.

As I sat under Dr. Peter's teaching about the Holy Spirit from a manual he had written, my spirit was refreshed by the living water and the washing of the water of the Word. The worship was never about anything but the Lord— no grand choir, worship team or gifted singers, just a CD of worship leader Terry MacAlmon or old standards like "I Surrender All," as we gathered Friday evenings to sing unto the Lord. As I became familiar with the church, I met Pastor Kate, who was also from Ghana, and a delight. She always had a radiant smile and a willingness to serve others at every turn. Pastor Kate would often bring powerful revelations and teachings born out of her own encounters with the Lord and the refiners' fire that had tested her faith. I was always amused by the stories Pastor Kate and Dr. Peter told about the Gold Coast and the delicious fruits enjoyed by their strong sense of family. Dr. Peters' strong Ghanaian dialect would make us laugh, as he would say things like, "James, you will go to Gold Coast with me and enjoy Maaaaangoo, juicy Maaaaaangoo."

He would often speak of his journey to the USA from his home continent of Africa and tell us how he loved to watch Roy Rogers' westerns and act like he was a real cowboy in Africa. Once he set foot on American soil, he went to The Stockyards in Ft. Worth and bought a cowboy hat and some fine leather boots. I always will remember during our Friday nights how he would stop in the middle of his teaching to walk over and greet the children and elders alike who happened to arrive late. He was a kind, gentle man with a mighty warrior spirit.

The other administrator of the church was the lovely, cheerful Cindy Lynn. Cindy was a real estate agent, who many times would bless us with her rendition of "Even So," as we entered worship. Cindy was always there, just like Pastor Kate, by Dr. Peter's side.

What you don't know is that in 2010 Dr. Peter suffered a near fatal auto accident on his way home from the church. Struck by a hummer, traveling on I-35, Dr. Peter was knocked unconscious and carried to Parkland Hospital to be treated for critical brain and spinal cord injuries. For months after he was admitted to the hospital, Pastor Kate and Cindy were right by his side. He was unable to walk or talk as the doctors monitored his frail condition. Of course, prayers were lifted up during this time, and a battery of tests was conducted to monitor any progress.

Months into this trial, Dr. Peter spoke to the nurses and said, "My doctor said I can go home."

The nurses replied, "We will see if the doctor confirms what you are telling us." By this time, Dr. Peter had regained his ability to stand and speak a little; however, it was not enough for the doctors, and the nurses replied,

"Your doctor did not say you could go home."

Sternly, Dr. Peter continued. "My doctor says I can go home." Again, the frustrated nurses checked, but no confirmation was given. Finally, after a tiresome exchange, the doctor came to Dr. Peter's room and said, "We cannot discharge you, because you cannot walk or talk."

"I am talking to you now, and I can stand," Dr. Peter quipped.

"You cannot leave, and none of your doctors have said you can go home," the doctor firmly countered.

Dr. Peter said, "My doctor, Jesus the Great Physician, has said I can go home." With that, the Parkland doctors made Dr. Peter sign a waiver that leaving on his own volition released the doctors of any liabilities should he die. Dr. Peter, knowing in his heart that the Lord had healed him, gladly signed the document and went straight to the church that evening to preach.

Dr. Peter was a man of faith. Yes, great Faith.

Recently, in July, Dr. Peter hosted evangelist Glenn Martin from California who worked and studied with Morris Cerrullo for the "Breaking the Chains" conference. Dr. Peter had been praying and fasting 40 days for this. The church printed postcards and campaigned to fill the small church for this important deliverance event. Dr. Peter seemed to vanish in the fast and was not very visible. He appeared a little weak in physical strength. I always saw him robust and full of vitality. I do not know if he was fasting water and food, but I knew he was spending much time in prayer.

Soon the event was upon us. We had people travel from all over the Metroplex to "Breaking the Chains." We gathered at the church and entered worship led by Pastor Daniel and his son. I am accustomed to contemporary Christian music and hymns but not to the African-style worship, which was exhilarating. It was a night of miracles on Friday that broke out even before the teaching. Several people were healed, physically and emotionally. Praise Yahweh. On Saturday, we returned, and Glenn Martin brought the Word, after much worship in the Spirit. Glenn taught the Word of God with fire about hanging on to your faith as if your life depended on it. We saw the glory of the Holy Spirit fall, as people were under the awesome presence of God. Afterward, we fellowshipped until early morning at Denny's restaurant. Our group included Carolyn, Andrew and Dr. Margaret.

Sunday morning came early, and I was back at Crossroads Tabernacle for my worship duties. I was impressed by the Holy Spirit to return to the final service of "Breaking the Chains" Sunday evening, knowing that my dialysis would come early at 5 a.m. Monday morning. *I anticipated the event all day.*

We arrived that Sunday evening, and the crowd was fiery, although it was a fraction of the Friday and Saturday attendance. What mattered is that we were pursuing the King of Kings and Lord of Lords.

I am currently building my nutrition and food network with the help of Beyond Organic. I have a wonderful team in Morris, Dr. Bard, OD; Carolyn and Vina; Blake and Chris; Charles and Devin; Eddie; Anthony; Teresa; Dr. Duncan, DC; Dr. Dan Pompa, DC; Warren Phillips; Dr. Josh Axe, DC; Susan and Bobbi; Tawni and Mark A.; and Beyond Organic founder Jordan Rubin. We are committed to helping others realize optimal health through daily consumption of organic, non-genetically modified foods and beverages, and we are off to a monumental start. I earned the position of vice president within my first 60 days, with the help of the wonderful people I mentioned above.

I am also praying for a fundraiser to allow me to receive stem cells to help repair my kidney function or a living donor kidney transplant, after dialyzing now for nine-and-a-half years. In this season, I have been blessed to move ahead, and I am able to move about with my newer car. Yes, I am confident that my only hope is in the Lord, as I cannot do it in my own strength, and he already knows my steps. It is all I can do to patiently wait upon him as he renews my strength. I also continue to stand for a Godly relationship. The one thing I can truly say is that music, in addition to scripture, has brought songs of hope to my spirit to refresh me in this season.

Making music for the Kingdom of God is a pure *joy* in how it can touch so many people beyond the muse of sex, drugs and rock 'n' roll. We are open to the Spirit of the Lord leading and opening doors, and I pray for restoration and provision of all things that I need for my health. For now, I am so excited about what the future holds for me. I am so thankful for the family I have around me at Crossroads Tabernacle. And for those who have been obedient, like Robbie Gustin, to knock on my door. My heart is set on the future to do great and mighty things for the Kingdom.

The title of this book, *A Wannabee Rock Star Who Finally Found the Rock*, couldn't be more appropriate for a child who grew up with great hopes and dreams, and then early on in childhood learned how to go on in fear and escapism, eventually running away from home, not being comfortable with who I was created to be, to the point that it almost cost me my life. Running back into the arms my mother, who would pray for me all those nights when I was out in the world wasn't that easy for me, with my pride and battle scars, but when it was life or death I heeded the Lord's call. And then the prodigal came home, learning that even though I was fatherless, my Father in Heaven loved me and still had a plan for me. I know there's great hope for me, and a wife, and children, and green pastures, touching many, many, many lives with His blessing. I am making the most of my "second chance."

So I was once a wannabee rock star, who thought, *"All that glitters is gold."* I have always loved this lyric from the Rush song "Spirit of the Radio":

Glittering prizes and endless compromises

Shatter the illusion of integrity.

That's what I thought it was about, but I found out it was more than that.

For me, in my life, the Lord became my Rock, and, yes, a wannabee rock star *finally* found the Rock.

I thank you all. God bless.

Restoration Observations

Second Chances

I idolized my big brother Jimmy and now have the greatest respect for the challenges he has faced. I remember when he left our home to run away, I think I was only 7 or 8 years old and crying over the circumstances, and he begged me to stop crying. He was my roommate, and all that I knew to look up to. Anything my bro was doing I did; I am sure I was an aggravating little brother. I remember in elementary thinking I was so cool for having a brother in rock 'n' roll. I and my friends wore the bandanas around our thighs and wrists like he did. I usually had the coolest ones because I used the same ones that James used. I totally felt I lost my world when Jimmy went to live with his dad. We might only be half brothers, but he is my brother at heart.

I was his greatest fan. I was able to go to clubs later in life when I was not old enough to be there, and it was such a cool experience. Not to be biased, but any band he was in was the greatest band in the world in my eyes, and I felt like I was a part of it. Whether it was Trees, July Alley (I think) or the Starplex, my big brother was rocking, and I never looked at him as lost. It took some growing up and death at the door for me to realize his path to destruction. I am just happy to have him. Later on, when I was able to become my brother's roommate again it was like we never stopped being brothers. We have had some great times, and I just can't say enough how proud I am of him. We have grown out of those things in the world that can only lead to destruction, and I thank God for allowing him another chance in life. I am very proud of his determination and faith.

Richard Howeth

As long as I can remember, my brother James played sports. We are five years apart, and when he was about 10 he was involved in sports, primarily football. As early as 5 years old, I was cheering him and his team on. I was into sports myself, so as we grew up I threw down the pom-poms and was involved in softball and soccer. At that time, he was in junior high playing football at school, and, since he was older, we didn't attend the same school for me to cheer for him and his team. He was 13, I believe, when he went to the doctor and found out that he had a disease that would prevent him from being able to play sports any longer. As I recall, he was pretty bummed. He began to get into music instead and immediately found another passion at which he would prove to be very talented. This would have been the mid 80s, and, of course, rock 'n' roll never goes out of style. His early years in high school he formed a band with his best friend, Brad Spalding, and a few other classmates. I recall them singing and practicing all the time at our house, as he wanted to really master his craft. His love for music and his desire to be a famous rock star led to contention between James and my mom and dad. He wanted to go his way, and, as a young teenager, he thought he had everything in place to do that. So, as it was, he left and moved into my dad's house. I would visit my dad regularly, where I might see James every now and then, if he was around. My dad and I saw him play a few times. Even when he was around, you got a sense that he didn't want to be there. He wanted to be with the rock-and-rollers and people who he thought "had it made" or "had arrived," so I let him do his thing.

I continued to go to school, and in my late teens I found out I was having a baby. I don't really know that I specifically shared that with my brother. I think he might have just heard it through the grapevine. Over the years, I would see him on special occasions, if ever, and never really knew him that well. His interest seemed elsewhere and not on his family, which was cool. I was too busy to worry about it, to tell you the truth. I always figured if he thought he could take care of himself, then that's what he was doing. I remember shortly after finding out about my pregnancy that we received a fateful call that our dad had passed away. I had always spent time with my dad, but I believed that James would have regrets about not having been around as much as he could have, or should have. We all live and learn. It seemed we may have gotten a little closer during that time period, but I was working and preparing to be a single parent, and James was still in search of his fame and fortune.

After being in different bands that always seemed to be on the cusp of "making it," he seemed like he was growing weary of waiting for fame, and the next thing I knew he was getting into nutrition. This could have been due to the fact that our dad had passed away at a young age and he wanted to make sure he maintained his own health and would not die young. James started working for a marketing company, and we would hear from him as he would share with us about his business and about the opportunities the business had for making extra money. Again, the visits were few and far between, and at this point we were both young adults living our lives, me being a mom, working full time and going to school, and him building his business. The next thing I knew, my mom was getting calls from him more frequently, and I began to realize that James was not doing well. I was with my mom when he called (at Frankie Ramirez's demand) when his body was filled with fluid and it was apparent something was severely wrong. I know my mom wanted nothing more than to reach out to her son who had been estranged from her for several years and help him in any way that she could. I rode over with her to an apartment complex in Carrollton, and when I looked at my brother I was devastated. He was very swollen and propped up on a chair with a pillow, just trying to breath. I recall him being in the back seat trying to get comfortable, and I could see the fear in his face. At that point, anything prior didn't matter. This was my brother, and we prayed to God that he would not die. We took him to the house where he called a doctor he knows who informed him to get to the hospital ASAP. I recall my mom calling ahead of time and telling them we were on our way and what his symptoms were. I knew she wanted to break down, but she stayed strong for him. He received the diagnosis that his kidneys were failing and they immediately started his treatment. After those eight days, he went back to my mom's to stay and begin his treatments. It was hard to see him go through that, and I had my own questions about why and what could have caused this to happen to someone like him. But, sometimes, we don't know the "whys" of life.

He had an old high school friend, Robbie Gustin, who had heard about what he had gone through and he had come by to see him. Robbie, too, had lived a life of rock 'n' roll, drugs, etc., and had recently rededicated his life to God. He encouraged my brother and asked him to go to church with him. My brother started to attend Crossroads Tabernacle and he too surrendered his life to God. Since then he has had many challenges but knows that he is not alone, that his God, his family and his friends are all with him.

In 2008, James began to contemplate having a kidney transplant. It was first discussed that possibly our mom would be a match, but in further discussing it and through researching other possibilities a research study came out at Northwestern in Chicago, and I told him I would be more than willing to be tested to see if I would match and could give him a kidney. We started that process, but due to some of the treatments that would have to be performed in that program, we did not continue. He is still currently contemplating a transplant, and we have begun the process with a transplant program in San Antonio. I say everything is in God's hands, God's timing. He will direct our paths if we don't lean on our own understanding, and I pray that He will continue to direct my brother into His perfect will, no matter what that is. We now enjoy a closer relationship, and he has gotten to know my daughter better over the last eight years. He continues to pursue his music and has God-given talent like no one I have ever seen playing the drums. But now he does it for God's glory, and not his own.

Marilyn McLester

I'm with the Band

I was "Jimmy" McLester's band director at North Richland Junior High. Even as a beginning trombonist, I could see that Jimmy had more musical aptitude than other students; it just came easy to him. He was a student who could do minimal practice and still excel on assignments. I also remember him as being a respectful and smart student. Teachers enjoy working with students like this as we know they will make a difference in the world. He was mature enough to joke around a little bit, but he never crossed the line of respect between teacher and student. I was always happy to see him walk into the room, as he brought positive energy in with him.

During his junior high days, Jimmy was more interested in rock music than the more classical style of music in his band lessons. He eventually did not want to play trombone in the band any more. Believe it or not, that didn't bother me, as my goal as a teacher has always been for each person to find his/her own musical voice, and Jimmy is certainly one who has done that!

Fred J. Allen
Director of Bands
Stephen F. Austin State University

Jimmy and I grew up on the same street and went to same junior high and high school together. I can remember him playing on his CB700 drum kit while I would jam out piano chords on our family upright. We were going to conquer the rock world and always said we would "make it" by the time we were 25. Our looks were everything, and we loved chasing the girls, thinking we were cool. We started our first bands together through school, eventually graduating to our 80s band ChazaRetta. We had about a three-year run and eventually parted ways. Through the years, we each made our travels and performed hundreds of shows with various bands and in 2010 found our way back to each other. He filled me in on his battle and asked me for some help to put piano to a single he had written. He then invited me to play some shows with his newest project, SNR. The show was at House of Blues, combining my keyboard work with their originals. I think we got together once or twice to rehearse. One of the other highlights was a show at Trees in Dallas, opening for legendary Christian rock band Stryper to a sold-out house. SNR's music is both moving and heartfelt, and I thoroughly enjoyed our reunion together as brothers in Christ and old friends.

Peter Nepo

I was only 18 years old when I gave birth to my firstborn son James. James' father and I married right after high school. His father had joined the Air Force and James was born at the base hospital in Glendale, Arizona. Shortly after his birth, his father was deployed to Vietnam for one year. On his return we settled in Fort Worth, and I hoped our lives would be happy. His father and I often listened to the music on the radio, and his father's favorite band was Chicago. I noticed early on that at a very young age James was memorizing the words to many songs. My mother had him record Barry Manilow's "I Can't Smile Without You" when he was very young. James also would emulate Elvis Presley at family gatherings by acting out "Hound Dog," as he would gyrate and roll around on the floor.

When James was 5, I gave birth to my daughter, Marilyn. Unfortunately, our marriage did not work out, and when James was 6 years old, we divorced. The marriage was riddled with abuse, alcoholism and strife, and on Valentine's Day 1973, I gathered the kids, and we left.

I remarried, and our lives went on. In the second marriage, I had another son, Richard. James was playing football in junior high, but that came to an end when he was diagnosed with Reiter's syndrome, which caused arthritic type symptoms, and the doctor said no more football. At that point, he joined the school band, playing the trombone. Eventually, he was turned on to rock and roll when he went to a rock concert. He decided he wanted to play drums. He really excelled in drumming, but his studies began to take second place to playing the drums.

James spent hours jamming with his friends, all of whom wanted to have a rock band. I was concerned, because I did not want him to fall into the trap of drugs, sex and rock and roll. As many young people do, he began to rebel and was determined to pursue his music. I was not against him playing drums, but I was concerned about the culture and the potential pitfalls of being in a hard rock band. In the summer after his sophomore year, he ran away to live with his father and to pursue his dream of being a rock star. This was heartbreaking, so I just began to pray to the Lord to take care of him. For the next 20 years we had a relationship but it was somewhat superficial. We never resolved what happened.

Although we would be together on holidays and special occasions, we didn't have a very close relationship. In addition to being in the bands and playing many venues and being very popular locally, he also began a career in nutrition and did very well. James has a great ability to reach out to people and an amazing gift of learning, retaining and sharing information, so he became quite successful in this endeavor.

In 2003, he began to call me more often and finally confessed that he had been told by the doctors that his kidneys may be in failure. He had not shared this with me before. His dreams and his world were crashing down around him, and he did not know what to do. After many years of praying, this was an opportunity for me to talk to him about the Lord and share scriptures with him. I told him to read Psalm 91 and encouraged him to turn his life to God. He was very ill and doctors were telling him to prepare to go on kidney dialysis, but he would not do it.

I convinced him to leave Dallas and move back to Fort Worth to live with me so he would have family support. By this time, he was carrying around 25 to 30 pounds of fluid due to the inability of his kidneys to work. Finally, one of the doctors that he most respected called and said he would have to immediately go to Presbyterian Hospital and start emergency dialysis or he could die. I took him to the hospital where he spent the next eight days being treated and dialyzed in order to save his life. We were afraid, but we were given grace through Jesus Christ to make it through this crisis. When James was discharged he came back to live at my house and was set up for treatments three times a week at the local dialysis center.

While he was recuperating, one of his high school musician friends heard he was sick and came by the house to see him. Robbie had survived a drug overdose himself and he had recommitted his life to the Lord. He was attending Crossroads Tabernacle in Fort Worth and invited James to their church service. On a Tuesday night when Crossroads held their weekly prayer meeting, he went to the altar and surrendered to the Lord. At that moment, a new journey began for him. He began playing drums with the praise and worship team, and he and Robbie formed a Christian Band called Supernova Remnant.

The Lord has restored our family relationships and healed hurts from the past. James continues to minister to people wherever he goes. He is always ready to share God's love and redeeming grace with hurting people. I believe you will be blessed as you read his story as it is a testimony of God's power to heal and restore.

Susan Howeth

When I met Jimmy McLester in seventh grade, it was through mutual girlfriends. They were always talking about how cute he was. Of course, I was a bit jealous but intrigued about this handsome drummer who was taking some of my action. Well, I met him at the skating rink, and we instantly became good friends—the kind of friends who shared everything and spent day and night together, thinking about and playing music. Jimmy had instant recall, so school came easy for him, and I could tell he was also easily bored. We would work on our music after school until we were able to play for the school talent show. This was when we got our first taste of the screaming girls, and our popularity skyrocketed.

We met up with other guys through the years and had many different lineups and bands. Once high school was on the horizon, I noticed Jimmy and some of the new band members getting into dangerous behaviors such as drugs and alcohol. This was something that didn't fly with me. I tried to stay connected; however, in the end I was forced to start a band without Jimmy, but it was a mutual split. I really missed that guy I grew up with as a young kid, and my heart was broken. I honestly felt betrayed. I really felt like my good friend was taking a path of destruction and he wasn't doing it alone. Most of the band members were headed down that same path, and it was unsettling to say the least.

I always knew that James would come out okay because he had a great family that loved him very much; I just didn't know when. It seemed to me that he was never at peace, and I couldn't make any sense out of who he was becoming. What happened to my bright eyed friend from eighth grade?

The thing I remember most about Jimmy is him wanting to stay with his dad because his parents were divorced. Jimmy's dad did everything for him. He allowed him whatever freedoms his staunch Christian mom would not. This had its pros and cons, to be sure. My account of Jimmy McLester is only of us as young adults, but I always held out hope one day he would realize just how much I loved and missed him as a dear friend and always wished we could have kept it together.

Eric Younkin

Not sure who took us to concert, but my Dad picked us up in the wee hours. It was my first rock concert as well and probably still in the top five of the best concerts I've seen. It was Bon Scott era AC/DC. They were not that well known at the time, I believe, and I know that we knew nothing of them beforehand. I think Journey was touring, supporting their Infinity album ("Lights," "Wheel in the Sky"). Though I loved Led Zeppelin and Van Halen, I wasn't much for the hair metal bands that followed in the ensuing years. We would read CREEM magazine, which would, in turn, spur the random Rush versus Clash arguments/discussions. I was very proud of you, James, when you started getting in bands and playing live. I remember seeing Outrageous, Solinger and some other band you were in that I don't remember the name of (I remember lots of candles on stage for that show). To this day, my favorite show of yours was when you were in Redhouse. I used to have a four-song cassette of that incarnation. I have searched for it in the last few years, but I haven't found it. "Which Lie" was a great song! Grunge came along in the nineties, and, in my opinion, saved rock 'n' roll. But we need something to come along in 2011 to give rock another life infusion. Rock has fallen behind rap, pop and country as the music of choice for young people. Sad but true.

Pump It Up,
High Voltage Cousin Steve

"I first met James McLester when he was around 14 at Christian Temple Church in Fort Worth. It was 1982, and I had just moved into the area with my wife and three children to begin a new job managing a music store. Coming from a musical family, I had been a professional drummer since the age of 12. As a young drummer, James asked me to help with syncopation basics. I immediately recognized James' talent and passion for music. That same talent and passion carried him many places.

Many years passed before our paths crossed again. I am still actively involved in music and the ministry and had an opportunity to see James play with his band, Supernova Remnant. I saw how his skill as a drummer had been honed to a high degree of excellence. Good musicians always appreciate other good musicians, and I enjoyed watching him play; however, beyond his excellence on the drums, his passion for Christ was even more obvious. Since reconnecting, James has shared with me his vision to help others, and I see the integrity he has in his calling. He is truly the "wannabee rock star who finally found the Rock."

Chuck Whitby
Fort Worth, Texas

James (known as Jimmy to me) was a constant in my son's life from the age of 13 into high school. Jimmy could be found at our home almost any hour of the day, always had a smile and a warm greeting for all. A consummate drummer, admired by fans and musicians alike, I saw Jimmy making a turn in the wrong direction in his late teens, gravitating to the darker side of rock 'n' roll; however, a devoted and spiritually enlightened mother had a covering awaiting Jimmy's hard left turn, and the rough edges he developed during those years have been smoothed and covered with blessings. My fondest memories of Jimmy are his passion for perfection in his musical performance, which has translated well to the walk his Savior. Jimmy has become a fine man and an Apostle of the Word, returning years ago with passion to His Promise."

Eric Younkin, Sr.

Wе had many parties at our carpet store, Skjolsvik's Floor Coverings. I was married to Jason Skjolsvik. His brother, Erik Skjolsvik, was really into graffiti art, and Jason gave him a huge wall on the outside of our store to express his art. Erik and his friends took full advantage of that wall, and we got to enjoy a constantly changing landscape of beautiful drawings and all the emotions that flowed through the artists that painted on "the wall."

Erik also arranged keg parties at our carpet warehouse, and James McLester's band, ChazaRetta, would play at the parties. The band had just started to come together, and we were all happy to be the test audience for the great music being created.

My brother, Sandy Satterfield, became interested in running lights for the bands, and learned the light boards at those "keggers." Sandy went on to start a career as a light tech and worked for many local bands, such as National Secrets, who played J. Gilligan's in Arlington. He was spotted by a local band, Pantera, who had produced two albums and had just been offered a record deal and tour with a major label. Sandy became the lighting engineer for Pantera and worked with them during their entire touring career. He still runs lights for many major bands all over the world. Erik also began his career creating artwork for album covers and backdrops for many bands including Pantera.

It is amazing have far we have come, and it creates hope for the greatness we all have inside, especially when we are given love, encouragement and a mind full of inspiration.

Sheila Skjolsvik

Marching to the Beat
of a Different Drummer

What can I say? I was a 30-something, recently divorced man looking to have some fun, and I always loved rock 'n' roll. So, what happened? I met some lovely ladies who just happened to be roommates with James and the guitar player of a rock band called Redhouse. I was living a dream; I was up close with members of a rock band. Then I got a house with one of the ladies (roommates only), and James moved in with us and we had a great time. We did a lot of things we probably shouldn't have, but we had fun, and the best part was going and seeing James play the drums at such local venues as Dallas City Limits, long gone, and The Basement, of which I have many fond memories, especially the dollar beer. Well, maybe too much dollar beer at times, but we had fun, the music was great and being right next to the stage was like a dream come true. James, I always loved it when you called me "Righteous" Wright, and, well, you know my other nicknames. I met some good friends from England, as well, whom I am happy to say are still very close friends. I still have the cassette you gave me, James, with the original Redhouse songs on it, as well as your other bands. Our friendship has lasted now for 20 years, and I am proud to call you my friend. I will always remember the trip to San Antonio, where we didn't get to play, but it was a fun trip anyway.

I love you, James. Peace and good heath to you in the future, as I know you continue your music career. Just throw in a song from Redhouse every now and then.

Bob "Righteous" Wright

So, James McLester calls me about a month ago and says, "Hey, do me a favor and write a paragraph about the old days (about 1983) on our time in the rock band Dirty Blonde. Days go by. James calls again: "Hey, did you write that paragraph?" Days go by. James calls again: same question. Days go by.

Today, Friday after Thanksgiving 2011, I'm sitting in my music room thinking "How can I possibly condense and convey a 30-year time span of trials, tribulations, relationships, intersecting paths, careers, families, etc., all of which are the cumulative reasons that we currently have such a different view and character than we did thirty years ago?" Impossible? Probably. But with the dilemma stated, here goes an attempt.

Sometime in the early 80s, I met James McLester because we had a common vision, desire and battle to win rock stardom, and in the heavily competitive field of rock/metal bands we were on a fast track to accomplishing that common goal (listed as an "A" band, Dirty Blonde performed in all the major rock venues in Texas and surrounding states). When I look back now, it's completely amazing to me that this group of four guys, ranging in age from 17 to 21, plus two or three various crew members, traversed across the southern part of the country every week in vans and box trucks, hauling tons of sound equipment, lighting equipment, pyrotechnics, etc., without any serious injury or death—and without the aid of cell phones, GPS or the Internet. The entire scenario now seems crazy from a mid-40s adult perspective, but we did just that, and every week!

James was the third drummer of Dirty Blonde because I, being the leader of the organization, was constantly in search of the perfect members to complete my perfect military type maneuver to conquer rock stardom. James (then known as Jamie Blaze) was a perfect fit: Bon Jovi physical features, hair that would make girls jealous, youth, power on the kit and bounding with charisma, which were exactly the qualities necessary for success in the 80s hair metal scene. The preceding list seems funny now, but it was crucial and very true during that time period.

So the band was doing great and conquering Texas, and this is the portion of the story where I tell a multitude of crazy rock 'n' roll road stories, right? Actually, not, sorry. Remember, James said a paragraph! But to fill in this part of history, I have to say that, truthfully, we were good looking young guys in positions of prestige and popularity, so, needless to say, decisions that were made back then are now viewed as lessons learned on the rocky path of youth to find ourselves. You live and you learn, right?

Anyway, years passed and James and I went our separate ways, both experiencing regional and minor national success in the music industry and other endeavors, but each not realizing that our personal desires, goals and agendas were being changed, molded and redirected by a powerful underlying force. During this time period, we went for up to 10 years at a time without any contact, but both of us going through somewhat parallel heavy life challenges (James' struggle with kidney issues and my struggle with incarceration/jail). We were each on our own personal life journey, being tested, strengthened, molded and redirected, but we were both headed for the same realization and view of life.

Fast-forward to today, sitting in my music room and skipping over tons of life's details, I look back in total amazement at the ever present and sometimes unseen presence of God, because about two years ago, after zero communication for years, I cross the path of "Jamie Blaze"…only he's not Jamie anymore—he's James Michael McLester, and something's changed in both of us. We don't have the same old goals and agendas in common anymore, but now there is a new much more powerful and rewarding common ground between us: God.

When he asked me to write this (paragraph), it seemed very hard, because those days back in the 80s seemed so distant and unimportant now. But I realized in writing this that we both have come full circle in this life journey, and I'm very pleased to see where we both are—still on the same path but a much smoother one with a better view.

Bryant Hunter

I've known James McLester, aka, "Jamie Powers" (stage name) since high school in the mid-80s, during the "golden times" of our youth! I was invited by a mutual friend, fellow guitarist Eric Younkin, to check out this flashy new drummer. So we went to Jamie's house one day after school, and he began to pound away at his fire-red Tama drums like a mad man wanting to stomp out multiple fires, and I was impressed! Since then, we've been friends and have crossed paths in various band projects along the way but never managed to collaborate on a musical venture. I've been playing guitar for 29 years and have always been inspired by drummers. One funny story that comes to mind is the time Jamie invited me to see him and his band Outrageous in concert at Dallas City Limits, one of the hottest clubs and music venues in Dallas at that time. All the major bands played there. My best friend Freddie and I went to see the show. It was a packed house on a Friday night. The band was tearing it up, and everybody was into the original music and covers they were playing. As the show went along, it was time for Jamie to do his drum solo. I remember the sound man was very good that night. Many people don't know this, but a sound man can make you or break you. If the sound man is no good, guess who is branded a terrible band?

Well, the reverb (sound effect) was set to high, along with the volume, and Jamie set the place on fire with all the tricks he had in his bag! All I remember is me saying to myself, "I gotta film this!" After the show, I went up to Jamie, and the first thing out of his mouth was, "How did it sound?"

I said, "Great!"

I asked him when he was playing again, and he said, "Next weekend, why?" I told him I wanted to film the show, especially his solo. He thought it was a great idea, so I borrowed my dad's monstrous Panasonic video camera to film the show. I was all geared up for the big show the following weekend. I had a lot of video equipment with me. My friend Freddie had to help me with it. So we went backstage before the show, and I started interviewing all the band members, as well as Jamie, and asked him if he was ready. He replied with an emphatic, "Yes!" The band started into their set just like the weekend before, only this time, no drum solo!

After the show, I went up to Jamie and asked, "What happened to the solo?"

He said, "We ran out of time, so we had to cut it out of the show. Sorry, Brother." Man, all that equipment and no solo! I did tape the show though, and it was a great memory of the fun times we had.

John Glen
Guitarist / songwriter / producer

———

In the fall of 1988, I attended TCJC (Tarrant County Junior College) to knock out some music and basic college courses. While taking a music theory and composition course, I met Brad Spalding, who was the soon to be lead guitarist of my new band. This friendship ultimately led to my auditioning and formation of the band Outrageous. Outrageous was an original four-man hard rock act in the Dallas area, consisting of myself on bass, Jamie on drums, Brad Spalding on guitar and Matt Story on vocals. This was the beginning of a long-lasting friendship with both Brad and Jamie.

With the largest light show in Dallas, which we brought in from Florida, and our unique black light stage design, our live show was indeed "outrageous" and set us apart from many of the Dallas bands during that time. After cutting a demo CD and touring local Texas venues, the name Outrageous was spreading across Texas successfully.

Unfortunately, like most locally successful bands, we soon hit a crux in our musical endeavors and were forced to make some not-so-desirable decisions. Under the leadership, direction and drive of our drummer Jamie, we maximized our network of contacts and soon acquired help from a notable name in the music scene, Kim Fowley. Kim was very impressed with Outrageous, seeing something promising with the core structure of the band, but he expressed to us that we needed to acquire a new frontman for the band in order for him to work with us and move forward. As to this, we sadly parted with singer Matt Story and finally found a voice that matched the music.

Madison, former singer for the Dallas-based band Katt Daquiri, tried out for our trio and fit in perfectly, leading to the formation of the new band, Redhouse. Although Kim was one of the main reasons we acquired a new frontman, our business relationship with him slowly dissipated over time. This really did not matter, because during this time the band was the essence of true brotherhood, and we all had our eyes set on the grand prize: "getting signed."

Redhouse was quite different than Outrageous in both music and performance. Through Brad's recent discovery and obsession with the blues, Redhouse was becoming a blues-based hard rock band under his influence. As a band, we focused more on the songwriting rather than putting on a theatrical show. The band cut two demo CDs, one of which was recorded at the famous Dallas Sound Lab, and got extensive airplay in Dallas. Like Outrageous, the band toured the local and regional circuit and was very successful until the band members began to pursue other ventures and slowly grew apart musically.

A few years into Redhouse, both Jamie and I were also playing as contract musicians in a band called The Crossing. Both Jamie and I had to manage time and emotion for over a year between Redhouse and The Crossing, which was clearly taking a toll on of the Redhouse band members, as well as on us. The Crossing required much of our time in the studio and for a short amount of time became a great focus of ours due to the simple fact that the music was indeed exceptional and new. Unfortunately, this musical masterpiece was ahead of its time, for it was the beginning of the "alternative" music scene. Although we cut a full CD, had some local airplay and were playing local gigs, the band began struggle due to personality conflicts. During this time, Redhouse had already called it quits, and my heart was no longer set on rock 'n' roll, which led to my mutual exit from the music scene.

Although my musical career was rather short, I would never change a thing about the many people I met and the time I spent jamming with all of these guys. To this day, those "dudes," who I spent countless nights with recording in both top-notch recording studios and practicing in dirty practice halls, will always be a part of my life. All of these guys, in a certain way that only band members can understand, will always be considered my "brothers." We learned many life lessons and shared many great times together that I still reflect on to this day.

Although it has been years since we have seen each other, Jamie, in particular, has indeed left a positive impression on me throughout my life. His dedication to his cause, drive and determination has subtly bled into my much of my successes in life. I suppose listening to that kick drum for so many years subconsciously embedded his solid rhythm section in my soul. Nonetheless, I have only met a few people in my life who I can say such things about. Although it would be a logistical nightmare, I do have a dream that someday all of us old friends can hook up again and share some laughs, stories and memories.

Steve Thompson

In the 80s I owned a booking agency called Golden Productions, which handled most of the prominent rock bands in the area. We were the largest agency in the DFW for entertainment. We also brought a bunch of National acts to the area: The Byrds, Pat Travers, Robin Trower, Foghat, Molly Hatchet, Grand Funk Railroad and others. I stumbled on to an up-and-coming rock band that caught my attention, "ChazaRetta." ChazaRetta had all the ingredients: great talent, looks, desire and an excellent live show. The leader of the band, was the drummer, Jimmy McLester. Jimmy and I had several meetings, and I was impressed by his "go get' em" attitude. He seemed like he had a vision to make it in this industry and was willing to work hard in reaching his goals. The band was very popular with the younger crowd, especially the ladies!

ChazaRetta ROCKED! Jimmy was a very nice person that everyone liked, and he was very professional in handling of the band. His smile was contagious. In my many years in this business, he was one of the most solid drummers around. I felt like Texas would really like ChazaRetta and their hard thumping sound, so I booked them in the largest rock club in the area, Savvy's on Lancaster in Fort Worth, Texas. The band was a huge success there. The crowd at Savvy's really related to their sound and their overall live performance. They were an instant hit at the largest venue Fort Worth had to offer. That showed me there might just be "something" to this band.

Time went on, and the band continued to gain a following. Regretfully, shortly after I had taken ChazaRetta under my wings, I decided to get completely out of the music business. My time had come to get into the corporate world. When I decided to close Golden Productions, I called Jimmy over to my house to tell him of my decision to leave the music industry. I thought so highly of Jimmy, and the way he handled himself in a professional manner, that I offered for him to continue Golden Productions on his own.

Jimmy thought about the offer, but at the time he was more concerned with making ChazaRetta a more known band, and he decided that running a booking agency really wasn't for him. I respected his wishes and we parted ways. But, I will add this: Not many in this crazy upside-down music business have remained in my thoughts, but through the years certain people, and Jimmy being one of them, I have never forgotten. There were few in this business that had morals and even a backbone, but Jimmy McLester was the exception. A good kid with a good heart, and he could play the drums like few rock drummers could.

Buck Judkins/SoundCheck International
Artist Management
Over 20 Years in the Music Industry

I remember as a small child I had received a small, single toy drum, which came with two wooden drum sticks. I was probably 6 or 7 years old. I cannot remember if or how often I may have played with it, but when I was in third grade I received an album from my uncle and the name of the group was Santana Abraxas. The second name I am not sure of the spelling, but he would also play a lot of Iron Butterfly music and Chicago. I guess listening to this music is when I started to become interested in the drums, and I would grab sticks or knives, whatever I could find to use as drums sticks, and I would beat on my mother's footstool while sitting on the floor next to what looked like back in those days a huge wooden box, and it had two speakers in front and two speakers, one on each side, and you would lift up the lid on top, and down inside was the record player, which played the big LPs and 45s. I think back then it was call a phonograph.

As the years went, by I decided I wanted to be in a band. I had discussed this with my mother, and she said, "Well, if you are going to be in a band, then I guess we will have to find a way to get you an instrument." I thought this was my chance to get a snare drum, and I would go down to our local music store at the mall and look at the drums. On the day that everybody met in band class, somewhere in the midst of all the confusion, all of a sudden, I remember the band director telling the class that the percussion part of the class was now full, and I found myself now sitting in the brass section of the band and would up playing the trombone.

Fast-forward to my freshman year in high school at 14 years old. I had a friend who I happen to be staying at his house one night, and we were messing around in their old barn. It was then that I happened to feast my eyes upon an incomplete set of dust-covered drums, and he said, "Yeah, but I don't ever play them anymore. I like the guitar." It was then that I started digging them out and wiping all the dust and dirt off of them and trying to put them together. Once we got them set up in his father's shed, we started horsing around and playing together—me and his drums and him and his guitar.

It was then that I said to Shane, "Hey, let's find a bass player and start a band. After all, Rush only has three members in their band." By this time, I was a huge Rush fan; after all they had none other than Neil Peart, the great, on drums. Well, eventually, this never worked out, so I ended up buying my friend's drums, and I remember spray painting them black, as the original color was gold.

I tried to save up some money during my freshmen year to add more pieces to the drum set, but I just couldn't seem to come up with the money. A short time later, I found myself in possession of my friend's electric guitar. At that time, I was also listening to a lot of Pat Benatar. I liked the way they sounded, and I was also interested in Billy Squire, so I had taken a few guitar lessons at the local music store and had a few years before become a huge Boston fan; all I wanted to do was play like Tom Scholtz of Boston.

It was around this time, the summer of 1980, when I called up my cousin James Michael McLester and asked him if he wanted my drums. I remember James driving up with his dad in the evening and loading up my drums and driving from Granbury, Texas, back to Fort Worth. I remember showing James at different times a few how-to things on the drums, and he went on from there and took some lessons of his own to become a really great and talented drummer.

I have seen him perform on stage over the years and have even been backstage with him, helping to set up his drums while they were opening up for some well-known bands, and I have even seen some intimidation from some of these big band drummers and saw it in their attitude towards James and his band. He is also I believe a gifted songwriter, and he is very dedicated to his music. I found that I could never stray too far from my own drums, as I have a pretty good-size drum set, as room permits me from setting the whole set up, and I have been playing off and on for 27 years now. But now I find myself asking James the best way to do a certain technique. Who would have ever thought we would be so alike, and that he would be as talented on the drums as he is? I have considered paying him for lessons. I heard a few times some years back that he might be one of the few top drummers around Dallas/Fort Worth.

Over the years of living the lifestyle that many rock bands fall into, James found, while drinking and partying for years, that he had developed high blood pressure, which over the years he simply brushed it off. I think that his high blood pressure, and maybe some other things, led to double kidney failure sometime around 2001. I believe that after getting admitted to a hospital, and possibly a near-death situation, that this was a turning point in James' life. He found himself at a crossroads. In the hospital, with no insurance and no money, which road to take is anybody's guess. I believe it was at this point in James' life that for the first time he reached out to the Lord Jesus Christ and put his trust in Him. He had to trust his faith in Jesus Christ and has never looked back.

He has since become a dedicated disciple and minister of the Lord, ministering to whomever may need to hear words of encouragement, words of truth quoted from the Bible or words of truth through his music. He has long since left the rock band scene and has dedicated his music now to worshipping God the Father. I have seen firsthand the things that God has changed in James' life. He has boldly stood up in public and made several testimonies of the life he had before he became saved through the shedding of blood from our Lord Jesus Christ, who said, "I am the way, the truth and the light. Anyone who believes in me and who I am shall be saved." James has now become a great man of God, putting his faith in God, while not forgetting about his own uncertainty but putting it aside to minister and try to reach others who may be lost and letting them know Jesus is waiting for them to call upon His name.

Some of us that know what the expression "finish the race" means from hearing it in church many times, know that when all the dust has settled and everything clears, James Michael McLester will have finished the race and stand in front of God the Father, who will say to James, "Well done my good and faithful servant."

Wade Thornton

Crossing Over

Many years ago, I had the pleasure to work with a group of very talented guys that called themselves The Crossing. James was the drummer of the band at the time. They had all the elements you like to hear in a promising band: great songs, a unique sound, strong vocals and killer all around musicianship. Unfortunately, as is the case with many talented groups, there seemed to be an abundance of energy but an inability to accurately focus it. It's too bad, because, of the many dozens of bands that came through the studio over the years, they were easily one of the more interesting ones and had a really cool sound.

Keith Rust
Studio Manager

Rock in a Hard Place

I've known James for nearly 20 years now. He is that certain kind of fellow that would give the shirt off his back to a complete stranger if need be. We have always been there for one another, through good times and bad. I remember his rock star days with his band Solinger, opening for the likes of superstars such as Alice Cooper. James was so good at his craft that it landed him in the Texas Drummers Hall Of Fame. No too shabby at all. He never let it go to his head though, and was always very humble. Since those days, James blossomed into a very successful businessman, making a number of companies much more profitable. He has also been stricken with an illness in recent years, which has severely hampered his ability to carry on a "normal" life. That being said, James has not let his disease get the best of him. His relationship with our Lord Jesus Christ has helped him through many dark days and nights. It is this relationship that has allowed James to persevere and to know that he will beat this sickness. J,as I call him, will be a brother to me for life.

Tom Vanderslice
Account Executive, Country Life Vitamins

Johnny Solinger and I were frat brothers in Denton. I knew he had some skills when I saw his band the Party Dolls. I first saw Solinger in 1989 at The Basement, and I was blown away! The music, the look and sounds spoke to me. I was hooked. The period from '89 to '91 was explosive, exciting and a little dangerous. By 1993, egos and too much partying were taking a toll on the band. Some new blood was needed. The first to go was Kirk on lead guitar. Sadly, Gray overdosed in the summer of '94. I truly miss his gentle soul. Tommy Hyatt filled the lead spot for about six months, and then Dave H. came in to fill the guitar spot permanently, and Jon M. became the bass player. Andre was the next to go, and was replaced by Jamie McLester. Johnny and John Mott were the only two originals left. This lineup brought new energy to the band, as well as a slightly different sound. The band played more shows and put out more new product than the original lineup. The emphasis was more on the music, as opposed to the after-show parties. My heart will always be with the original crew because of the close friendships, but the output and consistency of the band from '93 to '99 cannot be ignored. I really do miss going out every month or so to see the boys tear up a local club or open for a headliner. I am fortunate to have had open access to the band, and also to have had my camera with me to capture many magical moments. Music is medicine to me, and Solinger was some of the best!

Brandy Russel

In January of 1993, I went to The Basement, a rock/metal club in North Dallas, on a random Tuesday night just to have a few drinks and to go see some bands. I met and saw for the first time the band No Respect, with whom I became fast friends, and I went on to go to do several shows and tours with them. Later that year, I would begin an internship through my college with local rock station KEGL 97.1 FM, and at that job I would learn of another Dallas band KEGL 97.1 FM was playing at the time, Joey C. Jones and the Glory Hounds. Through the friendships I built with both bands, and going to their shows, plus just following the local scene through the Dallas Observer listings, I learned and heard about the local hard rock band of a similar style, Solinger. Since I was such good friends with No Respect and its members I sorta remember there being a little bit of a rivalry. With my allegiance to No Respect, I never caught a Basement or Dallas City Limits show of Solinger.

While at KEGL 97.1 FM, one of the jobs I acquired was assisting Chris Ryan with the very first Local Show on Sunday nights. This was the height of the grunge rock era, and Chris told me he wanted to play everything: alternative, metal, rock and punk bands. So the first time I heard Solinger was on the Local Show with the single "Sky Is Falling," and it really stuck out to me. I managed to get a copy of the record from the show and played the fire out of it, being a big fan of that style of hard rock music. As it got to be the mid-late 90s hair metal and real rock 'n' roll were suffering severe causalities in show attendance and major album release success. Even the majors started putting out weird grunge rock and alternative records, alienating the fans from the music they loved. It was kind of becoming a strange time for that style of music. I'm not sure how, but at the peak of things getting bleak, this band Solinger landed the opening slot on a bill at the biggest outside amphitheater venue in Dallas, opening for Alice Cooper and Scorpions. Since it was a KEGL 97.1 FM show, we had tickets, and that was the first, and actually last time, I would see the band Solinger.

Fast-forward four-and-a-half years, and I was running my own Metal Show on a station in LA. I had several hard rock and heavy metal magazine subscriptions for show preparations. Sitting on the couch in the DJ lounge reading one of the magazines, I see a little news blip about a new singer for Skid Row named Johnny Solinger. I stood up and said, "WHAT!? I know that guy!" Well, not personally as I had never met him, but years of knowing who his band was as the rival of No Respect. I knew that all the members of No Respect were huge fans of Skid Row and couldn't believe the news I had read. So I made sure to include a classic Skid Row song and a track from a CD that I had kept all that time from Solinger, and I spun "Sky Is Falling" on my show Cyber Thrash & Burn. I have also always wanted to catch the new Skid Row to see and finally meet Mr. Johnny Solinger. I have yet to meet him and see the new incarnation of Skid Row, but I have followed them still after seeing Skid Row's very first appearance in Dallas, opening for Bon Jovi on the New Jersey tour.

Now, let's fast-forward yet again another four-and-a-half years, and I meet a band through my current job at the time, as afternoon drive at 89.7 Power FM, and they come to my "other job" in the daytime, sit me down and play me this single "The Flame." I'm not even sure whom I met first, Robbie or James, but they were very persistent in getting their single on Power FM and telling me their story and personal testimonies of the band Supernova Remnant. Now, what is crazy, after talking and hanging at a few shows, we learned that we had many friends in common from the KEGL 97.1 FM days and even had been at shows in the same room, even at after-parties, and had never met until these many years later. I've come to travel with these two brothers and do countless shows with them. I can honestly say as a band, as musicians, and most important as men of God, I've seen them grow into a really powerful force for the Kingdom. The way they take to the streets to promote their shows the old school way is something that is lost on the current digital generation of new bands. I'm honored to know James and Robbie and thank God for their friendship and faithfulness. So, that is my story of how I know my brother James, and I'm sticking to it.

Mad Respects,

Drue Mitchell

I n the mid-nineties, I owned a marketing company for the music business called Real Cool Marketing (RCM) based in Dallas. The company represented for marketing a select number of national and regional artists, based on what we believed was true talent, marketability and potential. Solinger was one of the artists that we had the pleasure to work with. It was a time in the business when radio was moving in a different direction than their sound. The guys were the real deal and their fans knew it. Their live performances were slammin'...packed. They had a tremendous following and were true professionals. They just needed that one break to take them to the next level.

Roger Christian

What can I say? Jamie is just a little different than most drummers. We met in 1996 when I joined a band he was in. I noticed how his drum setup was not the usual thing you would see in those days. No big cage or huge rack of toms. But he had floor toms out to the side and low cymbals. But, man, he could wail on those things, so, as a bass player, I was impressed. Then the singer, whom I had known for years, pulls me to the side at my first rehearsal and explains to me that Jamie is really cool but he's just "kinda weird." It still makes me laugh. Though after getting to know him better, seeing how professional he is, reading the lyrics he wrote and understanding him as a person, I agree, kinda weird! Seriously though, one of the best people and one great drummer. I look forward to playing music together again.

Jonathan Mann

When I met Jamie back in the early 90s, around 1993, I believe, he was a long-haired rock star in the making. He showed a lot of promise not only as a drummer but also as a nutritionist, wild as I was as far as drinking, smoking and rock-n-roll (only I did not smoke). Funny how he could be so caught up in nutrition and still drink and smoke, but somehow he appeared to be very healthy and vibrant. The rock star side of him was a bit cocky; he was going places. This worked well because in 1996 he became one of Texas' elite drummers and probably in the USA and beyond when he became a Texas Tornado, which is equal to getting into the Hall of Fame.

James recorded three albums with the band that he was in at the time. He enjoyed lots of success with them until they split in 1999. Shortly thereafter, he and a long-lost friend who happened to pop back into his life again, by the name of Michael Madison, formed a band called Love Sound Revival, which produced one album in its two-year run. In 2003, it was the end of Love Sound Revival.

This was the pivotal point in James' life. This is when I found James in his apartment bedroom, on his bed, flat on his back. He was bloated, his skin was yellow, his feet looked like they belonged to Fred Flintstone. I could see the terror in his eyes, but he did not want to admit anything was wrong with him. It was obvious he was going to die. I asked him if he wanted me to take him to the hospital. He said no. That's when I told him, "I am either gonna take you myself, or I'm calling 911 or calling your mother. Which one do you prefer?" He said he wanted to call his mom. So that's what happened. His mom came and got him. He shared that apartment with Madison until that day, the day that changed James' life forever.

The next time I saw James was in the hospital. I was not allowed to enter the room. I was only able to observe him through a small window. His mother and sister met me in the hall and told me he had kidney failure. They were not sure he was going to make it. All I could do was hold back the tears. He had been a real good friend to me. I had seen him struggle throughout the years, with finances, girls, loneliness.

At one point he had absolutely nothing. It was the middle of winter, I guess, in 1995, he had no place to go or nothing to eat. He would call me, and I would come out and pick him up off the streets of Dallas, feed him, and then we would find a place to park and would stay in my car overnight so he would have company and shelter. This went on for several weeks until he got a job working at a health food store. Not too long after that he found himself an apartment and a girlfriend, and he was set. In 2000, if I'm not mistaken, he joined a marketing wellness company, in which he became an astute student and businessman, after a few years of learning and applying himself, he managed to retire. He was in that upper tax bracket we all struggle to get to. He enjoyed this for a good year, maybe a year-and-a-half, something like that.

Then came that day when I found him on that bed. He became a born-again Christian and had to begin living life hooked on that machine. Dialysis became a way of life. He had made it through the critical stage of kidney failure. About six months after that fateful day, he hooked up with another long lost friend by the name of Robbie Gustin to form a band called SuperNova Remnant and to this day, James still remains on dialysis and with Super-Nova Remnant. So, in short, the guy is resilient.

Frank Ramirez
October 3, 2011

Skid Row to the Penthouse

What's in a name?

I met James McLester in 1997 at a health food store. At that time he went by the name Jamie MC. We always had interesting and enjoyable conversations. Jamie was knowledgeable, friendly and exuded confidence.

After several months, Jamie introduced me to his friend Derek, with whom I eventually formed a partnership in a nutritional company. That enterprise became a very successful anti-aging and wellness company, in part, because of Jamie's involvement at the retail level and in network marketing. We saw his major leadership qualities from the very beginning.

Jamie MC became James McLester as the years passed. He not only matured as a business person but as one of God's faithful servants. James has done and is doing many positive things in his life. His success stems from his knowledge and sincerity. These two attributes are difficult to falsify. His spirituality has guided him on life's journey.

James is a testimonial to what a person is capable of, and can achieve, even when faced with a dire situation. We are not embarrassed or afraid to share that God has truly blessed both our lives.

So now we know: The Jamie MC of 1997 is James McLester of the present day…and I am proud to call him my friend.

Tom Wood

My wonderful relationship with James spans 10 years, to date. I first met him at Vital Nutrition where he worked helping people find the right nutritional supplements for their health. I trusted him right away because he was so knowledgeable in his field, and he introduced me to a product that he believed to be life transformational. The results I got inspired me to start sharing the product with others who needed a solution to their health problems. As my relationship with James grew and we worked the business together, the day finally came when he reached his goal of retiring from the store to be able to work the business full time.

On the day he retired, they rolled out the red carpet in front of the store with a limo waiting to escort him where he was taken on a celebration ride of dream building. We were all there to congratulate him on his success and the freedom he would now enjoy by being self employed. However, not too long after that the freedom he was enjoying came to an end because his health took a dramatic turn. In fact, many people had concerns for him which climaxed the day he was admitted to the hospital, near death from kidney failure.

By this time, James had developed many close relationships with the team he had built, and a few of his closest friends and family gathered by his bedside with hands joined in prayer asking God for a miracle and to spare his life. I remember several days that God had put him on my heart around the clock to intercede on his behalf, and I confirmed with others who knew him that they were doing the same. We all had a sense he was at heaven's door. Because music has such a healing effect, and such a large part of his life, I brought a

CD player with some specific songs for him to listen to that would help minister to him. I believe the angels of the Lord were encamped around him then and now to deliver him.

The Lord has His hand on James' life. And as he walked through the valley of the shadow of death several times, I have been witness to God's divine intervention and plan for James' during his journey to wholeness and healing. The friendship we developed has grown through the years, and since then I've had the privilege of watching him aspire to become the musician he has longed to be with his band SuperNova Remnant. He is an inspiration to countless people who hear not only his music but his story of great faith, strength, courage and hope. II Corinthians 1:3 says, "Praise be to the God and Father of our Lord Jesus Christ, the Father of compassion and the God of all comfort, who comforts us in all our troubles, so that we can comfort those in any trouble with the comfort we ourselves have received from God." That is his life and that is his vision—to minister and empower people as they walk with God on their own journey.

Georgia Bessett

I had the pleasure of playing bass/keys with James back in 2003–2004 in the band Love Sound Revival. We had many interesting gigs together. The one I remember most was an open mike at Club Dada. Our last song was called "Colors" (I think). We were all locked in and felt as one. I haven't felt that magic since.

Benjamin Law

Despite my good friend James McLester's modesty, even before he turned his life over to a higher purpose he was already a wonderful young man. When he first came into my life and others' lives with Ultimate Lifestyles, we were so blessed to have someone with his nutritional knowledge and years of experience to speak with us and further the education, training and interest in how our physical bodies worked and the importance of taking care of it. His focus was on good health, teaching others about nutrition and being a good friend. He has a gift of communication that he delivers with humor, and he puts you at ease when he speaks to you about subjects you more than likely can't spell. But listening to him talk about them you can easily understand what he means.

He's always had a mission to help others recognize, comprehend and appreciate how their bodies work and what they may need to keep them functioning optimally and strong for health and longevity. When James' own health crisis struck, what was taken from him on the one hand was given back to him in abundance on the other. His struggle became his salvation. He was a blessed man before he found his higher purpose, but since then he's truly become a rock of faith and conviction who has never stopped wanting to help others achieve excellent health and well being. Whether we were working together to educate others about their nutritional needs or off on a fishing trip, James is someone I've always been proud and blessed to call my friend.

Cathy Parolini
Dallas, Texas

Living Out Loud

James and I have spent time building the Living Out Loud concert ministry for SNR. Watching James battle kidney failure and still performing on stage like a rock star is inspiring. His prayer life is most impressive and speaks volumes to his warrior spirit and character. He is faithful that God will give him another kidney and allow him to walk as a living testament to the power of Jesus Christ.

James is wise and will not allow the world's clichés to be the model for his life, but rather the faithful resolve of the power of Jesus to heal first the soul and then everything else.

Living Life Large...Jude 1:20-23

Pastor Frank Lott

I was working with the youth group at FBCB when I met James and Robbie at the "Three Stripes and You're Saved" youth concert. It was my first time to see Supernova Remnant, and they blew me away! But, before I heard them play, I was already drawn to this dynamic duo, by the overwhelming presence of the Holy Spirit living within them. Within minutes, I felt I had made lasting friends, but I had no idea that I would be partnering with them in their ministry over the next few years. God has worked through them to help me and me to help them, and I feel like we've all grown in the process. These guys are "souled out for Christ," and I am so blessed for knowing them.

Lee "Mold Breaker" Cobb

Brother James. Prayer warrior. Human metronome. Master of the big beat! To have faith that he will be healed and to place all in the hands of the Lord is a true testimony of his walk with the Lord. Forgiveness is something a lot of folks struggle to bring into their hearts, and James does this with grace and humility. Having known what he has endured and suffered through with his dialysis treatments, it's easy to see how one could get down about the whole process, but he never misses a beat. I am blessed that I can call such an incredible musical talent my friend.

Doug Kovach

No Limitations, Only Inspiration and Hearts On Fire

It's been a pleasure to work with Jamie McLester over the last several months. Jamie is completely on fire for God and is passionate about using his musical gifts for ministry and evangelism. He is a great musician and talented drummer, but even more important, he is a wonderful person who is devoted to pursuing the heart of God. I look forward to continuing to work with him in the Christian music industry in the years to come, and supporting his band Supernova Remnant in their upcoming endeavors. I highly recommend him to anyone looking for a Christian musician, band or speaker.

Jesse Money

James McLester is one of the most passionate people I know in the music industry. He is definitely a force to be reckoned with. His mind is clearly focused and his heart is God-centered….

Dawn Henderson
PROMOTIONS DIRECTOR

I never understood why Jimmy would ever want me to consider writing about the day I met him, up until now. Thank you, Lord, for the revelation knowledge that you continue to lavish upon me so I can see….

So, it was around the summer before the ninth grade. My family had just moved, and I was trying to be reconciled to them after so many years of turmoil and struggle. I was in love with music and anyone who could relate I considered them family, even sometimes over my own. See, I was writing and playing guitar as a really young boy. I grew up at my grandfather's house, where music was being played 24 x 7.

I was at the mall hanging out with some friends, and I met a fellow youngster who was in love with music as well (John Eric Younkin, Jr.) and was invited to his house to come and hang out and watch his band rehearse.

So I went with these guys to Eric's house and walked into a bedroom full of music gear. Amps stacked to the ceiling, drums, PA, microphones everywhere. At 14 years of age I was really overwhelmed to see all of this stuff set up and ready to play for some of the guys that were my age. Well, when these guys started to play, I thought "Wow, pretty freaking cool!"

I remember like it was yesterday, Mrs. Younkin came into the room and said someone was at the door. So Eric said to his mother, "It's Jimmy McLester. Please let him in." After everyone was introduced, Jimmy asked Eric, humbly, if he could try a song on the drums . Eric and the rest of the band said sure. I couldn't believe it with my own eyes what was coming out of this guy when he played the drums.

Remember, we were all around the 13 to 15 and all in love with music. This Jimmy guy was so driven, so loud and aggressive, and so freaking awesome—he took the whole thing to another stratosphere.

290

Restoration Observations

I was really excited to call these guys my friends because I was going through so much stuff at my own house. I never wanted to be there, so I opted out to hang with them every chance I could.

I got some great news that my high school friends Eric Younkin and Jimmy were playing together in the original lineup of ChazaRetta. The band was playing sold-out teen clubs, keg parties, talent shows and making great original music. Unfortunately, not money, time or patience could keep these guys together, and, eventually, it imploded, and they all went their separate ways. Remember, we were all in high school and our dreams were still alive but volatile.

Fast-forward the music timeline to Teazer. I went to Free Beer Night with KZEW 98 FM and Chaz Mixon at The Ritz with a thousand scantily clad women. They let me in under age without an ID as the guitar tech for Brad. Staying out in DFW nightclubs in my teens became the norm. I was still playing guitar, and I was excited to be a part of the scene.

I wondered why they had a lead vocalist that vas vomiting on the side of the stage in a bucket instead of fronting the crowd. I thought, "Why did Jimmy go this way?" The band was good but just a stepping stone. Soon, I wanted to audition for Jimmy and Brad's new band. They held auditions for lead singers in Brad Spalding's garage, right behind the North Richland Hills Police Station.

One day, I went over to sing. With my rock 'n' roll looks and confidence, I would need to land the gig. They were into stage presence and vocal abilities, and a fellow rocker auditioned, but he would not come out of the closet for his bashfulness, so after some thought they decided to pass on both of us. My heart was crushed.

We stayed in touch and soon, in our senior year, with one semester left to graduate. Jimmy and Brad joined regional touring band Dirty Blonde, founded by guitarist Bryant Hunter. They took to the road, and I kept working at songwriting and playing guitar with some high school friends.

Brad and Jimmy returned from the road within a year, and with the skills they had learned on the road, birthed the second generation of ChazaRetta with Peter Nepo on vocals and Chad Allen on bass (Dirty Blonde). ChazaRetta partnered with booking agent Buck Judkins of Golden Productions and landed the house gig at Savvy's in Fort Worth.

In my own prison, after a bout with depression, I almost gave up on my own dreams of making music to change the world. I fell into drugs and alcoholism and promiscuity and began to hang out all hours of the night with people I did not know, not knowing where I would lay my head.

One day, I woke up saying, "I hate my life," and I hooked up with his girl from high school that ended in a pregnancy out of wedlock. I had angst pent up, and I needed a release for all these emotions that were buried in my life from early on.

I looked for an outlet, and I was soon blessed at 17 with a job from a close friend at C&S Music in their warehouse. I started pushing a broom in the warehouse, receiving gear and helping in the store. Soon, this job closed and they offered me a position at Brook Mays Pro Shop in Dallas, where I would learn from the likes of Tommy Nuckols, Kim Davis, John Scully and Ken Harris.

291

I also started a band called Regime, which produced a CD at Patrick Maguire Studio. We began to play out a couple of shows, but soon disbanded. With a new passion, I met a girl, Lori, whom I thought would be my saving grace to get me out of my dark hours.

I moved in with Lori, and my job was rocking. I worked at Brook Mays, a tanning salon and at All Texas Tees, working 70 hours a week. Driven to the money, I continued on and my music took a back seat. Lori and I brought our first child, Britney, into the world. Death would come to my door, as Britney almost died from a tonsillectomy. This was a major blessing of restoration.

I heard Jimmy was playing in a new band, Redhouse, and went to Dallas City Limits with my brother to see them. I noticed that Jimmy and Brad had evolved nicely from ChazaRetta and Outrageous and played very well together. We noticed something, just like Pantera did, that Redhouse was going places.

There is much left to be said, but as we stayed in touch I went to Guitar Center in Dallas to fuel my passion to work for a corporation that would pay me for what I had learned and what I was worth. During my tenure at Guitar Center, I won many sales awards and made many professional artist relationships.

In 1999, Jimmy (Jamie) James came to Guitar Center to promote his new hard rock band Solinger, who had been playing 200-plus shows a year. They culminated in an opening slot for Atlantic Recording Artists Scorpions and Alice Cooper, as well as Geffen recording artists Tesla, with KEGL 97.1. Solinger had amassed a major following and were playing the major venues. Jimmy brought me Chain Link Fence, Solinger's CD that was receiving rave reviews in Metal Edge and RIP magazines. They were getting ready to take the final step.

My wife Lori and I were trying to have our second child; however, after Garret was born I went to the NAMM show in Los Angeles because of all the pressure of awards and a piece of paper saying, "You are the man." Yet the only piece of paper I saw when I returned was a note from my wife that said, "You missed your daughter's first birthday, first words, etc. Is work really worth all this?" Soon, my wife's brother moved in, along with his drug addiction and alcoholism, after his divorce.

I began selling and doing the drugs and hiding them from my wife and everyone I knew. Eventually, I stopped going to work. I was shutting down. After failed attempts from my family to reach me, I came to Crossroads Tabernacle on NYE 2001. Calvin Hunt, a singer from Brooklyn Tabernacle Choir had been delivered from a crack/cocaine addiction and was featured on CBN's 700 Club, where Pastors Beth Ann and Corey Jones watched his testimony. Soon, they asked him to come to Crossroads to testify. It was this act of obedience that spoke to my hardened heart, as my arms were folded along the back wall of the sanctuary. Even though I got into my car on the way home and my wife was crying, "Tonight is supposed to be the night," expecting me to go to the altar, I refused.

I received an opportunity to get my job back, but I had to go to California. I reluctantly went, and as I was in my hotel room, I had an urge to use the restroom, and soon a gallon of blood left my innards into the toilet. I was rushed to Orange County Hospital. My lips turned blue, I weighed 138 pounds, and I was sticking my finger in my rib cage to ensure that my heart was beating. I was sick from the drugs. I went to sleep Friday at 3 a.m. and woke up Sunday, and I did not understand.

Restoration Observations

"You were in a drug induced coma," the doctor said. I did not know what that meant. All I knew was I wanted to get back home, after being convicted and torn up by what I had done to everyone. I just wanted to go back to Crossroads and make it all right.

I was discharged and got home Sunday at 4:30 p.m., and my mother called to let me know my wife had left with the kids and had taken everything out of the house. All she left me with were clothes and musical gear. I received a message from Crossroads, saying Jeremiah 29:11: "For I know the plans I have for you, plans to prosper you and give you a hope and a future." I asked my mom to buy me a suit so I could go back to Crossroads. I had tried everything, and now I realized fully that I needed a Savior.

I went back to Crossroads for a Tuesday night prayer meeting, my heart in a blender, seeking the feeling I knew as a kid at church camp, close to my Savior. I gave my life to the Lord at the altar, and I was on a new journey. All the bags of my past were falling off, slowly but surely, and God was birthing a new vision for me and my music.

I started journaling about my life and spent time at the church, after being served divorce papers that I really did not want. I hung out with brothers in Christ in the midnight hours, and studied Ephesians, praying, fasting and walking a new direction.

After testifying at Crossroads in front of thousands during the 2003 Miracles Still Happen, as the paralytic man, I heard rumors of my friend Jimmy (Jamie) James that he was dying of kidney failure and could die any day. My heart stopped ,and my heart returned to the moment when I was 14 at Eric Younkin's house. I said "Please, Lord, give me an opportunity to witness to him. " Please make a way. I want to share the miracle in my life with him."

Chad Allen had seen James at Bell Bottoms nightclub, where his band Touch played with Peter Nepo from ChazaRetta. James wanted to get out of the house, after being discharged from Presbyterian Hospital in February 2003. He wanted to see his friends and hear live music. Chad, who also worked with me at Guitar Center, called and said he saw James and he was deathly ill and dying.

I called to see what was up. I was surprised that my brother, who had run away from home at age 17, and had left his mom and had an estranged relationship, was back at his mom's without any hope of his own. I did not know anything except I wanted to share the goodness of God. I knew he was once a believer, as I was at church camp at age 11 when he gave his life to the Lord. I called him and soon I was "knocking" on his door to see if he was saved.

He shared with me his journey through the Valley of the Shadow of Death at Presbyterian Hospital those eight days before being miraculously released. He shared that God spoke to him in the basement of that cold dialysis unit and said on the seventh day, "James, you will live and not die and declare the works of the Lord." Psalm 118:17

I invited James to Crossroads for Tuesday night prayer service. He said he and his mom had been visiting area churches together but had not found a church home. James rode with me to Crossroads, and he was not able to drive and function very well. He knelt at the altar and surrendered his life to the Lord and came up a new man. Soon, he was at Crossroads serving as an usher, as well as serving in Miracles Still Happen 2004 as Lazarus and testifying to his life of sex, drugs and rock 'n' roll and what God had done for him. He also served as usher, while I played drums on the worship team. I know it was a humbling time

293

for us both.

We hung out, went to Starbucks, began writing songs in our journal and soon we were playing on the Worship Team at Crossroads. James went on to play Christ in Miracles Still Happen 2005-2009, while I worked with the Worship Team. I was also involved with 1,000 Guitars of Praise and guitar for Peter Fuhrler of Newsboys, Mylon Lefevre, Chuck Dennie's By The Tree, Stryper, Chris Tomlin and Mercy Me, to name a few. God had opened his floodgates of restoration and blessing.

Another tragedy came when I lost my father to a heart attack. James had been through this with his father when James was just 24 years old, when he suddenly received a call that had his father had passed away. I had a similar call to North Hills Hospital where my father, Butch, lay cold and gone. James and his mother rushed to North Hills to stand around my family and pray. We had both been through it. Looking back, I am thankful that prayers were answered for my father, as he began coming to Fellowship Church in Grapevine, Texas, and reserving a whole row of seats for James, me and my friends to worship the King together. My father loved the "sound."

In remembrance of my father and the journey of Supernova Remnant, James held a surprise birthday party for me with a full-blown Gibson Flying V cake and a shadow box of The Afterglow, Supernova Remnant's first CD, and aligned with pictures and words and a tribute to my father.

Supernova Remnant was born in 2003, after a random name search on Google for Remnant yielded "the Vela supernova remnant" on NASA's website. Thus, we shortened the name, and "Supernova Remnant" was born. We are still going strong, and these events are chronicled in this book.

To this day, even after decades interwoven with our lives, God has brought the inseparable fabric of Supernova Remnant together for life. And James admits mine was the best singing that day.

Robbie Gustin

Made in the USA
San Bernardino, CA
18 May 2014